Albert Harkness, William Randolph Hearst

**An introductory Latin book**

Intended as an elementary drill-book

Albert Harkness, William Randolph Hearst
**An introductory Latin book**
*Intended as an elementary drill-book*

ISBN/EAN: 9783337278144

Printed in Europe, USA, Canada, Australia, Japan

Cover: Foto ©Paul-Georg Meister /pixelio.de

More available books at **www.hansebooks.com**

AN

# INTRODUCTORY
# LATIN BOOK,

INTENDED AS AN

## ELEMENTARY DRILL-BOOK,

ON THE

INFLECTIONS AND PRINCIPLES OF THE LANGUAGE,

AND AS AN

## INTRODUCTION

TO THE

AUTHOR'S GRAMMAR, READER AND LATIN COMPOSITION.

BY

ALBERT HARKNESS,

*Professor in Brown University.*

AUTHOR OF "A LATIN GRAMMAR," "A LATIN READER," "A FIRST GREEK BOOK," ETC.

NEW YORK:
D. APPLETON AND COMPANY,
549 & 551 BROADWAY.
1876.

# PREFACE.

The volume now offered to the public is intended to furnish the pupil his first lessons in Latin. As an Elementary Drill-book, it aims to supply a want long felt in our schools. In no stage of a course of classical study is judicious instruction of more vital importance than in that which deals with the forms and elements of the Latin language. To the beginner, every thing is new, and requires minute and careful illustration. He must at the very outset become so familiar with all the grammatical inflections, with their exact form and force, that he will recognize them with promptness and certainty wherever they occur. He must not lose time in uncertain conjecture, where positive knowledge alone will be of any real value. Improvement on this point is one of the pressing needs of our schools. This volume is intended as a contribution to classical education in aid of this particular work. It aims to lighten the burden of the teacher in elementary drill, and to aid him in grounding his pupils in the first elements of the Latin language.

It is the unmistakable verdict of the class-room, that theory and practice must not be separated in the study of language. The true method of instruction will make ample provision for both. On the one hand, the pupil must, by a vigorous use of the memory, become master of all the grammatical forms and rules; while, on the other hand, he must not be denied the luxury of using the knowledge which he is so laboriously acquiring.

To this just and urgent demand of the class-room; the

author's First Latin Book, published fifteen years since, on the basis of Dr. Arnold's works, owed its origin. For the favor with which it was received, and for the generous interest with which it has so long been regarded, the author desires here to express his sincere thanks to the numerous classical instructors whose fidelity in its use has contributed so largely to its success. In the conviction, however, that it has now done its appointed work, he begs leave to offer them the present volume as its successor.

The great objection to most First Latin Books, that, however excellent they may be in themselves, they are not especially adapted to any particular Grammar, and that they accordingly fill the memory of the pupil with rules and statements which must, as far as possible, be unlearned as soon as he passes to his Grammar, is entirely obviated in this volume. All the grammatical portions of it, even to the numbering of the articles, are introduced in the exact form and language of the author's Grammar. Indeed, the paradigms are not only the same as in the Grammar, but also occupy the same place on the page; so that even the local associations which the beginner so readily forms with the pages of his first book may be transferred directly to the Grammar.

This work is intended to be complete in itself. It comprises a distinct outline of Latin Grammar, Exercises for Double Translation, Suggestions to the Learner, Notes and Vocabularies. As an Introduction to the author's Grammar, Reader and Latin Composition, it discusses and illustrates precisely those points which are deemed most essential as a preparation for the course of study presented in those works.

PROVIDENCE, R.I., June, 1866.

# CONTENTS.

## PART FIRST.

### ORTHOGRAPHY.

|  | Page. |
|---|---|
| Alphabet | 1 |
| Sounds of Letters | 2 |
| Exercise I. | 3 |
| " II. | 4 |
| " III. | 5 |
| Syllables | 6 |
| Quantity | 6 |
| Accentuation | 7 |
| Exercise IV. | 7 |

## PART SECOND.

### ETYMOLOGY.

### CHAPTER I.

#### NOUNS.

| | |
|---|---|
| Gender | 8 |
| Person and Number | 9 |
| Cases | 9 |
| Declensions | 10 |
| First Declension | 11 |
| Exercise V. | 11 |
| Second Declension | 13 |
| Exercise VI. | 14 |
| " VII. | 16 |
| Third Declension | 17 |
| Exercise VIII. | 23 |
| " IX. | 25 |
| Fourth Declension | 26 |
| Exercise X. | 27 |

vi                           CONTENTS.

|                                  | Page. |
|----------------------------------|-------|
| Fifth Declension                 | 28    |
| Exercise XI.                     | 29    |

## CHAPTER II.
### ADJECTIVES.

| First and Second Declensions | 30 |
| Exercise XII.                | 33 |
| Third Declension             | 35 |
| Exercise XIII.               | 37 |
| Comparison of Adjectives     | 38 |
| Exercise XIV.                | 39 |
| Numeral Adjectives           | 40 |
| Exercise XV.                 | 42 |

## CHAPTER III.
### PRONOUNS.

| Personal Pronouns | 43 |
| Possessive        | 44 |
| Demonstrative     | 44 |
| Relative          | 45 |
| Interrogative     | 46 |
| Indefinite        | 46 |
| Exercise XVI.     | 47 |

## CHAPTER IV.
### VERBS.

| Voices           | 48 |
| Moods            | 49 |
| Tenses           | 50 |
| Numbers          | 50 |
| Persons          | 51 |
| Conjugation      | 51 |
| The Verb Sum     | 52 |
| Exercise XVII.   | 56 |
| "   XVIII.       | 57 |
| "   XIX.         | 60 |
| First Conjugation | 62 |
| Exercise XX.     | 6ƒ |

|  |  | Page. |
|---|---|---|
| Exercise XXI. | . . . . . . . . | 67 |
| " XXII. | . . . . . . . . | 69 |
| " XXIII. | . . . . . . . . | 71 |
| " XXIV. | . . . . . . . . | 73 |
| " XXV. | . . . . . . . . | 74 |
| " XXVI. | . . . . . . . . | 75 |
| " XXVII. | . . . . . . . . | 76 |
| Second Conjugation | . . . . . . . . | 78 |
| Exercise XXVIII. | . . . . . . . | 82 |
| " XXIX. | . . . . . . . . | 83 |
| " XXX. | . . . . . . . . | 84 |
| " XXXI. | . . . . . . . . | 85 |
| " XXXII. | . . . . . . . . | 86 |
| " XXXIII. | . . . . . . . . | 87 |
| " XXXIV. | . . . . . . . . | 88 |
| Third Conjugation | . . . . . . . . | 90 |
| Exercise XXXV. | . . . . . . . . | 94 |
| " XXXVI. | . . . . . . . . | 95 |
| " XXXVII. | . . . . . . . . | 96 |
| " XXXVIII. | . . . . . . . | 97 |
| " XXXIX. | . . . . . . . . | 97 |
| " XL. | . . . . . . . . | 98 |
| " XLI. | . . . . . . . . | 99 |
| Fourth Conjugation | . . . . . . . . | 100 |
| Exercise XLII. | . . . . . . . | 104 |
| " XLIII. | . . . . . . . . | 104 |
| " XLIV. | . . . . . . . . | 105 |
| " XLV. | . . . . . . . . | 106 |
| " XLVI. | . . . . . . . . | 107 |
| " XLVII. | . . . . . . . . | 107 |
| " XLVIII. | . . . . . . . | 108 |
| Verbs in io | . . . . . . . . | 110 |
| Exercise XLIX. | . . . . . . . | 112 |

## PART THIRD.

### SYNTAX.

#### CHAPTER I.

SYNTAX OF SENTENCES.

Section.
I. Classification of Sentences . . . . . . . 114
II. Simple Sentences . . . . . . . . 115

## CHAPTER II.

### SYNTAX OF NOUNS.

| Section. | | Page. |
|---|---|---|
| I. | Agreement of Nouns | 117 |
| | Exercise L. | 117 |
| | " LI. | 119 |
| II. | Nominative | 120 |
| | Exercise LII. | 120 |
| III. | Vocative | 121 |
| | Exercise LIII. | 121 |
| IV. | Accusative | 122 |
| | Exercise LIV. | 123 |
| | " LV. | 124 |
| | " LVI. | 125 |
| V. | Dative | 126 |
| | Exercise LVII. | 127 |
| | " LVIII. | 129 |
| VI. | Genitive | 130 |
| | Exercise LIX. | 131 |
| | " LX. | 132 |
| VII. | Ablative | 133 |
| | Exercise LXI. | 135 |
| | " LXII. | 137 |
| | " LXIII. | 138 |
| | " LXIV. | 140 |
| VIII. | Cases with Prepositions | 141 |
| | Exercise LXV. | 142 |
| Suggestions to the Learner | | 143 |
| Latin-English Vocabulary | | 147 |
| English-Latin Vocabulary | | 157 |

# EXPLANATION OF REFERENCES AND ABBREVIATIONS.

The numerals refer to articles in this work.

The following abbreviations occur:

| | | | |
|---|---|---|---|
| abl. . . . . . . | ablative. | n. . . . . . | neuter. |
| acc. . . . . . . | accusative. | nom. . . . . | nominative. |
| act. . . . . . . | active. | p. . . . . . | page. |
| adv. . . . . . . | adverb. | part. . . . . | particle. |
| conj. . . . . . | conjunction. | pass. . . . . | passive. |
| dat. . . . . . . | dative. | pers. . . . . | person. |
| f. . . . . . . . | feminine. | plur., *or* pl. . . | plural. |
| gen. . . . . . . | genitive. | prep. . . . . | preposition. |
| indef. . . . . . | indefinite. | rel. . . . . . | relative. |
| interrog. . . . | interrogative. | sing. . . . . | singular. |
| m. . . . . . . . | masculine. | voc. . . . . | vocative. |

# INTRODUCTORY LATIN BOOK.

1. **Latin Grammar** treats of the principles of the Latin language.

## PART FIRST.

## ORTHOGRAPHY.[1]

### ALPHABET.

2. The Latin alphabet is the same as the English, with the omission of *w*.

3. **Classes of Letters.** — Letters are divided into two classes:

    I. *Vowels* . . . . . . . . a, e, i, o, u, y.
    II. *Consonants:* —
        1. Liquids . . . . . . . l, m, n, r.
        2. Spirants . . . . . . h, s.
        3. Mutes: 1) Labials . . . . . p, b, f, v.
                 2) Palatals . . . . c, g, k, q, j.
                 3) Linguals . . . . t, d.
        4. Double Consonants . . . . x, z.

4. **Combinations of Letters.** — We notice here,

1. *Diphthongs,* — combinations of two vowels in one syllable. The most common are *ae, oe, au.*

2. *Double Consonants,* — $x = cs$ or $gs$; $z = ds$ or $ts$.

3. *Ch, ph, th,* are best treated, not as combinations of letters, but only as aspirated forms of *c, p,* and *t,* as *h* is only a breathing.

---

[1] Orthography treats of the letters and sounds of the language.

## SOUNDS OF LETTERS.

**5.** Scholars in different countries generally pronounce Latin substantially as they do their own languages. In this country, however, two distinct systems are recognized, generally known as the *English* and the *Continental Method*.[1] For the convenience of the instructor, we add a brief outline of each.

### I. ENGLISH METHOD.

#### 1. *Sounds of Vowels.*

**6.** Vowels generally have their *long* or *short* English sounds.

**7. Long Sound.** — Vowels have their long English sounds — *a* as in *fate*, *e* in *mete*, *i* in *pine*, *o* in *note*, *u* in *tube*, *y* in *type* — in the following situations:

1. In final syllables ending in a vowel:[2] *se, si, ser'-vi, ser'-vo, cor'-nu, mi'-sy.*

2. In all syllables before a vowel or diphthong: *de'-us, de-o'-rum, de'-ae, di-e'-i, ni'-hi-lum.*[3]

3. In penultimate[4] and unaccented syllables, not final, before a single consonant, or a mute with *l* or *r : pa'-ter, pa'-tres, A'-thos, O'-thrys, do-lo'-ris.* But

1) *A unaccented* has the sound of *a final* in America: *men'-sa.*

**8. Short Sound.** — Vowels have the short English sound — *a* as in *fat*, *e* in *met*, *i* in *pin*, *o* in *not*, *u* in *tub*, *y* in *myth* — in the following situations:

---

[1] Strictly speaking, there is no Continental Method, as every nation on the continent of Europe has its own method.

[2] Some give to *i* in both syllables of *tibi* and *sibi* the short sound.

[3] In these rules, no account is taken of *h*, as that is only a breathing: hence the first *i* in *nihilum* is treated as a vowel before another vowel: for the same reason, *ch, ph*, and *th* are treated as single mutes; thus *th* in *Athos* and *Othrys.*

[4] Penultimate, the last syllable but one.

1. In final syllables ending in a consonant: *a'-mat, a'-met, rex'-it, sol, con'-sul, Te'-thys;* except *post, es final,* and *os final* in plural cases: *res, di'-es, hos, a'-gros.*

2. In all syllables before *x*, or any two consonants except a mute with *l* or *r* (7, 3): *rex'-it, bel'-lum, rex-e'-runt, bel-lo'-rum.*

3. In all accented syllables before one or more consonants, except the penultimate: *dom'-i-nus, pat'-ri-bus.* But

1) *A, e,* or *o,* before a single consonant (or a mute with *l* or *r*) followed by *e, i,* or *y,* before another vowel, has the long sound: *a'-ci-es, a'-cri-a, me'-re-o, do'-ce-o.*

2) *U,* in any syllable not final, before a single consonant, or a mute with *l* or *r,* except *bl,* has the long sound: *Pu'-ni-cus, sa-lu'-bri-tas.*

## 2. *Sounds of Diphthongs.*

9. *Ae* and *oe* are pronounced like e:

   1) long: *Cae'-sar* (Ce'-sar), *Oe'-ta* (E'-ta).
   2) short: *Daed'-ă-lus* (Ded'-a-lus), *Oed'-i-pus.*

*Au* as in author: *au'-rum.*
*Eu* . . neuter: *neu'-ter.*[1]

### Exercise I.

*Give the sounds of the Vowels and Diphthongs in the following words.*

1. Men'-sam,[2] men'-sas, men'-sis, men'-sae,[3] men-sa'-rum.[4]
2. Ho'-ram,[5] ho'-ras, ho'-ris, ho'-rae,[6] ho-ra'-rum.[7] 3. Scho'-la,[8] scho'-lam, scho'-las, scho'-lis, scho'-lae, scho-la'-rum.
4. Co-ro'-na,[8] co-ro'-nam, co-ro'-nas, co-ro'-nis, co-ro'-nae.[9]

---

[1] *Ei* and *oi* are seldom diphthongs; but, when so used, they have the long sound of *i:* hei, cui.

[2] 8, 2; 8, 1.     [5] 7, 3; 8, 1.     [8] 7, 3; 7, 3, 1).
[3] 8, 2; 9; 7, 1.     [6] 7, 3; 9; 7, 1.     [9] 7, 3; 9; 7, 1.
[4] 8, 2; 7, 3; 8, 1.     [7] 7, 3; 8, 1.

## 3. *Sounds of Consonants.*

**10.** The consonants are pronounced in general as in English; but a few directions may aid the learner.

**11. C, G, S, T,** and **X** are generally pronounced with their ordinary English sounds. Thus,

1. *C* and *g* are *soft* (like s and j) before *e, i, y, ae,* and *oe;* and *hard* in other situations: *ce'-do* (sedo), *ci'-vis, Cy'-rus, cae'-do, coe'-na, a'-ge* (a-je), *a'-gi; ca'-do* (ka'do), *co'-go, cum, Ga'-des.*

2. *S* generally has its regular English sound as in son, thus: *sa'-cer, so'-ror, si'-dus.* But

1) *S final* after *e, ae, au, b, m, n, r,* is pronounced like *z: spes, praes, laus, urbs, hi'-ems, mons, pars.*

3. *T* has its regular English sound as in time: *ti'-mor, to'-tus.*

4. *X* has generally its regular English sound like *ks: rex'-i* (rek'-si), *ux'-or* (uk'-sor).

**12. C, S, T,** and **X — Aspirated.** — Before *i*, preceded by an accented syllable and followed by a vowel, *c, s, t,* and *x* are aspirated, — *c, s,* and *t* taking the sound of *sh*, x that of *ksh: so'-ci-us* (so'-she-us), *Al'-si-um* (Al'-she-um), *ar'-ti-um* (ar'-she-um); *anx'-i-us* (ank'-she-us). *C* has also the sound of *sh* before *eu* and *yo,* preceded by an accented syllable: *ca-du'-ce-us* (ca-du'-she-us), *Sic'-y-on* (Sish'-e-on).

**13. Silent Consonants.** — An initial consonant, with or without the aspirate *h*, is sometimes silent: *Cne'-us* (Ne'-us).

### Exercise II.

*Give the sounds of the Letters in the following words.*

1. Ci'-vis,[1] civ'-i-um, civ'-i-bus. 2. Car'-men,[2] car'-mi-nis, car'-mi-ne.[3] 3. Rex,[4] re'-gis,[5] re'-gi, re'-gum.[5] 4. Ca'-put,[6] cap'-i-tis, cap'-i-tum. 5. A'-ci-em,[7] a'-ci-e, a'-ci-es.[8] 6. Ars,[8] ar'-tis, ar'-tes,[8] ar'-ti-um.[9]

---

[1] 11, 1 and 2; 7, 3; 8, 1.
[2] 11, 1; 8, 2; 8, 1.
[3] 8, 3; 7, 3; 7, 1.
[4] 11, 4.
[5] 11, 1; 7, 3; 8, 1.
[6] 11, 1, and 3.
[7] 8, 3, 1); 12; 8, 1.
[8] 11, 2, 1).
[9] 12.

ORTHOGRAPHY. — SOUNDS OF LETTERS. 5

## II. CONTINENTAL METHOD.[1]

### 1. *Sounds of Vowels.*

**14.** Each vowel has in the main one uniform sound;[2] but the length or duration of the sound depends upon the quantity of the vowel. See 20.

The vowel-sounds are as follows:

*a* like ä in father: e.g., *a'-ra.*
*e* " ā made: " *ple'-bes.*
*i* " ē me: " *i'-ri.*
*o* " ō no: " *o'-ro.*
*u* " ô do: " *u'-num.*
*y* " ē me; " *Ny'-sa.*

### 2. *Sounds of Diphthongs.*

**15.** *Ae* and *oe* like a in made: e.g., *ae'-tas, coe'-lum.*
 *au* " ou " out: " *au'-rum.*[3]

### 3. *Sounds of Consonants.*

**16.** The pronunciation of the consonants is similar to that of the English method; but it varies somewhat in different countries.

### EXERCISE III.

*Give the sounds of the Letters in the following words, according to the Continental Method.*

1. Hŏ'-ră, hŏ'-răm, hŏ'-rās, hŏ'-rīs, hŏ'-rae, hŏ-rā'-rŭm.
2. Glŏ'-rĭ-ă, glŏ'-rĭ-ŭm, glŏ'-rĭ-ae. 3. Dŏ'-nŭm, dŏ'-nī, dŏ-

---

[1] If the *English Method* is adopted as the standard in the school, this outline of the *Continental Method* should be omitted.

[2] These sounds sometimes undergo slight modifications in uniting with the various consonants.

[3] In other combinations, the two vowels are generally pronounced separately; but *ei* and *eu* occur as diphthongs, with nearly the same sound as in English.

nō, dŏ'-nă, dō-nō'-rŭm, dō'-nis. 4. Cī'-vĭs, cī'-vī, cī'-vĕm, cī'-vēs, cīv'-ĭ-ŭm, cīv'-ĭ-bŭs.

## SYLLABLES.

17. In the pronunciation of Latin, every word has as many syllables as it has vowels and diphthongs; thus the Latin words *more, vice, acute,* and *persuade* are pronounced, not as the same words are in English, but with their vowel-sounds all heard in separate syllables; thus: *mo'-re, vi'-ce, a-cu'-te, per-sua'-de.*

## QUANTITY.

20. Syllables are, in quantity or length, either long, short, or common.[1]

21. **Long.**— A syllable is long in quantity,

1. If it contains a diphthong: *haec.*

2. If its vowel is followed by *j, x, z,* or any two consonants, except a mute with *l* or *r : rex, mons.*

22. **Short.**— A syllable is short if its vowel is followed by another vowel or a diphthong: *di'-es, vi'-ae, ni'-hil.*[2]

23. **Common.** — A syllable is common, if its vowel, naturally[3] short, is followed by a mute with *l* or *r : a'-gri.*

24. The signs ¯, ˘, ˇ, denote respectively that the syllables over which they are placed are long, short, or common : *ă-grō-rŭm.*[4]

---

[1] Common; i.e., sometimes long, and sometimes short.

[2] No account is taken of the breathing *h.* See 7, 2, note 3.

[3] A vowel is said to be *naturally* short when it is short in its own *nature;* i.e., in itself, without reference to its position.

[4] By referring to 14, it will be seen, that, in the Continental Method, *quantity* and *sound* coincide with each other: a vowel long in quantity is long in sound, and a vowel short in quantity is short in sound. But, by referring to 7 and 8, it will be seen, that, in the English Method, the quantity of a vowel does not at all affect its sound, except in determining the accent (26). Hence, in this method, a vowel long in quantity is often short in sound, and a vowel short in quantity is often long in sound. Thus, in *rēx, ūrbs, ārs, sōl,* the vowels are all long in quantity;

## ACCENTUATION.

### I. Primary Accent.

**25.** Monosyllables are treated as accented syllables: *mons, nos.*

**26.** Other words are accented as follows:[1]

1. *Words of two syllables* — always on the first: *men'-sa.*
2. *Words of more than two syllables* — on the *penult*[2] if that is long in quantity, otherwise on the *antepenult:*[2] *ho-nō'-ris, con'-sŭ-lis.*

### II. Secondary Accents.

**27.** A second accent is placed on the second or third syllable before the primary accent, — on the second, if that is the first syllable of the word, or is long in quantity; otherwise on the third: *mon'-u-e'-runt, mon'-u-e-ra'-mus, in-stau'-ra-ve'-runt.*

**28.** In the same way, a third accent is placed on the second or third syllable before the second accent: *hon'-o-rif'-i-cen-tis'-sĭ-mus.*

### Exercise IV.

*Accent and pronounce the following Words.*

1. Cŏrōnă,[3] cŏrōnae, cŏrōnārŭm.[4]  2. Gemmae,[5] gemmărum, gemmārŭm.  3. Săpientiae,[6] ămīcĭtiae, justĭtiae, glōriae.[7]

---

but by 8, 1, they all have the short English sounds: while in *ăvĕ, mărĕ,* the vowels are all short in quantity; but by 7, 1, and 3, they all have the long English sounds. Hence, in pronouncing according to the English Method, determine the place of the accent by the quantity (according to 26), and then determine the sounds of the letters irrespective of quantity (according to 7–12).

[1] In the subsequent pages, the pupil will be expected to accent words in pronunciation according to these rules. The quantity of the penult in words of more than two syllables will therefore be marked (unless determined by 21 and 22), to enable him to ascertain the place of the accent.

[2] Penult, last syllable but one; antepenult, the last but two.

[3] 26, 2; 7, 3, 1).  [5] 11, 1; 26, 1.  [7] 11, 1; 8, 3, 1).
[4] 26, 2; 27.  [6] 27; 8, 3, 1); 12.

4. Săpientiăm, ămīcĭtiăm, justĭtiăm, glōriăm. 5. Săpientiă, ămīcītiă, justĭtiă, glōriă.

# PART SECOND.

# ETYMOLOGY.

**29.** ETYMOLOGY treats of the classification, inflection, and derivation of words.

**30.** The Parts of Speech[1] are — *Nouns, Adjectives, Pronouns, Verbs, Adverbs, Prepositions, Conjunctions,* and *Interjections.*

## CHAPTER I.

### NOUNS.

**31.** A Noun, or Substantive, is a name, as of a person, place, or thing: *Cicĕro*, Cicero; *Rōma*, Rome; *puer*, boy; *dŏmus*, house.

1. A **Proper Noun** is a proper name, as of a person or place: *Cicĕro, Rōma.*

2. A **Common Noun** is a name common to all the members of a class of objects: *vir*, man; *ĕquus*, horse.

**32.** Nouns have *Gender, Number, Person, and Case.*

### GENDER.

**33.** There are three genders,[2] — *Masculine, Feminine,* and *Neuter.*

---

[1] Thus in Latin, as in English, words are divided, according to their use, into eight classes, called *Parts of Speech.*

[2] In English, *Gender* denotes *sex.* Accordingly, masculine nouns denote *males;* feminine nouns, *females;* and neuter nouns, objects which are *neither male nor female.* In Latin, however, this natural distinction

34. In some nouns, gender is determined by signification; in others, by endings.

35. GENERAL RULES FOR GENDER.

I. MASCULINES.

1. Names of *Males*: *Cicĕro* ; *vir*, man; *rex*, king.
2. Names of *Rivers*, *Winds*, and *Months*: *Rhēnus*, Rhine; *Nŏtus*, south wind; *Aprīlis*, April.

II. FEMININE.

1. Names of *Females*: *mulier*, woman; *leaena*, lioness.
2. Names of *Countries*, *Towns*, *Islands*, and *Trees*: *Aegyptus*, Egypt; *Rōma*, Rome; *Dēlos*, Delos; *pĭrus*, pear-tree.

## PERSON AND NUMBER.

37. The Latin, like the English, has three persons and two numbers. The first person denotes the speaker; the second, the person spoken to; the third, the person spoken of. The singular number denotes one, the plural more than one.

## CASES.

38. The Latin has six cases:[1]

| Names. | English Equivalents. |
|---|---|
| Nominative, | Nominative. |
| Genitive, | Possessive, or Objective with *of*. |
| Dative, | Objective with *to* or *for*. |
| Accusative, | Objective. |
| Vocative, | Nominative Independent. |
| Ablative, | Objective with *from*, *by*, *in*, *with*. |

---

of gender is applied only to the names of *males* and *females;* while, in all other nouns, gender depends upon an artificial distinction, according to grammatical rules.

[1] The *case* of a noun shows the relation which that noun sustains to other words; as, *John's book.* Here the *possessive case* (*John's*) shows that John sustains to the book the relation of *possessor.*

**1. Oblique Cases.** — In distinction from the Nominative and Vocative (casus recti, right cases), the other cases are called *oblique* (casus obliqui).

**2. Case-Endings.** — In form, the several cases are, in general, distinguished from each other by certain terminations called *case-endings*: Nom. *mensa*, Gen. *mensae*, &c.

**3. Cases alike.** — But certain cases are not distinguished in form. Thus,

1) The *Nominative, Accusative,* and *Vocative, in neuters,* are alike, and in the plural end in *a*.

2) The *Nominative* and *Vocative* are alike in all nouns, except those in *us* of the second declension (45).

3) The *Dative* and *Ablative Plural* are alike.

## DECLENSIONS.

39. The formation of the several cases is called Declension.

40. **Five Declensions.** — In Latin, there are five declensions, distinguished from each other by the following

*Genitive Endings.*

| Dec. I. | Dec. II. | Dec. III. | Dec. IV. | Dec. V. |
|---|---|---|---|---|
| ae, | ī, | ĭs, | ūs, | eī.[1] |

41. **Stem and Endings.** — In any noun, of whatever declension,

1. The stem[2] may be found by dropping the ending of the genitive singular.

2. The several cases may be formed by adding to this stem the case-endings.

---

[1] See 119, 1.

[2] The *stem* is the basis of the word, or the part to which the several endings are added to form the various cases. Thus in the forms, *mensă, mensae, mensăm, mensĭs,* &c., given under 42, it will be observed that *mens* remains unchanged; and that, by the addition of the endings, *a, ae, am, is,* &c., to it, the several cases are formed. Here *mens* is the *stem;* and *a, ae, am, is,* &c., are the *case-endings.*

## FIRST DECLENSION.

**42.** Nouns of the first declension end in

ă and ĕ, — *feminine ;* ās and ēs, — *masculine.*[1]

But pure Latin nouns end only in *a*, and are declined as follows:

SINGULAR.

| | | | |
|---|---|---|---|
| Nom. | mensă, | a table, | ă |
| Gen. | mensae, | of a table, | ae |
| Dat. | mensae, | to, for, a table, | ae |
| Acc. | mensăm, | a table, | ăm |
| Voc. | mensă, | O table, | ă |
| Abl. | mensā, | with, from, by, a table, | ā |

PLURAL.

| | | | |
|---|---|---|---|
| Nom. | mensae, | tables, | ae |
| Gen. | mensārŭm, | of tables, | ārŭm |
| Dat. | mensīs, | to, for, tables, | īs |
| Acc. | mensās, | tables, | ās |
| Voc. | mensae, | O tables, | ae |
| Abl. | mensīs, | with, from, by, tables, | īs. |

1. **Case-Endings.** — From an inspection of this example, it will be seen that the several cases are distinguished from each other by the case-endings placed on the right.

2. **Examples for Practice.** — With these endings decline:

*Ala,* wing; *ăqua,* water; *causa,* cause; *fortūna,* fortune; *porta,* gate; *victōria,* victory.

EXERCISE V. 5 Five fünf

### I. *Vocabulary.*

| | | |
|---|---|---|
| Amīcĭtĭă, | ae,[2] *f.*[3] | *friendship.* |
| Cŏrōnă, | ae, *f.* | *crown.* |

---

[1] That is, nouns of this declension in *a* and *e* are feminine, and those in *as* and *es* are masculine.

[2] The ending *ae* is the case-ending of the Genitive: *amicitia;* Gen., *amicitiae.*

[3] Gender is indicated in the vocabularies by *m.* for *masculine, f.* for *feminine,* and *n.* for *neuter.*

| | | |
|---|---|---|
| Gemmă | ae, *f.* | *gem.* |
| Glōriă, | ae, *f.* | *glory.* |
| Hōră, | ae, *f.* | *hour.* |
| Justĭtiă, | ae, *f.* | *justice.* |
| Săpientiă, | ae, *f.* | *wisdom.* |
| Schŏlă, | ae, *f.* | *school.* |

## II. *Translate into English.*

1. Corōnă,[1] corōnā, corōnae,[2] corōnam, coronārum, corōnis, corōnas. 2. Gemmă, gemmā, gemmae, gemmam, gemmārum, gemmis, gemmas. 3. Sapientiă, amicitiă, justitiă, gloriă. 4. Sapientiam, amicitiam, justitiam, gloriam. 5. Sapientiā, amicitiā, justitiā, gloriā. 6. Scholārum, horārum. 7. Scholis, horis. 8. Scholas, horas.

## III. *Translate into Latin.*

1. Friendship, friendships. 2. Of[3] friendship, of friendships. 3. To friendship, to friendships. 4. By friendship, by friendships. 5. Justice, by justice, of justice, to justice. 6. Wisdom, glory. 7. With wisdom, with glory. 8. To wisdom, to glory. 9. Of wisdom, of glory. 10. Of a[4] crown, of a gem. 11. Crowns, gems. 12. With the[4] crowns, with the gems. 13. Of crowns, of gems.

---

[1] As the Latin has no article, a noun may, according to the connection in which it is used, be translated (1) without the article; as, *corōna*, crown; (2) with the indefinite article *a* or *an*; as, *corōna*, a crown; (3) with the definite article *the*; as, *corōna*, the crown.

[2] When the same Latin form may be found in two or more cases, the pupil is expected to give the meaning for each case. Thus *corōnae* may be in the Genitive or Dative Singular, or in the Nominative or Vocative Plural.

[3] The pupil will observe that the English prepositions, *of, to, by*, may be rendered into Latin by simply changing the ending of the word. Thus *friendship*, amicitia; *of friendship*, amicitiae.

[4] The pupil will remember that the English articles, *a, an*, and *the*, are not to be rendered into Latin at all. *Crown, a crown,* and *the crown,* are all rendered into Latin by the same word.

## SECOND DECLENSION.

**45.** Nouns of the second declension end in

ĕr, ĭr, ŭs, os, — *masculine;* ŭm, on, — *neuter.*

But pure Latin nouns end only in *er, ir, us, um,* and are declined as follows:

Servus, *slave.* Puer, *boy.* Ager, *field.* Templum, *temple.*

### SINGULAR.

| | | | |
|---|---|---|---|
| *N.* servŭs | puĕr | ăgĕr | templŭm |
| *G.* servī | puĕrī | ăgrī | templī |
| *D.* servō | puĕrō | ăgrō | templō |
| *A.* servŭm | puĕrŭm | ăgrŭm | templŭm |
| *V.* servĕ | puĕr | ăgĕr | templŭm |
| *A.* servō | puĕrō | ăgrō | templō |

### PLURAL.

| | | | |
|---|---|---|---|
| *N.* servī | puĕrī | ăgrī | templă |
| *G.* servōrŭm | puĕrōrŭm | ăgrōrŭm | templōrŭm |
| *D.* servīs | puĕrīs | ăgrīs | templīs |
| *A.* servōs | puĕrōs | ăgrōs | templă |
| *V.* servī | puĕrī | ăgrī | templă |
| *A.* servīs | puĕrīs | ăgrīs | templīs |

**1. Case-Endings.** — From an inspection of the paradigms, it will be seen that they are declined with the following

*Case-endings.*

1. ŭs.   2. ĕr.   3. ŭm.

### SINGULAR.

| | 1 | 2 | 3 |
|---|---|---|---|
| *N.* | ŭs | —[1] | ŭm |
| *G.* | ī | ī | ī |
| *D.* | ō | ō | ō |
| *A.* | ŭm | ŭm | ŭm |
| *V.* | ĕ | —[1] | ŭm |
| *A.* | ō | ō | ō |

---

[1] The endings for the Nom. and Voc. Sing. are wanting in nouns in *er:* thus *puer* is the stem without any case-ending; the full form would be *puĕrŭs.*

PLURAL.

|   |      |      |      |
|---|------|------|------|
| N.| ī    | ī    | ă    |
| G.| ōrŭm | ōrŭm | ōrŭm |
| D.| īs   | īs   | īs   |
| A.| ōs   | ōs   | ă    |
| V.| ī    | ī    | ă    |
| A.| īs.  | īs.  | īs.  |

2. **Examples for Practice.** — Like SERVUS: *annus*, year; *domĭnus*, master. — Like PUER: *gĕner*, son-in-law; *sŏcer*, father-in-law. — Like AGER: *făber*, artisan; *magister*, master. — Like TEMPLUM: *bellum*, war; *regnum*, kingdom.

3. **Paradigms.** — Observe

1) That *puer* differs in declension from *servus* only in dropping the endings *us* and *e* in the Nom. and Voc.: Nom. *puer* for *puĕrus*, Voc. *puer* for *puĕre*.

2) That *ager* differs from *puer* only in dropping *e* before *r*.

3) That *templum*, as a neuter noun, has the Nom., Accus., and Voc. alike, ending in the plural in *a*. See 38, 3.

### Exercise VI.

#### I. *Vocabulary.*

| | |
|---|---|
| Dōnŭm, ī, *n.* | *gift.* |
| Gĕnŏr, gĕnĕrī, *m.* | *son-in-law.* |
| Lĭbĕr, lĭbrī, *m.* | *book.* |
| Ocŭlŭs, ī, *m.* | *eye.* |
| Praeceptŭm, ī, *n.* | *rule, precept.* |
| Sŏcĕr, sŏcĕrī, *m.* | *father-in-law.* |
| Tўrannŭs, ī, *m.* | *tyrant.* |
| Verbŭm, ī, *n.* | *word.* |

#### II. *Translate into English.*

1. Ocŭlus, ocŭli, ocŭlo, ocŭlum, ocŭle, oculōrum, ocŭlis, ocŭlos. 2. Socer, socĕri, socĕro, socĕrum, socerōrum, socĕris, socĕros. 3. Servi, tyranni. 4. Puĕri, genĕri. 5. Agri, libri. 6. Templi, doni. 7. Servo, tyranno. 8. Puĕrum, genĕrum. 9. Agrōrum, librōrum. 10. Templa, dona. 11. Servum, servos. 12. Genĕri, generōrum. 13. Agri, agrō-

ruin. 14. Dono, donis. 15. Verbum, praeceptum. 16. Verbi, praecepti.

### III. *Translate into Latin.*

1. The slave, the slaves. 2. For the slave, for the slaves. 3. Of the slave, of the slaves. 4. Of the father-in-law, of the son-in-law. 5. Of the fathers-in-law, of the sons-in-law. 6. For the fathers-in-law, for the sons-in-law. 7. The boy, the field. 8. The boys, the fields. 9. The gift, the gifts. 10. With the gift, with the gifts. 11. The tyrant, the boy, the book, the precept. 12. Of the tyrant, of the boy, of the book, of the precept.

## SECOND DECLENSION — CONTINUED.

### RULE II. — Appositives.

363. An Appositive agrees with its Subject in CASE:[1]

*Cluilius rex mŏrĭtur, Cluilius the king dies.* Liv. *Urbes Carthāgo atque Nŭmantia, the cities Carthage and Numantia.* Cic.

### I. DIRECTIONS FOR PARSING.

In parsing a Noun, Adjective, or Pronoun,
1. Name the Part of Speech to which it belongs.
2. Decline[2] it.
3. Give its Gender, Number, Case, &c.
4. Give its Syntax,[3] and the Rule for it.

---

[1] A noun or pronoun used to explain or identify another noun or pronoun, denoting the same person or thing, is called an *appositive;* as, *Cluilius rex,* Cluilius the king. Here *rex,* the king, is the appositive, showing the rank or office of Cluilius, — *Cluilius the king.* The noun or pronoun to which the appositive is added — *Cluilius* in the example — is called the *subject* of the appositive.

[2] Adjectives in the Comparative or in the Superlative degree (160) should also be compared (162).

[3] By the *Syntax* of a word is meant the Grammatical construction of it. Thus we give the Syntax of *regīna,* under the Model, by stating that it is in apposition with its subject, *Artemisia.*

MODEL.

Artĕmīsiă rēgīnă, *Artemisia the queen.*

*Regina* is a noun (31) of the First Declension (42), as it has *ae* in the Genitive Singular (40); STEM, *regīn* (41). Singular: *regīna, regīnae, regīnae, regīnam, regīnā, regīnā.* Plural: *regīnae, regīnārum, regīnis, regīnas, regīnae, regīnis.* It is of the Feminine gender, as the names of females are feminine by 35, II. 1. It is in the Nominative Singular, in apposition with its subject *Artemisia*, with which it agrees in *case*, according to Rule II.: "An Appositive agrees with its Subject in CASE."

EXERCISE VII.

I. *Vocabulary.*

| | |
|---|---|
| Cāiŭs, ii, *m.* | *Caius*, a proper name. |
| Fīliă, ae, *f.* | *daughter.* |
| Hastă, ae, *f.* | *spear.* |
| Pīsistrătŭs, ī, *m.* | *Pisistratus*, Tyrant of Athens. |
| Rāmŭs, ī, *m.* | *branch.* |
| Rēgīnă, ae, *f.* | *queen.* |
| Tulliă, ae, *f.* | *Tullia*, a proper name. |
| Victōria, ae, *f.* | *Victoria*, Queen of England. |

II. *Translate into English.*

1. Ramus, hastă. 2. Rami, hastae. 3. Ramo, hastae. 4. Ramum, hastam. 5. Ramo, hastā. 6. Ramōrum, hastārum. 7. Ramis, hastis. 8. Ramos, hastas. 9. Tyranni, tyrannōrum. 10. Verbum, verba. 11. Verbo, verbis. 12. Templum, templa. 13. Templi, templōrum. 14. Pisistrătus tyrannus.[1] 15. Pisistrăti tyranni. 16. Pisistrăto tyranno. 17. Tulliă filiă. 18. Tulliae filiae. 19. Tulliam filiam.

II. *Translate into Latin.*

1. The tyrant, the crown. 2. The tyrants, the crowns.

---

[1] *Tyrannus* is an appositive, in the Nominative, in agreement with its subject, *Pisistrătus*, according to Rule II. 363.

3. Of the tyrant, of the crown. 4. Of the tyrants, of the crowns. 5. To the tyrant, to the crown. 6. To the tyrants, to the crowns. 7. The book, the books. 8. With the book, with the books. 9. Of Pisistratus, for Pisistratus. 10. Of the queen, for the queen. 11. Caius the slave.[1] 12. Of Caius the slave. 13. For Caius the slave. 14. Victoria the queen. 15. For Victoria the queen. 16. Of Victoria the queen.

## THIRD DECLENSION.

48. Nouns of the third declension end in

a, e, i, o, y, c, l, n, r, s, t, x.

I. MASCULINE ENDINGS:[2]

o, or, os, er, es *increasing in the genitive.*

II. FEMININE ENDINGS:

as, is, ys, x, es *not increasing in the genitive; s preceded by a consonant.*

III. NEUTER ENDINGS:

a, e, i, y, c, l, n, t, ar, ur, us.

49. Nouns of this declension may be divided into two classes:

I. Nouns which have a case-ending in the Nominative Singular. These all end in *e*, *s*, or *x*.

II. Nouns which have no case-ending in the Nominative Singular.

In Class II., the Nom. Sing. is either the same as the stem, or is formed from it by dropping or changing one or more letters of the stem: *consul*, Gen. consŭlis; stem, *consul*, a consul: *leo*, leōnis; stem, *leon* (Nom. drops n), lion: *carmen*, carmĭnis; stem, *carmĭn* (Nom. changes in to en), song.

---

[1] See Rule II. 363.

[2] That is, nouns with these endings are masculine.

**50. Class I. — With Nominative Ending.**

I. Nouns in **es, is, s** *impure*,[1] and **x**: — *with stem unchanged in Nominative.*

| Nubes, *f.* | Avis, *f.* | Urbs, *f.* | Rex, *m.* |
| cloud. | bird. | city. | king. |

SINGULAR.

| | | | |
|---|---|---|---|
| *N.* nūbĕs | ăvĭs | urbs | rex[2] |
| *G.* nubĭs | avĭs | urbĭs | rĕgĭs |
| *D.* nubī | avī | urbī | regī |
| *A.* nubĕm | avĕm | urbĕm | regĕm |
| *V.* nubĕs | avĭs | urbs | rex |
| *A.* nubĕ | avĕ | urbĕ | regĕ |

PLURAL.

| | | | |
|---|---|---|---|
| *N.* nubēs | avēs | urbēs | regēs |
| *G.* nubĭŭm | avĭŭm | urbĭŭm | regŭm |
| *D.* nubĭbŭs | avĭbŭs | urbĭbŭs | regĭbŭs |
| *A.* nubēs | avēs | urbēs | regēs |
| *V.* nubēs | avēs | urbēs | regēs |
| *A.* nubĭbŭs. | avĭbŭs. | urbĭbŭs. | regĭbŭs. |

II. Nouns in **es, is, s** *impure*, and **x**: — *with stem changed in Nominative.*

| Miles, *m.* | Lapis, *m.* | Ars, *f.* | Judex, *m.* and *f.* |
| soldier. | stone. | art. | judge. |

SINGULAR.

| | | | |
|---|---|---|---|
| *N.* mīlĕs | lăpĭs | ars | jūdex[2] |
| *G.* milĭtĭs | lapĭdĭs | artĭs | judĭcĭs |
| *D.* milĭtī | lapĭdī | artī | judĭcī |
| *A.* milĭtĕm | lapĭdĕm | artĕm | judĭcĕm |
| *V.* milĕs | lapĭs | ars | judex |
| *A.* milĭtĕ | lapĭdĕ | artĕ | judĭcĕ |

PLURAL.

| | | | |
|---|---|---|---|
| *N.* milĭtēs | lapĭdēs | artēs | judĭcēs |
| *G.* milĭtŭm | lapĭdŭm | artĭŭm | judĭcŭm |

---

[1] *Impure;* i.e., preceded by a consonant.

[2] X in rex = *gs;* *g* belonging to the stem, and *s* being the Nom. ending: but in judex, x = *cs;* *c* belonging to the stem, and *s* being the Nom. ending.

ETYMOLOGY. — THIRD DECLENSION.

| | | | |
|---|---|---|---|
| D. milit**ĭbŭs** | lapid**ĭbŭs** | art**ĭbŭs** | judic**ĭbŭs** |
| A. milītēs | lapĭdēs | artēs | judĭcēs |
| V. milītēs | lapĭdēs | artēs | judĭcēs |
| A. milit**ĭbŭs.** | lapid**ĭbŭs.** | art**ĭbŭs.** | judic**ĭbŭs.** |

III. Nouns in **as, os, us,** and **e**: — *those in* as, os, *and* us *with stem changed, those in* e *with stem unchanged.*

| Civĭtas, *f.* | Nepos, *m.* | Virtus, *f.* | Mare, *n.* |
|---|---|---|---|
| *state.* | *grandson.* | *virtue.* | *sea.* |

SINGULAR.

| N. civĭtās | nĕpōs | virtūs | mărĕ |
|---|---|---|---|
| G. civitātĭs | nepōtĭs | virtūtĭs | marĭs |
| D. civitātī | nepōtī | virtūtī | marī |
| A. civitātĕm | nepōtĕm | virtūtĕm | marĕ |
| V. civĭtās | nepōs | virtūs | marĕ |
| A. civitātĕ | nepōtĕ | virtūtĕ | marī [2] |

PLURAL.

| N. civĭtātēs | nepōtēs | virtūtēs | marĭă |
|---|---|---|---|
| G. civĭtāt**ŭm** [1] | nepōt**ŭm** | virtūt**ŭm** | marĭŭm |
| D. civitat**ĭbŭs** | nepot**ĭbŭs** | virtut**ĭbŭs** | mar**ĭbŭs** |
| A. civitātēs | nepōtēs | virtūtēs | marĭă |
| V. civitātēs | nepōtēs | virtūtēs | marĭă |
| A. civitat**ĭbŭs.** | nepot**ĭbŭs.** | virtut**ĭbŭs.** | mar**ĭbŭs.** |

**51. Class II. — Without Nominative Ending.**

I. Nouns in **l** and **r**: — *with stem unchanged in Nominative.*

| Sol, *m.* | Consul, *m.* | Passer, *m.* | Vultur, *m.* |
|---|---|---|---|
| *sun.* | *consul.* | *sparrow.* | *vulture.* |

SINGULAR.

| N. sōl | consŭl | passĕr | vultŭr |
|---|---|---|---|
| G. sōlĭs | consŭlĭs | passĕrĭs | vultŭrĭs |
| D. sōlī | consŭlī | passĕrī | vultŭrī |
| A. sōlĕm | consŭlĕm | passĕrĕm | vultŭrĕm |
| V. sōl | consŭl | passĕr | vultŭr |
| A. sōlĕ | consŭlĕ | passĕrĕ | vultŭrĕ |

PLURAL.

| N. sōlēs | consŭlēs | passĕrēs | vultŭrēs |
|---|---|---|---|
| G. | consŭl**ŭm** | passĕr**ŭm** | vultŭr**ŭm** |
| D. sōl**ĭbŭs** | consul**ĭbŭs** | passer**ĭbŭs** | vultur**ĭbŭs** |

---

[1] Sometimes *civitatiŭm.*  [2] Sometimes *mare* in poetry.

| A. sŏlēs | consŭlēs | passĕrēs | vultŭrēs |
| V. sŏlēs | consŭlēs | passĕrēs | vultŭrēs |
| A. sŏlĭbŭs. | consulĭbŭs. | passerĭbŭs. | vulturĭbŭs. |

II. Nouns in **o** and **r**: — *with stem changed in Nominative.*

| Leo, *m.* | Virgo, *f.* | Pater, *m.* | Pastor, *m.* |
| lion. | maiden. | father. | shepherd. |
| | SINGULAR. | | |
| N. leo | virgo | pătĕr | pastŏr |
| G. leōnĭs | virgĭnĭs | pătrĭs | pastōrĭs |
| D. leōnī | virgĭnī | patrī | pastōrī |
| A. leōnĕm | virgĭnĕm | patrĕm | pastōrĕm |
| V. leo | virgo | patĕr | pastŏr |
| A. leōnĕ | virgĭnĕ | patrĕ | pastōrĕ |
| | PLURAL. | | |
| N. leōnēs | virgĭnēs | patrēs | pastōrēs |
| G. leōnŭm | virgĭnŭm | patrŭm | pastōrŭm |
| D. leonĭbŭs | virgĭnĭbŭs | patrĭbŭs | pastorĭbŭs |
| A. leōnēs | virgĭnēs | patrēs | pastōrēs |
| V. leōnēs | virgĭnēs | patrēs | pastōrēs |
| A. leonĭbŭs. | virginĭbŭs. | patrĭbŭs. | pastorĭbŭs. |

III. Nouns in **en, us,** and **ut**: — *with stem changed in Nominative.*

| Carmen, *n.* | Opus, *n.* | Corpus, *n.* | Capŭt, *n.* |
| song. | work. | body. | head. |
| | SINGULAR. | | |
| N. carmĕn | ŏpŭs | corpŭs | căpŭt |
| G. carmĭnĭs | opĕrĭs | corpŏrĭs | capĭtĭs |
| D. carmĭnī | opĕrī | corpŏrī | capĭtī |
| A. carmĕn | opŭs | corpŭs | capŭt |
| V. carmĕn | opŭs | corpŭs | capŭt |
| A. carmĭnĕ | opĕrĕ | corpŏrĕ | capĭtĕ |
| | PLURAL. | | |
| N. carmĭnă | opĕră | corpŏră | capĭtă |
| G. carmĭnŭm | opĕrŭm | corpŏrŭm | capĭtŭm |
| D. carminĭbŭs | operĭbŭs | corporĭbŭs | capitĭbŭs |
| A. carmĭnă | opĕră | corpŏră | capĭtă |
| V. carmĭnă | opĕră | corpŏră | capĭtă |
| A. carminĭbŭs. | operĭbŭs. | corporĭbŭs. | capitĭbŭs. |

**52. Case-Endings.** — From an inspection of the paradigms, it will be seen,

1. That the nouns belonging to Class II. differ from those of Class I. only in taking no case-ending in the Nominative and Vocative Singular.

2. That all nouns of both classes are declined with the following

*Case-Endings.*

SINGULAR.

|  | Masc. and Fem. | Neuter. |
|---|---|---|
| *Nom.* | s[1] (es, is) ——[2] | ĕ ——[2] |
| *Gen.* | ĭs | ĭs |
| *Dat.* | ī | ī |
| *Acc.* | ĕm (ĭm)[3] | like Nom. |
| *Voc.* | like Nom. | " " |
| *Abl.* | ĕ, ī | ĕ, ī |

PLURAL.

|  | Masc. and Fem. | Neuter. |
|---|---|---|
| *Nom.* | ēs | ă, iă |
| *Gen.* | ŭm, iŭm | ŭm, iŭm |
| *Dat.* | ĭbŭs | ĭbŭs |
| *Acc.* | ēs | ă, iă |
| *Voc.* | ēs | ă, iă |
| *Abl.* | ĭbŭs. | ĭbŭs. |

**53. Declension.** — To apply these endings in declension, we must know, besides the Nominative Singular,

1. *The Gender*, as that shows which set of endings must be used.

2. *The Genitive Singular* (or some oblique case), as that contains the *stem* (41) to which these endings must be added.

---

[1] In nouns in *x* (= cs or gs), *s* is the case-ending, and the *c* or *g* belongs to the stem.

[2] The dash here implies that the case-ending is sometimes wanting, as in all nouns of Class II.

[3] The enclosed endings are less common than the others.

## 54. Examples for Practice:

### Class I.

| | | | | | |
|---|---|---|---|---|---|
| Rūpes, | *Gen.* rupis, f. | *rock;* | hospes, | *Gen.* hospĭtis, m. | *guest.* |
| vestis, | vestis, f. | *garment;* | cuspis, | cuspĭdis, f. | *spear.* |
| trabs, | trăbis, f. | *beam;* | mons, | montis, m. | *mountain.* |
| lex, | lēgis, f. | *law;* | ăpex, | apĭcis, m. | *summit.* |
| libertas, | libertātis, f. | *liberty;* | sălus, | salūtis, f. | *safety.* |
| sedīle, | sedĭlis, n. | *seat;* | | | |

### Class II.

| | | | | | |
|---|---|---|---|---|---|
| Exsul, | *Gen.* exsŭlis, m. and f. | *exile;* | dŏlor, | *Gen.* dolōris, m. | *pain.* |
| actio, | actiōnis, f. | *action;* | īmāgo, | imagĭnis, f. | *image.* |
| anser, | ansĕris, m. | *goose;* | frăter, | fratris, m. | *brother.* |
| nōmen, | nomĭnis, n. | *name;* | tempus, | tempŏris, n. | *time.* |

## RULE XVI. — Genitive.

395. Any Noun, not an Appositive, qualifying the meaning of another noun, is put in the Genitive:[1]

Cătōnis ōrātiōnes, *Cato's orations.* Cic. Castra hostium, *the camp of the enemy.* Liv. Mors Hămilcăris, *the death of Hamilcar.* Liv.

#### MODEL FOR PARSING.

Cătōnis ōrātiōnēs, *Cato's orations.*

*Catōnis* is a proper noun, as it is the name of a person (31, 1). It is of the Third Declension, as it has *is* in the Genitive Singular (40); of Class II., as it has no Nominative Ending (49, II. and 51, II.): STEM, *Catōn* (41); Nom. *Cato* (*n* dropped, 49, II.). Singu-

---

[1] The Appositive (363, p. 15) and this qualifying Genitive resemble each other in the fact that they both qualify the meaning of another noun: *Cluilius rex,* Cluilius the king; *Catōnis oratiōnes,* Cato's orations, *or* the orations of Cato. Here the Appositive *rex* qualifies, or limits, the meaning of Cluilius by showing *what* Cluilius is meant, — *Cluilius the king.* In a similar manner, the Genitive *Catōnis* qualifies, or limits, the meaning of *oratiōnes* by showing *what* orations are meant, — *the orations of Cato.* Yet the Appositive and the Genitive are readily distinguished by the fact that the former qualifies a noun denoting the *same* person or

lar:[1] *Cato, Catōnis, Catōni, Catōnem, Cato, Catōne.* It is of the Masculine gender, as the names of males are masculine by 35, I. 1. It is in the Genitive Singular, depending upon *orātiōnes*, according to Rule XVI.: "Any noun, not an Appositive, qualifying the meaning of another noun, is put in the Genitive."

## THIRD DECLENSION — CONTINUED. — CLASS I.[2]

### EXERCISE VIII.

#### I. *Vocabulary.*

| | |
|---|---|
| Cĭvĭs, cīvĭs, *m.* and *f.* | *citizen.* |
| Lex, lēgĭs, *f.* | *law.* |
| Mors, mortĭs, *f.* | *death.* |
| Pax, pācĭs, *f.* | *peace.* |

#### II. *Translate into English.*

1. Nubis, nubium. 2. Nubem, nubes. 3. Avis, aves. 4. Avi, avĭbus. 5. Urbs, urbes. 6. Urbi, urbĭbus. 7. Rex, reges. 8. Regis, regum. 9. Nubēs, mīlĕs. 10. Nubis, mīlĭtis. 11. Nubem, mīlĭtem. 12. Rex, judex. 13. Regis, judĭcis. 14. Reges, judĭces. 15. Cīvĭtas, cīvĭtātes. 16. Virtus, virtūtes. 17. Mors regis.[3] 18. Morte regis. 19. Mortes regum. 20. Virtus judĭcis. 21. Pacis gloria.

#### III. *Translate into Latin.*

1. The citizen, to the citizen, of the citizen, of citizens, for citizens. 2. A cloud, clouds, of a cloud, of clouds, with a cloud, with clouds. 3. A king, a law. 4. Kings, laws.

---

thing as itself, while the Genitive qualifies a noun denoting a *different* person or thing. Thus, in the examples above, *Cluilius* and the Appositive *rex* denote the *same* person; while *orationes* and the Genitive *Catōnis* denote entirely *different* objects.

[1] As *Cato* is the name of a person, the Plural is seldom used.

[2] This exercise furnishes practice in the declension of nouns belonging to Class I. of the Third Declension. See 50.

[3] *Regis* is in the Genitive, and qualifies the meaning of *mors*, according to Rule XVI. 395.

5. Of the king, of the law.  6. Of the kings, of the laws.
7. To the king, to the law.  8. To the kings, to the laws.
9. The law of the state.[1]  10. The laws of the state.

## THIRD DECLENSION — Continued. — Class II.
### Prepositions.

**RULE XXXII.** — Cases with Prepositions.

432. The Accusative and Ablative may be used with Prepositions.[2]

Ad ămīcum scripsi, *I have written to a friend.* Cic. In cūriam, *into the senate-house.* Liv. In Itălĭā,[3] *in Italy.* Nep. Pro castris, *before the camp.*

### MODEL FOR PARSING.

Ad ămīcŭm, *To a friend.*

*Amīcum* is a noun (31) of the Second Declension (45), as it has *i* in the Genitive Singular (40); STEM, *amīc* (41). Singular: *amīcus, amīci, amīco, amīcum, amīce, amīco.* Plural: *amīci, amīcōrum, amīcis, amīcos, amīci, amīcis.* It is of the Masculine gender by 45, is in the Accusative Singular, and is used with the preposition *ad*, according to Rule XXXII.: "The Accusative and Ablative may be used with Prepositions." The Accusative is used with *ad*.

---

[1] The Latin word for *of the state* will be in the Genitive, according to Rule XVI. 395.

[2] The Preposition is the part of speech which shows the relations of objects to each other: *in Italia esse*, to be in Italy; *ante me*, before me. Here *in* and *ante* are prepositions. In the Vocabularies, each preposition, as it occurs, will be marked as such; and the case which may be used with it will be specified. It has not been thought advisable at this early stage of the course to burden the memory of the learner with a list of prepositions and their cases.

[3] Here the Ablative *Italia* is used with *in*; though, in the second example, the Accusative *curiam* is used with the same preposition. The rule is, that the Latin preposition *in* is used with the *Accusative* when it means *into*, and with the Ablative when it means *in*.

## Exercise IX.

### I. Vocabulary.

| | |
|---|---|
| Ad, *prep. with acc.* | *to, towards.* |
| Cĭcĕrŏ, Cĭcĕrōnĭs, *m.* | *Cicero, the Roman orator.* |
| Consŭl, consŭlĭs, *m.* | *consul.*[1] |
| Contrā, *prep. with acc.* | *against, contrary to.* |
| Exsŭl, exsŭlĭs, *m.* and *f.* | *exile.* |
| Frāter, frātrĭs, *m.* | *brother.* |
| Nōmĕn, nōmĭnĭs, *n.* | *name.* |
| Orātĭŏ, ōrātĭōnĭs, *f.* | *oration, speech.* |
| Orātŏr, ōrātōrĭs, *m.* | *orator.* |
| Victŏr, victōrĭs, *m.* | *victor, conqueror.* |

### II. Translate into English.

1. Leo, leōnis, leōnes. 2. Virgo, virgĭnis, virgĭnes. 3. Solis, solem, soles. 4. Consŭlis, consŭlem, consŭles. 5. Solĭbus, consulĭbus. 6. Passĕris, vultŭris. 7. Passĕrum, vultŭrum. 8. Patri, pastōri. 9. Patres, pastōres. 10. Carmen, carmĭna. 11. Caput, capĭta. 12. Opĕris, corpŏris. 13. Cicerōnis[2] oratio. 14. Cicerōnis oratiōnes. 15. Oratiōne consŭlis. 16. Ad gloriam.[3] 17. Contra regem.

### III. Translate into Latin.

1. The exile, the exiles. 2. For the exile, for the exiles. 3. Of an exile, of the exiles. 4. The shepherd, the orator. 5. Of shepherds, of orators. 6. Shepherds, orators. 7. Of a shepherd, of an orator. 8. A song, a name. 9. Songs,

---

[1] The *consuls* were joint presidents of the Roman commonwealth. They were elected annually, and were two in number.

[2] See Rule XVI. 395, and Model.

[3] The Accusative *gloriam* is here used with the preposition *ad*, according to Rule XXXII. 432.

names. 10. Of songs, of names. 11. Father, brother. 12. To¹ the father, to the brother. 13. Contrary to the law.² 14. Contrary to the laws of the state.

## FOURTH DECLENSION.

**116.** Nouns of the fourth declension end in

**us,** — *masculine;* **u,** — *neuter.*

They are declined as follows:

Fructus, *fruit.*     Cornu, *horn.*     Case-Endings.

**SINGULAR.**

| | | | |
|---|---|---|---|
| N. fructŭs | cornū | ŭs | ū |
| G. fructūs | cornūs | ūs | ūs |
| D. fructuī | cornū | uī | ū |
| A. fructŭm | cornū | ŭm | ū |
| V. fructŭs | cornū | ŭs | ū |
| A. fructū | cornū | ū | ū |

**PLURAL.**

| | | | |
|---|---|---|---|
| N. fructūs | cornuă | ūs | uă |
| G. fructuŭm | cornuŭm | uŭm | uŭm |
| D. fructĭbŭs | cornĭbŭs | ĭbŭs (ŭbŭs) | ĭbŭs (ŭbŭs) |
| A. fructūs | cornuă | ūs | uă |
| V. fructūs | cornuă | ūs | uă |
| A. fructĭbŭs. | cornĭbŭs. | ĭbŭs (ŭbŭs). | ĭbŭs (ŭbŭs). |

1. **Case-Endings.**—Nouns of this declension are declined with the case-endings placed on the right.

2. **Examples for Practice.**—*Cantus* song; *currus,* chariot; *cursus,* course; *versus,* verse; *gĕnu,* knee.

---

¹ *To* should still be regarded as a sign of the Dative, though it may sometimes be rendered by the preposition *ad.*

² See Rule XXXII. 432. The words *contrary to* are to be rendered by a single Latin preposition.

ETYMOLOGY. — FOURTH DECLENSION.

## Exercise X.

### I. *Vocabulary.*

| | |
|---|---|
| Adventŭs, ūs, *m.* | *arrival, approach.* |
| Antĕ, *prep. with acc.* | *before.* |
| Caesăr, Caesărĭs, *m.* | *Caesar,* a Roman surname. |
| Cantŭs, ūs, *m.* | *singing, song.* |
| Conspectŭs, ūs, *m.* | *sight, presence.* |
| Exercĭtŭs, ūs, *m.* | *army.* |
| Hostĭs, hostĭs, *m.* and *f.* | *enemy.* |
| Impĕtŭs, ūs, *m.* | *attack.* |
| In, *prep.* | *into* with acc., *in* with abl. |
| Luscĭnĭă, ae, *f.* | *nightingale.* |
| Occāsŭs, ūs, *m.* | *the setting,* as of the sun. |
| Post, *prep. with acc.* | *after.* |
| Ver, vērĭs, *n.* | *spring.* |

### II. *Translate into English.*

1. Fructus, cantus.  2. Fructĭbus, cantĭbus.  3. Cantus lusciniae.[1]  4. Cantu lusciniae.  5. Cantĭbus luscĭniārum.  6. Adventus veris.  7. Post adventum[2] veris.[1]  8. Solis occāsus.  9. Post solis occāsum.  10. Caesăris adventu.  11. Ante adventum Caesăris.  12. Impĕtus hostium.  13. Impĕtu hostium.  14. In conspectu exercĭtus.

### III. *Translate into Latin.*

1. The army, the armies.  2. For the army, for the armies.  3. Of the army, of the armies.  4. The arrival of the army.  5. Before the arrival of the army.  6. After[3]

---

[1] Genitive, according to Rule XVI. See p. 22.

[2] Used with *post,* according to Rule XXXII. See p. 24.

[3] See Rule XXXII. 432, p. 24. The pupil will remember that the English prepositions, *to, for, with, from, by,* are generally rendered into Latin by merely putting the noun in the proper case, i.e. in the Dative for *to* or *for,* and in the Ablative for *with, from, by.* Other English prepositions, *before, after, behind, between,* etc., are rendered into Latin by corresponding Latin prepositions.

the arrival of the consul. 7. The singing of the nightingale. 8. After the setting of the sun. 9. Before the attack of the enemy. 10. After the attack of the enemy.

## FIFTH DECLENSION.

**119.** Nouns of the fifth declension end in **es**, — *feminine*, and are declined as follows:

Dies, *day*.[1]   Res, *thing*.   Case-Endings.

|  | | |
|---|---|---|
| *SINGULAR.* | | |
| N. diēs | rēs | ēs |
| G. diēī | rěī | ēī |
| D. diēī | rěī | ēī |
| A. diěm | rěm | ěm |
| V. diēs | rēs | ēs |
| A. diē | rē | ē |
| *PLURAL.* | | |
| N. diēs | rēs | ēs |
| G. diērŭm | rērŭm | ērŭm |
| D. diēbŭs | rēbŭs | ēbŭs |
| A. diēs | rēs | ēs |
| V. diēs | rēs | ēs |
| A. diēbŭs. | rēbŭs. | ēbŭs. |

**1. Case-Endings.** — Nouns of this declension are declined with the case-endings placed on the right.

*E* in *ei* is generally short when preceded by a consonant, otherwise long.

**2. Examples for Practice.**[2] — *Acies*, battle-array; *effigies*, effigy; *facies*, face; *series*, series; *species*, form; *spes*, hope.

---

[1] *Dies*, day, is an exception in Gender, as it is generally *masculine*, though sometimes *feminine* in the singular.

[2] Nouns of this declension, except *dies* and *res*, want, in the Plural, the Genitive, Dative, and Ablative. These cases must, therefore, be omitted in declining these examples.

# COMPARATIVE VIEW OF THE FIVE DECLENSIONS.

**121. Case-Endings of Latin nouns.**[1]

### SINGULAR.

| | Dec. I. Fem. | Dec II. Masc., | Neut. | Dec. III. M. & F. | Neut. | Dec. IV. Masc. | Neut. | D. V. Fem. |
|---|---|---|---|---|---|---|---|---|
| N. | ă | ŭs —[2] | ŭm | s (es, is)[3] | — ĕ — | ŭs | ū | ēs |
| G. | ae | ī | ī | ĭs | ĭs | ūs | ūs | ēī |
| D. | ae | ō | ō | ī | ī | uī | ū | ēī |
| A. | ăm | ŭm | ŭm | ĕm (ĭm) | like nom. | ŭm | ū | ĕm |
| V. | ă | ĕ — | ŭm | like nom. | like nom. | ŭs | ū | ēs |
| A. | ā | ō | ō | ĕ (ī) | ĕ (ī) | ū | ū | ē |

### PLURAL.

| | | | | | | | | |
|---|---|---|---|---|---|---|---|---|
| N. | ae | ī | ă | ēs | ă (iă) | ūs | uă | ēs |
| G. | ārŭm | ōrŭm | ōrŭm | ŭm (iŭm) | ŭm (iŭm) | uŭm | uŭm | ērŭm |
| D. | īs | īs | īs | ĭbŭs | ĭbŭs | ĭbŭs (ŭbŭs) | ĭbŭs (ŭbŭs) | ēbŭs |
| A. | ās | ōs | ă | ēs | ă (iă) | ūs | uă | ēs |
| V. | ae | ī | ă | ēs | ă (iă) | ūs | uă | ēs |
| A. | īs | īs | īs | ĭbŭs | ĭbŭs | ĭbŭs (ŭbŭs) | ĭbŭs (ŭbŭs) | ēbŭs |

## EXERCISE XI.

### I. *Vocabulary.*

| | |
|---|---|
| Acĭēs, ăcĭēī, *f.* | *battle-array, army.* |
| Amīcŭs, ī, *m.* | *friend.* |
| Cĭbŭs, ī, *m.* | *food.* |
| Dē, *prep. with abl.* | *concerning.* |
| Dĭēs, dĭēī, *m.* and *f.* | *day.* |
| Făcĭēs, făcĭēī, *f.* | *face, appearance.* |
| Nŭmĕrŭs, ī, *m.* | *number, quantity.* |
| Rēs, rĕī, *f.* | *thing, affair.* |
| Spĕcĭēs, spĕcĭēī, *f.* | *appearance.* |
| Spēs, spĕī, *f.* | *hope.* |
| Victōrĭă, ae, *f.* | *victory.* |

---

[1] This table presents the endings of all nouns in the Latin language, except a few derived from the Greek.

[2] The dash denotes that the case-ending is sometimes wanting: *er* and *ir* in Dec. II., it will be remembered, are not case-endings, but parts of the stem (45, 1).

[3] The enclosed endings are less common than the others.

II. *Translate into English.*

1. Diēi, diērum, diēbus. 2. Aciēi, aciem, acie. 3. Diem, speciem. 4. Die, specie. 5. Res, spes. 6. Rei, spei. 7. Victoriae spes. 8. Victoriae spe. 9. Diēi horae. 10. Numĕrus diērum. 11. Gloria, cibus, nubes, cantus, facies. 12. Gloriae, cibi, nubis, cantus, faciēi. 13. Gloriam, cibum, nubem, cantum, faciem.

III. *Translate into Latin.*

1. A day, days. 2. Of the day, of the days. 3. For the day, for the days. 4. The thing, the things. 5. With the thing, with the things. 6. Concerning the thing, concerning the things. 7. Of the thing, of the things. 8. Concerning the battle-array. 9. Wisdom, friend, citizen, fruit, hope. 10. For wisdom, for a citizen, for hope.

---

## CHAPTER II.

### ADJECTIVES.

146. The adjective is that part of speech which is used to qualify nouns: *bŏnus*, good; *magnus*, great.

The form of the adjective in Latin depends in part upon the gender of the noun which it qualifies; *bonus puer*, a good boy; *bona puella*, a good girl; *bonum tectum*, a good house. Thus *bonus* is the form of the adjective when used with masculine nouns, *bona* with feminine, and *bonum* with neuter.

147. Some adjectives are partly of the first declension and partly of the second, while all the rest are entirely of the third declension.

I. FIRST AND SECOND DECLENSIONS.

148. Adjectives of this class have in the nominative singular the endings:

## ETYMOLOGY. — ADJECTIVES.

Masc., Dec. II.   Fem., Dec. I.   Neut., Dec. II.
us —[1],           a,              um.

They are declined as follows:

### Bŏnus, *good.*

#### SINGULAR.

|      | Masc.  | Fem.   | Neut.  |
|------|--------|--------|--------|
| Nom. | bŏnŭs  | bŏnă   | bŏnŭm  |
| Gen. | bonī   | bonae  | bonī   |
| Dat. | bonō   | bonae  | bonō   |
| Acc. | bonŭm  | bonăm  | bonŭm  |
| Voc. | bonĕ   | bonă   | bonŭm  |
| Abl. | bonō   | bonā   | bonō ; |

#### PLURAL.

|      | Masc.    | Fem.     | Neut.    |
|------|----------|----------|----------|
| Nom. | bonī     | bonae    | bonă     |
| Gen. | bonōrŭm  | bonārŭm  | bonōrŭm  |
| Dat. | bonīs    | bonīs    | bonīs    |
| Acc. | bonōs    | bonās    | bonă     |
| Voc. | bonī     | bonae    | bonă     |
| Abl. | bonīs    | bonīs    | bonīs.   |

### Līber, *free.*

#### SINGULAR.

|      | Masc.    | Fem.     | Neut.    |
|------|----------|----------|----------|
| Nom. | lībĕr    | lībĕră   | lībĕrŭm  |
| Gen. | libĕrī   | libĕrae  | libĕrī   |
| Dat. | libĕrō   | libĕrae  | libĕrō   |
| Acc. | libĕrŭm  | libĕrăm  | libĕrŭm  |
| Voc. | libĕr    | libĕră   | libĕrŭm  |
| Abl. | libĕrō   | libĕrā   | libĕrō ; |

#### PLURAL

|      | Masc.     | Fem.      | Neut.     |
|------|-----------|-----------|-----------|
| Nom. | libĕrī    | libĕrae   | libĕră    |
| Gen. | liberōrŭm | liberārŭm | liberōrŭm |
| Dat. | libĕrīs   | libĕrīs   | libĕrīs   |
| Acc. | libĕrōs   | libĕrās   | libĕră    |
| Voc. | libĕrī    | libĕrae   | libĕră    |
| Abl. | libĕrīs   | libĕrīs   | libĕrīs.  |

---

[1] The dash indicates that the ending is sometimes wanting. See 45, 1.

## Aeger, *sick*.

### SINGULAR.

|       | Masc.   | Fem.    | Neut.   |
|-------|---------|---------|---------|
| Nom.  | aegĕr   | aegră   | aegrŭm  |
| Gen.  | aegrī   | aegrae  | aegrī   |
| Dat.  | aegrō   | aegrae  | aegrō   |
| Acc.  | aegrŭm  | aegrăm  | aegrŭm  |
| Voc.  | aeger   | aegră   | aegrŭm  |
| Abl.  | aegrō   | aegrā   | aegrō ; |

### PLURAL.

|       | Masc.    | Fem.     | Neut.    |
|-------|----------|----------|----------|
| Nom.  | aegrī    | aegrae   | aegră    |
| Gen.  | aegrōrŭm | aegrārŭm | aegrōrŭm |
| Dat.  | aegrīs   | aegrīs   | aegrīs   |
| Acc.  | aegrōs   | aegrās   | aegră    |
| Voc.  | aegrī    | aegrae   | aegră    |
| Abl.  | aegrīs   | aegrīs   | aegrīs.  |

1. *Bonus* is declined in the Masc. like *servus* of Dec. II. (45), in the Fem. like *mensa* of Dec. I. (42), and in the Neut. like *templum* of Dec. II. (45).

2. *Liber* differs in declension from *bonus* only in dropping *us* and *e* in the Nom. and Voc. (45, 3, 1). *Aeger* differs from *liber* only in dropping *e* before *r* (45, 3, 2).

3. Most adjectives in *er* are declined like *aeger*.

### RULE XXXIII.—Agreement of Adjectives.

438. An Adjective agrees with its Noun in GENDER, NUMBER, and CASE:

Fortūna caeca est, *Fortune is blind*.[1] Cic. Vērae ămīcĭtiae, *true friendships*. Cic. Măgister optĭmus, *the best teacher*. Cic.

---

[1] Here the adjective *caeca* is in the feminine gender, in the singular number, and in the nominative case, to agree with *fortūna*. It is declined like BONUS: *caecus, caeca, caecum*.

## MODEL FOR PARSING.

Vērae ămīcĭtiae, *True friendships.*

*Verae* is an adjective (146) of the First and Second Declensions (147): STEM, *ver* (41, 148, 1). Singular: N. *verus, veră, verum;* G. *veri, verae, veri;* D. *vero, verae, vero;* A. *verum, veram, verum;* V. *vere, verā, verum;* A. *vero, verā, vero.* Plural: N. *veri, verae, vera;* G. *verōrum, verārum, verōrum;* D. *veris, veris, veris;* A. *veros, veras, vera;* V. *veri, verae, vera;* A. *veris, veris, veris.* It is in the Nominative Plural Feminine, and agrees with its noun *amicitiae,* according to Rule XXXIII: "An Adjective agrees with its Noun in GENDER, NUMBER, and CASE."

## EXERCISE XII.

### I. *Vocabulary.*

| | |
|---|---|
| Annŭlŭs, ī, *m.* | *ring.* |
| Aureŭs, ă, ŭm,[1] | *golden.* |
| Beātŭs, ă, ŭm, | *happy, blessed.* |
| Bŏnŭs, ă, ŭm, | *good.* |
| Egrĕgĭŭs, ă, ŭm, | *distinguished.* |
| Fīdŭs, ă, ŭm, | *faithful.* |
| Grātŭs, ă, ŭm, | *acceptable, pleasing.* |
| Magnŭs, ă, ŭm, | *great.* |
| Multŭs, ă, ŭm, | *much, many.* |
| Puellă, ae, *f.* | *girl.* |
| Pulchĕr, pulchră, pulchrŭm, | *beautiful.* |
| Rēgīnă, ae, *f.* | *queen.* |
| Rēgnŭm, ī, *n.* | *kingdom.* |
| Vērŭs, ă, ŭm, | *true.* |
| Vītă, ae, *f.* | *life.* |

---

[1] The endings *a* and *um* belong respectively to the feminine and to the neuter. Thus *aureus, aurea, aureum,* like *bonus,* 148.

II. *Translate into English.*

1. Amīcus fidus.¹ 2. Amīci fidi. 3. Amīco fido. 4. Amīcum fidum. 5. Amīce fide. 6. Amicōrum fidōrum. 7. Amīcis fidis. 8. Amīcos fidos. 9. Corōnă aureă. 10. Corōnae aureae. 11. Corōnam auream. 12. Corōnā aureā. 13. Coronārum aureārum. 14. Corōnis aureis. 15. Corōnas aureas. 16. Donum gratum. 17. Doni grati. 18. Dono grato. 19. Dona grata. 20. Donōrum gratōrum. 21. Donis gratis. 22. Ager pulcher. 23. Puellă pulchră. 24. Donum pulchrum. 25. Agri pulchri. 26. Puellae pulchrae. 27. Dona pulchra. 28. Beătă vită. 29. Aureus annŭlus. 30. Aurei annŭli. 31. Magnă gloriă. 32. Egregiă victoriă.

III. *Translate into Latin.*

1. A true² friend. 2. The true² friends. 3. For a true friend. 4. For true friends. 5. Of the true friend. 6. Of true friends. 7. True glory. 8. With true glory. 9. Of true glory. 10. An acceptable word. 11. Acceptable words. 12. With acceptable words. 13. Of acceptable words. 14. A beautiful book. 15. The beautiful books. 16. With a beautiful book. 17. Of beautiful books. 18. The beautiful queen. 19. The crown of the beautiful queen. 20. The beautiful crown of the queen. 21. A good king, a good queen, a good kingdom. 22. The brothers of the good king.

---

¹ In Latin the adjective generally follows its noun, as in this example; though sometimes it precedes it, as in English. When emphatic, the adjective is placed before its noun; as, *Verae amicitiae,* true friendships. *Fidus* agrees with *amīcus,* according to Rule XXXIII.

² Be sure and put the adjective in the right form to agree with its noun, according to Rule XXXIII.

## II. ADJECTIVES OF THE THIRD DECLENSION.

**150.** Adjectives of the third declension may be divided into three classes:

I. Those which have in the nominative singular three different forms, — one for each gender.

II. Those which have two forms, — the masculine and feminine being the same.

III. Those which have but one form, — the same for all genders.

**151. I. Adjectives of Three Endings** of this declension have in the nominative singular:

| Masc. | Fem. | Neut. |
|---|---|---|
| **er,** | **is,** | **e.** |

They are declined as follows:

### Acer, *sharp*.

SINGULAR.

| | Masc. | Fem. | Neut. |
|---|---|---|---|
| N. | ăcĕr | ācrĭs | ācrĕ |
| G. | acrĭs | acrĭs | acrĭs |
| D. | acrī | acrī | acrī |
| A. | acrĕm | acrĕm | acrĕ |
| V. | acĕr | acrĭs | acrĕ |
| A. | acrī | acrī | acrī ; |

PLURAL.

| | Masc. | Fem. | Neut. |
|---|---|---|---|
| N. | acrēs | acrēs | acriă |
| G. | acriŭm | acriŭm | acriŭm |
| D. | acrĭbŭs | acrĭbŭs | acrĭbŭs |
| A. | acrēs | acrēs | acriă |
| V. | acrēs | acrēs | acriă |
| A. | acrĭbŭs | acrĭbŭs | acrĭbŭs. |

**152. II. Adjectives of Two Endings** have in the nominative singular:

|  | M. and F. | Neut. |  |
|---|---|---|---|
| 1. | is | e, | for positives. |
| 2. | ior (or) | ius (us), | for comparatives. |

They are declined as follows:

Tristis, *sad*.          Tristior, *more sad*.[1]

### SINGULAR.

| M. and F. | Neut. | M. and F. | Neut. |
|---|---|---|---|
| N. tristĭs | tristĕ | N. tristiŏr | tristiŭs |
| G. tristĭs | tristĭs | G. tristiōrĭs | tristiōrĭs |
| D. tristī | tristī | D. tristiōrī | tristiōrī |
| A. tristĕm | tristĕ | A. tristiōrĕm | tristiŭs |
| V. tristĭs | tristĕ | V. tristiŏr | tristiŭs |
| A. tristī | tristī ; | A. tristiōrĕ (ī) | tristiōrĕ (ī) ; |

### PLURAL.

| M. and F. | Neut. | M. and F. | Neut. |
|---|---|---|---|
| N. tristēs | tristĭă | N. tristiōrēs | tristiōră |
| G. tristĭŭm | tristĭŭm | G. tristiōrŭm | tristiōrŭm |
| D. tristĭbŭs | tristĭbŭs | D. tristiōrĭbŭs | tristiōrĭbŭs |
| A. tristēs | tristĭă | A. tristiōrēs | tristiōră |
| V. tristēs | tristĭă | V. tristiōrēs | tristiōră |
| A. tristĭbŭs | tristĭbŭs. | A. tristiōrĭbŭs | tristiōrĭbŭs. |

**153. III. Adjectives of One Ending.**—All other adjectives have but one form in the nominative singular for all genders. They generally end in *s* or *x*, sometimes in *l* or *r*, and are declined in the main like nouns of the same endings. The following are examples:

Felix, *happy*.          Prudens, *prudent*.

### SINGULAR.

| M. and F. | Neut. | M. and F. | Neut. |
|---|---|---|---|
| N. felix | felix | N. prudens | prudens |
| G. felicĭs | felicĭs | G. prudentĭs | prudentĭs |
| D. felicī | felicī | D. prudentī | prudentī |
| A. felicĕm | felix | A. prudentĕm | prudens |
| V. felix | felix | V. prudens | prudens |
| A. felicĕ (ī) | felicĕ (ī) ; | A. prudentĕ (ī) | prudentĕ (ī) ; |

---

[1] Comparative. See 160.

## ETYMOLOGY. — ADJECTIVES.

PLURAL.

| | | | |
|---|---|---|---|
| N. felicēs | felicia | N. prudentēs | prudentia |
| G. feliciŭm | feliciŭm | G. prudentium | prudentium |
| D. felicibŭs | felicibŭs | D. prudentibus | prudentibus |
| A. felicēs | felicia | A. prudentēs | prudentia |
| V. felicēs | felicia | V. prudentēs | prudentia |
| A. felicibŭs | felicibŭs. | A. prudentibus | prudentibus. |

### Exercise XIII.

#### I. *Vocabulary.*

| | |
|---|---|
| Acĕr, ācris, ācrĕ, | *sharp, severe.* |
| Anĭmăl, ănĭmālis, *n.* | *animal.* |
| Brĕvĭs, ĕ, | *short, brief.* |
| Crūdēlĭs, ĕ, | *cruel.* |
| Dŏlŏr, dŏlōrĭs, *m.* | *pain, grief.* |
| Dux, dŭcĭs, *m.* | *leader.* |
| Fertīlĭs, ĕ, | *fertile.* |
| Fortĭs, ĕ, | *brave.* |
| Năvālĭs, ĕ, | *naval.* |
| Omnĭs, ĕ, | *every, all, whole.* |
| Pugnă, ae, *f.* | *battle.* |
| Săpiens, săpientĭs, | *wise.* |
| Singŭlārĭs, ĕ, | *singular, remarkable.* |
| Utīlĭs, ĕ, | *useful.* |

#### II. *Translate into English.*

1. Dolor acer. 2. Dolōres acres. 3. Lex acris. 4. Legĭbus acrĭbus. 5. Hostis crudēlis. 6. Hostem crudēlem. 7. Miles fortis. 8. Virtus milĭtis[1] fortis. 9. Virtūte milĭtum[1] fortium. 10. Ager fertĭlis. 11. In agro fertĭli. 12. Agros fertĭles. 13. In agris fertilĭbus. 14. Post vitam brevem. 15. Pugnae navāles. 16. Post pugnas navāles. 17. Singulāris virtus. 18. Singulāri virtūte. 19. Omne anĭmal. 20. Omnia animalia.

---

[1] Genitive, according to Rule XVI.

### III. *Translate into Latin.*

1. A useful citizen. 2. Of useful citizens. 3. For a useful citizen. 4. For useful citizens. 5. Of a useful citizen. 6. The wise judge. 7. Wise judges. 8. For the wise judge. 9. For wise judges. 10. Brave soldiers. 11. For brave soldiers. 12. A brave soldier. 13. Of the brave soldier. 14. The brave leader. 15. Brave leaders. 16. The word of the brave leader. 17. By the words of the brave leader.

### COMPARISON OF ADJECTIVES.

**160.** Adjectives have three forms to denote different degrees of quality. They are usually called the Positive, the Comparative, and the Superlative degree: *altus, altior, altissĭmus*,[1] high, higher, highest.

Comparatives and superlatives are sometimes best rendered into English by *too* and *very*, instead of *more* and *most: doctus*, learned; *doctior*, more learned, *or* too learned; *doctissĭmus*, most learned, *or* very learned.

**161.** The Latin, like the English, has two modes of comparison:

I. *Terminational Comparison* — by endings.
II. *Adverbial Comparison* — by adverbs.

### I. TERMINATIONAL COMPARISON.

**162.** Adjectives are regularly compared by adding to the stem of the positive the endings:

| Comparative. | | | Superlative. | | |
|---|---|---|---|---|---|
| *M.* | *F.* | *N.* | *M.* | *F.* | *N.* |
| iŏr, | iŏr, | iŭs. | issĭmŭs, | issĭmă, | issĭmŭm. |

---

[1] Each of these forms of the adjective is declined. Thus *altus* and *altissĭmus* are declined like *bonus*, 148: *altus, a, um; alti, ae, i,* etc.; *altissĭmus, a, um; altissĭmi, ae, i,* etc. *Altior* is declined like *tristior*, 152: *altior, altius; altiōris,* etc.

#### EXAMPLES.

Altus, altior, altissĭmus: *high, higher, highest.*
lēvis, levior, levissĭmus: *light, lighter, lightest.*

## II. ADVERBIAL COMPARISON.

**170.** Adjectives which want the terminational comparison form the comparative and superlative, when their signification requires it, by prefixing the adverbs *măgis*, more, and *maxĭme*, most, to the positive:

Arduus, măgis arduus, maxĭme arduus.
*Arduous, more arduous, most arduous.*

#### MODEL FOR PARSING.

Ōrātŏr clāriŏr, *A more renowned orator.*

*Clarior* is an adjective (146) in the Comparative degree (160, 162), from the positive *clarus*, which is of the First and Second Declensions (148). Positive, *clārus;* STEM, *clār;* Comparative, *clarior;* Superlative, *clarissĭmus.* *Clarior* is an adjective of the Third Declension, declined like *tristior* (152). Singular: N. *clarior, clarius;* G. *clariōris, clariōris,* etc.[1] It is in the Nominative Singular Masculine, and agrees with its noun *orātor,* according to Rule XXXIII.[2]

### EXERCISE XIV.

#### I. *Vocabulary.*

| | |
|---|---|
| Altŭs, ă, ŭm, | *high, lofty.* |
| Clārŭs, ă, ŭm, | *distinguished, renowned.* |
| Intĕr, *prep. with acc.* | *among, in the midst of.* |
| Mons, montĭs, *m.* | *mountain.* |

#### II. *Translate into English.*

1. Orātor clarus. 2. Orātor clarior.[3] 3. Orātor clarissĭmus. 4. Oratōres clari. 5. Oratōres clariōres.[3] 6. Ora-

---

[1] Decline through all the cases of both numbers.

[2] Give the Rule.

[3] Declined like *tristior,* 152. Comparatives and superlatives, as well as positives, must agree with their nouns, according to Rule XXXIII. p. 32.

tōres clarissĭmi. 7. Beāta vita. 8. Beatior vita. 9. Beatissĭma vita. 10. Donum gratum. 11. Donum gratius. 12. Donum gratissĭmum. 13. Dona grata. 14. Dona gratiōra. 15. Dona gratissĭma. 16. Milĭtes fortissĭmi. 17. Liber utĭlis. 18. Libri utĭliōres. 19. Libris utilissĭmis. 20. Mons altus. 21. Montes altiōres.

### III. *Translate into Latin.*

1. A fertile field. 2. A more fertile field. 3. The most fertile field. 4. Fertile fields. 5. More fertile fields. 6. A useful life. 7. A more useful life. 8. The most useful life. 9. Useful lives. 10. More useful lives. 11. The most useful lives. 12. A pleasing song. 13. A more pleasing song. 14. The most pleasing song.

## NUMERALS.

**171.** Numerals comprise numeral adjectives and numeral adverbs.

### I. NUMERAL ADJECTIVES.

**172.** Numeral adjectives comprise three principal classes:

1. CARDINAL NUMBERS:[1] *ūnus*, one; *duo*, two.
2. ORDINAL NUMBERS:[1] *prīmus*, first; *secundus*, second.
3. DISTRIBUTIVES:[1] *singŭli*, one by one; *bīni*, two by two, two each, two apiece.

**174.** TABLE OF NUMERAL ADJECTIVES.

| CARDINALS. | ORDINALS. | DISTRIBUTIVES. |
|---|---|---|
| 1. ūnŭs, ūnă, ūnŭm, | prīmŭs, *first*, | singŭli, *one by one*. |
| 2. duŏ, duae, duŏ, | sĕcundŭs, *second*, | bīni, *two by two*. |
| 3. trēs, triă, | tertiŭs, *third*, | ternī (trīnī). |
| 4. quattuŏr, | quartŭs, *fourth*, | quăternī. |
| 5. quinquĕ, | quintŭs, *fifth*, | quīnī. |
| 6. sex, | sextŭs, | sēnī. |

[1] *Cardinals* denote simply the *number* of objects: *ūnus*, one; *duo*, two. *Ordinals* denote the *place* of an object in a series: *prīmus*, first; *secundus*,

## ETYMOLOGY. — NUMERAL ADJECTIVES.

| | | |
|---|---|---|
| 7. septĕm, | septĭmŭs, | septēnī. |
| 8. octō, | octāvŭs, | octōnī. |
| 9. nŏvĕm, | nōnŭs, | nŏvēnī. |
| 10. dĕcĕm, | dĕcĭmŭs, | dēnī. |
| 11. undĕcĭm, | undĕcĭmŭs, | undēnī. |
| 12. duŏdĕcĭm, | duŏdĕcĭmŭs, | duŏdēnī. |
| 13. trĕdĕcĭm, or dĕcĕm ĕt trēs, | tertiŭs dĕcĭmŭs, | ternī dēnī. |
| 20. vīgintī, | vīcēsĭmŭs, | vīcēnī. |
| 21. { vīgintī ūnŭs, ūnŭs ĕt vīgintī, | vīcēsĭmŭs prīmŭs, ūnŭs ĕt vīcēsĭmŭs, | vīcēnī singŭlī. singŭlī ĕt vīcenī |
| 30. trīgintā, | trīcēsĭmŭs, | trīcēnī. |
| 40. quadrāgintā, | quadrāgēsĭmŭs, | quadrāgēnī. |
| 50. quinquāgintā, | quinquāgēsĭmŭs, | quinquāgēnī. |
| 100. centŭm, | centēsĭmŭs, | centēnī. |
| 200. dūcentī, ae, ă, | dūcentēsĭmŭs, | dūcēnī. |
| 1000. millĕ, | millēsĭmŭs, | singŭlă milliă, |

## DECLENSION OF NUMERAL ADJECTIVES.

### 1. *Cardinals.*

**175.** On the declension of cardinals, observe,

1. That the units, *ūnus, duo,* and *tres,* are declined.
2. That the other units, all the tens, and *centum,* are indeclinable.
3. That the hundreds are declined.[1]
4. That *mille* is sometimes declined.[2]

**176.** The first three cardinals are declined as follows:

### 1. Unus, *one.*

| | Singular. | | | Plural. | |
|---|---|---|---|---|---|
| *N.* ūnŭs, | ūnă, | ūnŭm, | ūnī, | ūnae, | ūnă, |
| *G.* unīŭs, | unīŭs, | unīŭs, | unōrŭm, | unārŭm, | unōrŭm, |
| *D.* unī, | unī, | unī, | unīs, | unīs, | unīs, |
| *A.* unŭm, | unăm, | unŭm, | unōs, | unās, | ună, |
| *V.* unĕ, | ună, | unŭm, | | | |
| *A.* unō, | unā, | unō; | unīs, | unīs, | unīs. |

---

second. *Distributives* denote the *number* of objects taken at a time: *singŭli,* one by one; *bini,* two by two.

[1] These are declined like the plural of *bonus* (148); *ducenti, ae, a,* two hundred.

[2] Though only in the plural, and only when used substantively. It is then declined like the plural of *mare* (50); *millia, millium, millibus.*

2. Duo, *two*.  3. Tres, *three*.

| | | | | |
|---|---|---|---|---|
| *N.* duŏ, | duae, | duŏ, | trēs, *m.* and *f.* | triă, *n.* |
| *G.* duōrŭm, | duārŭm, | duōrŭm, | triŭm, | triŭm, |
| *D.* duōbŭs, | duābŭs, | duōbŭs, | trĭbŭs, | trĭbŭs, |
| *A.* duŏs, duŏ, | duās, | duŏ, | trēs, | triă, |
| *A.* duōbŭs, | duābŭs, | duōbŭs. | trĭbŭs, | trĭbŭs. |

## Exercise XV.

### I. *Vocabulary.*

Annŭs, 1, *m.* — *year.*
Classĭs, classĭs, *f.* — *fleet.*
Fortĭtūdŏ, fortĭtūdĭnĭs, *f.* — *fortitude, bravery.*
Impĕriŭm, iĭ, *n.* — *reign, power.*
Nāvĭs, nāvĭs, *f.* — *ship.*
Proeliŭm, iĭ, *n.* — *battle.*
Vĭr, vĭrĭ, *m.* — *man, hero.*

### II. *Translate into English.*

1. Unus[1] liber. 2. Duo[1] libri. 3. Liber primus.[1] 4. Liber secundus. 5. Tres libri. 6. Tertius liber. 7. Tria bella. 8. Post tria bella. 9. Post tertium bellum. 10. Ante quartum bellum. 11. Quattuor[2] anni. 12. Post bellum quinque annōrum. 13. Decem[2] dies. 14. Decĭmus dies.[3] 15. Decem horae. 16. Decĭma hora. 17. Decem proelia. 18. Decĭmum proelium. 19. Horā diēi decĭmā.

### III. *Translate into Latin.*

1. Five friends. 2. Of five friends. 3. The fifth year. 4. The fifth day. 5. The fifth present. 6. With five presents. 7. Eight books. 8. With eight books. 9. The eighth book. 10. Before the eighth book. 11. The bravery of two soldiers. 12. By the bravery of two soldiers.

---

[1] Numeral adjectives agree with their nouns, like other adjectives.

[2] The indeclinable numeral adjectives (175, 2) may be used without change of form with nouns of any gender, and in any case.

[2] *Dies*, it will be remembered, is generally *masculine*.

## CHAPTER III.

### PRONOUNS.

182. The Pronoun is that part of speech which properly supplies the place of nouns: *ĕgo*, I; *tu*, thou.

183. Pronouns are divided into six classes:

1. Personal Pronouns: *tu*, thou.
2. Possessive Pronouns: *meus*, my.
3. Demonstrative Pronouns: *hic*, this.
4. Relative Pronouns: *qui*, who.
5. Interrogative Pronouns: *quis*, who?
6. Indefinite Pronouns: *alĭquis*, some one.

#### I. Personal Pronouns.

184. Personal Pronouns, so called because they designate the person of the noun which they represent, are *ĕgo*, I; *tu*, thou; *sui* (Nom. not used), of himself, herself, itself. They are declined as follows:

SINGULAR.

| | | | |
|---|---|---|---|
| N. | ĕgŏ | tū | |
| G. | meī | tuī | suī |
| D. | mĭhĭ | tĭbĭ | sĭbĭ |
| A. | mē | tē | sē |
| V. | | tū | |
| A. | mē; | tē; | sē; |

PLURAL.

| | | | |
|---|---|---|---|
| N. | nōs | vōs | |
| G. | nostrŭm / nostrī | vestrŭm / vestrī | suī |
| D. | nōbīs | vōbīs | sĭbĭ |
| A. | nōs | vōs | sē |
| V. | | vōs | |
| A. | nōbīs. | vōbīs | sē. |

1. **Substantive Pronouns.** — Personal pronouns are also called *Substantive* pronouns, because they are always used as substantives.

2. **Reflexive Pronoun.** — *Sui*, from its reflexive signification, *of himself*, etc., is often called the *Reflexive* pronoun.

## II. Possessive Pronouns.

**185.** From *Personal* pronouns are formed the *Possessives*:

| | |
|---|---|
| meus, *my*, | noster, *our*. |
| tuus, *thy, your*, | vester, *your*. |
| suus, *his, her, its*, | suus, *their*. |

They are declined as adjectives of the first and second declensions;[1] *meus, mea, meum; noster, nostra, nostrum*: but *meus* has in the vocative singular masculine generally *mi*, sometimes *meus*.

## III. Demonstrative Pronouns.

**186.** Demonstrative Pronouns, so called because they specify the objects to which they refer, are

*Hic, ille, iste, ipse, is, idem.*

They are declined as follows:

### Hic, *this*.

| | SINGULAR. | | | PLURAL. | | |
|---|---|---|---|---|---|---|
| | *M.* | *F.* | *N.* | *M.* | *F.* | *N.* |
| *N.* | hĭc | haec | hŏc | hī | hae | haec |
| *G.* | hujŭs | hujŭs | hujŭs | hōrŭm | hārŭm | hōrŭm |
| *D.* | huic | huic | huic | hīs | hīs | hīs |
| *A.* | hunc | hanc | hŏc | hōs | hās | haec |
| *V.* | | | | | | |
| *A.* | hōc | hāc | hōc; | hīs | hīs | hīs. |

### Illĕ, *he* or *that*.

| | SINGULAR. | | | PLURAL. | | |
|---|---|---|---|---|---|---|
| | *M.* | *F.* | *N.* | *M.* | *F.* | *N.* |
| *N.* | illĕ | illă | illŭd | illī | illae | illă |
| *G.* | illiŭs | illiŭs | illiŭs | illōrŭm | illārŭm | illōrŭm |
| *D.* | illī | illī | illī | illīs | illīs | illīs |
| *A.* | illŭm | illăm | illŭd | illōs | illās | illă |
| *V.* | | | | | | |
| *A.* | illō | illā | illō; | illīs | illīs | illīs. |

---

[1] See *bonus* and *aeger*, 148.

ETYMOLOGY. — PRONOUNS.

Istĕ, *that*.

Istĕ, *that*, is declined like *illĕ*. It usually refers to objects which are present to the person addressed, and sometimes expresses contempt.

Ipsĕ, *self, he*.

| | SINGULAR. | | | | PLURAL. | |
|---|---|---|---|---|---|---|
| | *M.* | *F.* | *N.* | *M.* | *F.* | *N.* |
| *N.* | ipsĕ | ipsă | ipsŭm | ipsī | ipsae | ipsă |
| *G.* | ipsīŭs | ipsīŭs | ipsīŭs | ipsōrŭm | ipsārŭm | ipsōrŭm |
| *D.* | ipsī | ipsī | ipsī | ipsīs | ipsīs | ipsīs |
| *A.* | ipsŭm | ipsăm | ipsŭm | ipsōs | ipsās | ipsă |
| *V.* | | | | | | |
| *A.* | ipsō | ipsā | ipsō ; · | ipsīs | ipsīs | ipsīs. |

Is, *he, that*.

| | SINGULAR. | | | | PLURAL. | |
|---|---|---|---|---|---|---|
| | *M.* | *F.* | *N.* | *M.* | *F.* | *N.* |
| *N.* | ĭs | eă | ĭd | iī | eae | eă |
| *G.* | ejŭs | ejŭs | ejŭs | eōrŭm | eārŭm | eōrŭm |
| *D.* | eī | eī | eī | iīs (eīs) | iīs (eīs) | iīs (eīs) |
| *A.* | eŭm | eăm | ĭd | eōs | eās | eă |
| *V.* | | | | | | |
| *A.* | eō | eā | eō ; | iīs (eīs) | iīs (eīs) | iīs (eīs). |

Idem, *the same*.

Idem, compounded of *is* and *dem*, is declined like *is*, but shortens *isdem* to *īdem*, and *iddem* to *ĭdem*, and changes *m* to *n* before the ending *dem ;* thus :

| | SINGULAR. | | | | PLURAL. | |
|---|---|---|---|---|---|---|
| | *M.* | *F.* | *N.* | *M.* | *F.* | *N.* |
| *N.* | ĭdĕm | eădĕm | ĭdĕm | iīdĕm | eaedĕm | eădĕm |
| *G.* | ejusdĕm | ejusdĕm | ejusdĕm | eōrundĕm | eārundĕm | eōrundĕm |
| *D.* | eīdĕm | eīdĕm | eīdĕm | iisdĕm | iisdĕm | iisdĕm |
| *A.* | eundĕm | eandĕm | ĭdĕm | eōsdĕm | eāsdĕm | eădĕm |
| *V.* | | | | | | |
| *A.* | eōdĕm | eādĕm | eōdĕm ; | iisdĕm | iisdĕm | iisdĕm. |

IV. RELATIVE PRONOUNS.

187. The Relative *qui*, who, so called because it relates to some noun or pronoun, expressed or understood, called its antecedent, is declined as follows :

|  | SINGULAR. |  |  | PLURAL. |  |
|---|---|---|---|---|---|
| *M.* | *F.* | *N.* | *M.* | *F.* | *N.* |
| N. quī | quae | quŏd | quī | quae | quae |
| G. cujŭs | cujŭs | cujŭs | quōrŭm | quārŭm | quōrŭm |
| D. cuī | cuī | cuī | quĭbŭs | quĭbŭs | quĭbŭs |
| A. quĕm | quăm | quŏd | quōs | quās | quae |
| V. |  |  |  |  |  |
| A. quō | quā | quō; | quĭbŭs | quĭbŭs | quĭbŭs. |

### V. Interrogative Pronouns.

188. Interrogative Pronouns are used in asking questions. The most important are

*Quis* and *qui*, with their compounds.

*Quis* (who, which, what?) is generally used substantively, and is declined as follows:

|  | SINGULAR. |  |  | PLURAL. |  |
|---|---|---|---|---|---|
| *M.* | *F.* | *N.* | *M.* | *F.* | *N.* |
| N. quĭs | quae | quĭd | quī | quae | quae |
| G. cujŭs | cujŭs | cujŭs | quōrŭm | quārŭm | quōrŭm |
| D. cuī | cuī | cuī | quĭbŭs | quĭbŭs | quĭbŭs |
| A. quĕm | quăm | quĭd | quōs | quās | quae |
| V. |  |  |  |  |  |
| A. quō | quā | quō; | quĭbŭs | quĭbŭs | quĭbŭs. |

*Qui* (which, what?) is generally used adjectively, and is declined like the *relative qui*.

### VI. Indefinite Pronouns.

189. Indefinite Pronouns do not refer to any definite persons or things. The most important are

*Quis* and *qui*, with their compounds.

190. *Quis*, any one, *qui*, any one, any, are the same in form and declension as the interrogatives *quis* and *qui*.[1]

191. From *quis* and *qui* are formed

I. *The Indefinites:*

| aliquis, | aliqua, | aliquid | *or* aliquod, | *some, some one.* |
| quispiam, | quaepiam, | quidpiam | *or* quodpiam, | *some, some one.* |
| quidam, | quaedam, | quiddam | *or* quoddam, | *certain, certain one.* |
| quisquam, |  | quidquam, |  | *any one.* |

---

[1] But after *si, nisi, ne*, and *num*, the Feminine Singular and the Neuter Plural have *quae* or *qua; si quae, si qua*. In like manner, *aliquis* has *aliqua* in the Feminine Singular and in the Neuter Plural.

## II. The General Indefinites:

| | | | | |
|---|---|---|---|---|
| quisque, | quaeque, | quidque | or quodque, | *every, every one.* |
| quivis, | quaevis, | quidvis | or quodvis, | *any one you please.* |
| quilibet, | quaelibet, | quidlibet | or quodlibet, | *any one you please.* |

### Exercise XVI.

#### I. Vocabulary.

| | |
|---|---|
| Consĭlĭŭm, ĭi, *n.* | *design, plan.* |
| Epistŏlă, ae, *f.* | *letter.* |
| Ex, *prep. with abl.* | *from.* |
| Insŭlă, ae, *f.* | *island.* |
| Părens, părentĭs, *m.* and *f.* | *parent.* |
| Pars, partĭs, *f.* | *part, portion.* |
| Pătrĭă, ae, *f.* | *country, native country.* |
| Praeclārŭs, ă, ŭm, | *distinguished.* |
| Prātŭm, ĭ, *n.* | *meadow.* |
| Prō, *prep. with abl.* | *for, in behalf of.* |
| Quīvīs, quaevīs, quodvīs, | *whoever, whatever.* |

#### II. Translate into English.

1. Mihi, tibi, sibi. 2. Ad me,[1] ad te. 3. Contra nos, contra se. 4. Ante vos, ante nos. 5. Pro vobis.[1] 6. Meă[2] vită. 7. Patriă tuă. 8. Pro patriă tuă.[2] 9. Contra patriam tuam. 10. Nostra consilia. 11. Nostris[2] consiliis. 12. Vestri patres. 13. In nostrā patriā. 14. Hic[2] puer, hi pueri. 15. Haec corōnă, hae corōnae. 16. Hoc donum, haec dona. 17. Haec urbs praeclară. 18. Ex hac vită. 19. Illīus libri. 20. In eā pugnā. 21. In eōdem prato. 22. Quae[2] urbs?

---

[1] See 184, 1. Substantive pronouns are used in the several cases like nouns, and are parsed by the same rules. See Rule XXXII. 432. Other pronouns are sometimes used as nouns, and parsed in the same way.

[2] The *Possessive*, the *Demonstrative*, and the *Interrogative* pronouns, in this exercise, are all used as *adjectives*, and agree with their nouns, like any other adjectives, according to Rule XXXIII. 438, p. 32. Hence *meă* is in the Nominative Singular Feminine, to agree with *vită;* *nostris*, in the Dative or Ablative Plural Neuter, to agree with *consiliis;* *hic*, in the Nominative Singular Masculine, to agree with *puer*.

### III. *Translate into Latin.*

1. We, you. 2. You, me, himself. 3. For you, for me, for himself. 4. Of himself, of you. 5. Against you, against me. 6. My book, your book, his book. 7. My books, your books, his books. 8. Our parents, your parents, their parents. 9. This letter, that letter. 10. These letters, those letters. 11. This city, that city. 12. These cities, those cities. 13. After that victory. 14. The same words. 15. With the same words.

## CHAPTER IV.

### VERBS.

**192.** Verbs in Latin, as in English, express existence, condition, or action: *est*, he is; *dormit*, he is sleeping; *lĕgit*, he reads.

**193.** Verbs comprise two principal classes:

I. TRANSITIVE VERBS, — which admit a direct object of their action: *servum*[1] *verbĕrat*, he beats the slave.

II. INTRANSITIVE VERBS, — which do not admit such an object: *puer currit*, the boy runs.

**194.** Verbs have *Voice, Mood, Tense, Number*, and *Person*.

### I. VOICES.

**195.** There are two Voices:[2]

I. THE ACTIVE VOICE, — which represents the subject as acting or existing: *păter filium amat*, the father loves his son; *est*, he is.

---

[1] Here *servum*, the slave, is the direct object of the action denoted by the verb *beats: beats* (what?) *the slave.*

[2] *Voice* shows whether the subject *acts* (Active Voice), or is *acted upon* (Passive Voice).

II. The Passive Voice, — which represents the subject as acted upon by some other person or thing: *filius a patre amātur*, the son is loved by his father.

## II. Moods.

196. Moods[1] are either Definite or Indefinite:

I. The **Definite** or **Finite Moods** make up the Finite Verb; they are:

1. The Indicative Mood, — which either asserts something as a *fact*, or inquires after the fact: *lĕgit*, he is reading; *legitne*, is he reading?

2. The Subjunctive Mood, — which expresses, not an actual fact, but a *possibility* or *conception*, often rendered by *may*, *can*, etc.: *lĕgat*, he may read, let him read.

3. The Imperative Mood, — which expresses a *command* or an *entreaty*: *lĕge*, read thou.

II. The **Indefinite Moods** express the meaning of the verb in the form of nouns or adjectives; they are:

1. The Infinitive, — which, like the English Infinitive, gives the simple meaning of the verb, without any necessary reference to person or number: *legĕre*, to read.

2. The Gerund, — which gives the meaning of the verb in the form of a verbal noun of the second declension, used only in the *genitive, dative, accusative*, and *ablative singular*. It corresponds to the English participial noun in ing: *amandi*, of loving; *amandi causā*, for the sake of loving.

3. The Supine, — which gives the meaning of the verb in the form of a verbal noun of the fourth declension, used only in the *accusative* and *ablative singular: amātum*, to love, for loving; *amātu*, to be loved, in loving.

4. The Participle, — which, like the English Participle, gives the meaning of the verb in the form of an adjective.

---

[1] *Mood*, or *Mode*, means *manner*, and relates to the manner in which the meaning of the verb is expressed, as will be seen by observing the force of the several Moods.

A Latin verb may have four participles: two in the Active, the Present and Future, — *amans*, loving; *amaturus*, about to love: and two in the Passive, the Perfect and Future, — *amatus*, loved; *amandus*, deserving to be loved.

## III. Tenses.

**197.** There are six tenses:[1]

I. Three Tenses for Incomplete Action:
1. Present: *amo*, I love.
2. Imperfect: *amābam*, I was loving.
3. Future: *amābo*, I shall love.

II. Three Tenses for Completed Action:
1. Perfect: *amāvi*, I have loved, I loved.
2. Pluperfect: *amavĕram*, I had loved.
3. Future Perfect: *amavĕro*, I shall have loved.

### 198. Remarks on Tenses.

1. **Present Perfect and Historical Perfect.** — The Latin Perfect sometimes corresponds to our Perfect with *have* (*have loved*), and is called the *Present Perfect*, or *Perfect Definite;* and sometimes to our Imperfect or Past (*loved*), and is called the *Historical Perfect,* or *Perfect Indefinite.*

2. **Principal and Historical.** — Tenses are also distinguished as

1) *Principal:* — Present, Present Perfect, Future, and Future Perfect.

2) *Historical:* — Imperfect, Historical Perfect, and Pluperfect.

3. **Tenses Wanting.** — The Subjunctive wants the Future and Future Perfect; the Imperative has only the Present and Future; the Infinitive, only the Present, Perfect, and Future.

## IV. Numbers.

**199.** There are two Numbers:[2] Singular and Plural.

---

[1] *Tense* means *time*, and is employed to designate the *time* of an action or event.

[2] *Number* in verbs corresponds, it will be observed, to number in nouns. See 37.

## V. Persons.

**200.** There are three Persons:[1] First, Second, and Third.

## CONJUGATION.

**201.** Regular verbs are inflected, or conjugated, in four different ways, and are accordingly divided into Four Conjugations, distinguished from each other by the

INFINITIVE ENDINGS.

| Conj. I. | Conj. II. | Conj. III. | Conj. IV. |
|---|---|---|---|
| āre, | ēre, | ĕre, | īre. |

**202. Principal Parts.** — Four forms of the verb — the Present Indicative, Present Infinitive, Perfect Indicative, and Supine [2] — are called, from their importance, the *Principal Parts* of the verb.

**203. Entire Conjugation.** — In any regular verb,

1. The Verb-Stem may be found by dropping the Infinitive Ending: *amāre;* stem, *am.*

2. The Principal Parts may be formed from this stem by means of proper endings.

3. The Entire Conjugation of the verb through all its parts may be readily formed from these Principal Parts by means of the proper endings.[3]

---

[1] *Person* in verbs corresponds, it will be observed, to person in nouns. See 37.

[2] In the Active Voice, all these four forms are usually given as Principal Parts; but, in the Passive, only the first three.

[3] In the Paradigms of regular verbs, the endings, both those which distinguish the Principal Parts and those which distinguish the forms derived from those parts, are separately indicated, and should be carefully noticed.

## 204. Sum, *I am.*

*Sum* is used as an auxiliary in the passive voice of regular verbs. Accordingly, its conjugation, though quite irregular, must be given at the outset.

### PRINCIPAL PARTS.

| Pres. Ind. | Pres. Inf. | Perf. Ind. | Supine. |
|---|---|---|---|
| sŭm, | essĕ, | fŭi, | —.[1] |

### INDICATIVE MOOD.

#### PRESENT TENSE.
*I am.*

| SINGULAR. | | PLURAL. | |
|---|---|---|---|
| sŭm, | *I am,* | sŭmŭs, | *we are,* |
| ĕs, | *thou art,*[2] | estĭs, | *you are,* |
| est, | *he is;* | sunt, | *they are.* |

#### IMPERFECT.
*I was.*

| ĕrăm, | *I was,* | ĕrămŭs, | *we were,* |
|---|---|---|---|
| ĕrās, | *thou wast,* | ĕrātĭs, | *you were,* |
| ĕrăt, | *he was;* | ĕrant, | *they were.* |

#### FUTURE.
*I shall or will be.*

| ĕrŏ, | *I shall be,* | ĕrĭmŭs, | *we shall be,* |
|---|---|---|---|
| ĕrĭs, | *thou wilt be,* | ĕrĭtĭs, | *you will be,* |
| ĕrĭt, | *he will be;* | ĕrunt, | *they will be.* |

#### PERFECT.
*I have been, was.*

| fŭi, | *I have been,* | fŭĭmŭs, | *we have been,* |
|---|---|---|---|
| fŭistĭ, | *thou hast been,* | fŭistĭs, | *you have been,* |
| fŭĭt, | *he has been;* | fŭērunt, } fŭērĕ, } | *they have been.* |

#### PLUPERFECT.
*I had been.*

| fŭĕrăm, | *I had been,* | fŭĕrāmŭs, | *we had been,* |
|---|---|---|---|
| fŭĕrās, | *thou hadst been,* | fŭĕrātĭs, | *you had been,* |
| fŭĕrăt, | *he had been;* | fŭĕrant, | *they had been.* |

#### FUTURE PERFECT.
*I shall or will have been.*

| fŭĕrŏ, | *I shall have been,* | fŭĕrĭmŭs, | *we shall have been,* |
|---|---|---|---|
| fŭĕrĭs, | *thou wilt have been,* | fŭĕrĭtĭs, | *you will have been,* |
| fŭĕrĭt, | *he will have been;* | fŭĕrint, | *they will have been.* |

[1] The Supine is wanting in this verb.

[2] Or, *you are*: *thou* is confined mostly to solemn discourse: in ordinary English, *you are* is used both in the singular and in the plural.

## SUBJUNCTIVE.

### PRESENT.

*I may or can be.*[1]

| SINGULAR. | | PLURAL. | |
|---|---|---|---|
| sĭm, | *I may be,* | sīmŭs, | *we may be,* |
| sīs, | *thou mayst be,* | sītĭs, | *you may be,* |
| sĭt, | *he may be;* | sint, | *they may be.* |

### IMPERFECT.

*I might, could, would, or should be.*

| essĕm, | *I might be,* | essēmŭs, | *we might be,* |
| essēs, | *thou mightst be,* | essētĭs, | *you might be,* |
| essĕt, | *he might be;* | essent, | *they might be.* |

### PERFECT.

*I may or can have been.*

| fuĕrĭm, | *I may have been,* | fuĕrĭmŭs, | *we may have been,* |
| fuĕrĭs, | *thou mayst have been,* | fuĕrĭtĭs, | *you may have been,* |
| fuĕrĭt, | *he may have been;* | fuĕrint, | *they may have been.* |

### PLUPERFECT.

*I might, could, would, or should have been.*

| fuissĕm, | *I might have been,* | fuissēmŭs, | *we might have been,* |
| fuissēs, | *thou mightst have been,* | fuissētĭs, | *you might have been,* |
| fuissĕt, | *he might have been;* | fuissent, | *they might have been.* |

## IMPERATIVE.

| PRES. | ĕs, | *be thou,* | estĕ, | *be ye.* |
| FUT. | estō, | *thou shalt be,*[2] | estōtĕ, | *ye shall be,* |
| | estō, | *he shall be;* | suntō, | *they shall be.* |

## INFINITIVE.

| PRES. | essĕ, | *to be.* |
| PERF. | fuissĕ, | *to have been.* |
| FUT. | fŭtūrŭs[3] essĕ, | *to be about to be.* |

## PARTICIPLE.

| FUT. | fŭtūrŭs,[3] | *about to be.* |

---

[1] The Subjunctive is sometimes best rendered by *let:* sit, *he may be, may he be, let him be.*

[2] The Future is sometimes best rendered like the Present, or with *let:* esto, *thou shalt be,* or *be thou;* sunto, *they shall be,* or *let them be.*

[3] *Futŭrus* is declined like *bonus;* N. *futŭrus, a, um,* G. *futŭri, ae, i;* so in the Infinitive: *futŭrus, a, um esse.*

## RULE XXXV.—Verb with Subject.

460. A Finite[1] Verb agrees with its Subject[2] in NUMBER and PERSON:

Deus mundum aedǐfǐcāvit,[3] *God made the world.* Cic. Ego rēges ejēci, vos tȳrannos intrōdūcǐtis, *I have banished kings, you introduce tyrants.* Cic.

1. PARTICIPLES IN COMPOUND TENSES.—These agree with the subject, according to Rule XXXIII. page 32:
Thēbāni accūsāti sunt,[4] *The Thebans were accused.* Cic.
2. SUBJECT OMITTED.—The subject is generally omitted—
1) When it is a Personal Pronoun, or can be readily supplied from the context:
Discǐpǔlos mǒneo,[5] ut stǔdia ǎment,[5] *I instruct pupils to love*[6] *their studies.* Quint.

---

[1] See 196, I.

[2] With the Active Voice of a Transitive Verb, the *Subject* represents the person (or thing, one or more) who *performs* the action; as, *Deus* in the first example, *God made:* but, with the Passive Voice, it represents the person (or thing, one or more) who *receives* the action, i.e. *is acted upon*, as, *Thebāni*, 460, 1: *the Thebans were accused.*

[3] *Aedificāvit* is in the Third Person and in the Singular Number, because its subject *deus* is in that person and number. *Ejēci* is in the First Person Singular, to agree with its subject *ego;* and *introducǐtis* in the Second Person Plural, to agree with its subject *vos.*

[4] The verb *accusāti sunt* is in the Third Person Plural, to agree with its subject *Thebāni*, according to Rule XXXV.; but the participle *accusāti*, which is one element of the verb, is in the Nominative Plural Masculine, to agree with its noun *Thebāni*, according to Rule XXXIII.

[5] The subject of *moneo* is *ego*. It is omitted, because it is a Personal Pronoun, and is, accordingly, fully implied in the verb, as the ending *eo* shows, as we shall soon see, that the subject cannot be *you, he,* or *they*, but must be *I*.

*Ut—ament* means literally *that they may love.* The subject of *ament* is the pronoun *ii*, they, referring to *discipǔlos*. It is omitted, partly because it is implied in the ending *ent*, but more especially because it can be so readily supplied from *discipǔlos*, which shows *who* are here meant by *they*

[6] *To love*, or, more literally, *that they may love.*

ETYMOLOGY. — VERB SUM. 55

The Pronoun may be expressed for emphasis or contrast, as in the second example under the rule.

### I. Directions for Parsing Verbs.

In parsing a verb,

1. Tell whether it is transitive or intransitive (193), name the Conjugation to which it belongs, give the Present Indicative Active and the Stem (203).

2. Give the Principal Parts (202), and inflect the tense in which the given form is found.[1]

3. Give the voice, mood, tense, number, and person.

4. Name the subject, and give the Rule for agreement.

MODELS FOR PARSING THE VERB SUM.

#### 1. *Sum with Subject.*

Nōs[2] ĕrāmŭs,  *We were.*

*Erāmus* is an intransitive irregular[3] verb, from *sum*. Principal Parts: *sum, esse, fui,* —— [4]. Inflection of tense (Imperfect Indicative): *eram, eras, erat, erāmus, erātis, erant.* The form *erāmus* is found in the *Indicative* mood, *Imperfect* tense, *First* person, *Plural* number, and agrees with its *subject nos,* according to Rule XXXV.: "A Finite Verb agrees with its Subject in NUMBER and PERSON."

#### 2. *Sum without Subject.*[5]

Fuī, *I have been.*

*Fui* is an intransitive irregular verb, from *sum*. Principal Parts: *sum, esse, fui*. Inflection of tense (Perfect Indicative): *fui, fuisti,*

---

[1] That is, if the form occurs in a given tense of the Indicative, give the several forms for the different persons and numbers in that tense and mood. The teacher may also find it convenient to require the synopsis of the mood till the required tense is found.

[2] *Nos* is the Subject. With an intransitive verb, the Subject represents the person (or thing) who is in the condition, or state, denoted by the verb.

[3] Hence it does not belong to either of the regular conjugations.

[4] The *Supine* is wanting.

[5] That is, without any subject expressed.

*fuit; fuĭmus, fuistis, fuērunt,* or *fuēre.* The form *fui* is found in the *Indicative* mood, *Perfect* tense, *First* person, *Singular* number, and agrees with its subject *ego* omitted (though fully implied[1] in the ending *i* of *fui*), according to Rule XXXV.

## Exercise XVII.

### I. *Translate into English.*

1. Sum, sumus, sunt.[2] 2. Es, est, estis. 3. Eram, erāmus.[2] 4. Erat, erant. 5. Eris, crĭtis.[2] 6. Erit, erunt. 7. Fui, fuĕram, fuĕro. 8. Fuĭmus, fuerāmus, fuerĭmus. 9. Fuisti, fuistis. 10. Fuit, fuĕrunt. 11. Fuĕrat, fuĕrant. 12. Fuĕrit, fuĕrint. 13. Sim, simus. 14. Sit, sint. 15. Essem, essēmus. 16. Esset, essent. 17. Fuĕrim, fuissem. 18. Fuerĭmus, fuissēmus. 19. Fuĕrit, fuĕrint. 20. Fuisset, fuissent. 21. Es, este.

### II. *Translate into Latin.*

1. He[3] is, they[3] are. 2. He has been, they have been. 3. He will be, they will be. 4. He was, they were. 5. He will have been, they will have been. 6. He had been, they had been. 7. I[3] was, you were. 8. We have been, you have been. 9. You may be, they may be. 10. He would be, they would be. 11. I might have been, we might have been.

---

[1] See Rule XXXV., 2, together with the note.

[2] In parsing the forms contained in this Exercise, observe the second Model just given. If the verb is of the first person, supply, as subject, the personal pronoun (184) of the first person; i.e., *ego* for the singular, and *nos* for the plural. If the verb is of the second person, supply the personal pronoun of the second person; i.e., *tu* for the singular, and *vos* for the plural. If the verb is of the third person, supply the demonstrative pronoun *is* (186) for the singular, and *ii* for the plural, as the personal pronoun *sui* is not used in the Nominative: hence, *ego sum, nos sumus, ii sunt.*

[3] The English pronouns in this Exercise are not to be rendered by the corresponding Latin pronouns, as the latter may be implied in the ending of the verb, as in the Latin forms above: hence, *he is = est.*

## SUM WITH SUBJECT AND ADJECTIVE.

### RULE III.—Subject Nominative.

367. The Subject of a Finite[1] Verb is put in the Nominative:

Servius[2] regnāvit, *Servius reigned.* Liv. Pătent portae, *The gates are open.* Cic. Rex vīcit, *The king conquered.* Liv.

1. The Subject is always a substantive, a pronoun, or some word or clause used substantively:

Ego rēges ejēci, *I have banished kings.* Cic.

2. SUBJECT OMITTED. See 460, 2; page 54.

#### MODEL FOR PARSING SUBJECTS.

Rex vĭcĭt, *The king conquered.*

*Rex* is a noun (31) of the Third Declension, as it has *is* in the Genitive Singular (40); of Class I., as it has a nominative ending *s* (x = g-s, of which *s* is the ending, as *g* belongs to the *stem.* See 50, I. note); STEM, *reg.* Singular: *rex, regis, regi, regem, rex, rege.* Plural: *reges, regum, regĭbus, reges, reges, regĭbus.* It is of the Masculine gender, by 35, I. 1.; is in the Nominative Singular; and is the subject of *vicit,* according to Rule III.: "The Subject of a Finite Verb is put in the Nominative."

### EXERCISE XVIII.

#### I. *Vocabulary.*

| | |
|---|---|
| Cătŏ, Cătōnĭs, *m.* | *Cato, a distinguished Roman.* |
| Crūdŭs, ă, ŭm, | *unripe.* |
| Dīlĭgens, Dīlĭgentĭs, | *diligent.* |
| Discĭpŭlŭs, ī, *m.* | *pupil.* |

---

[1] See 196, I.
[2] In these examples, the *subjects* are *Servius, portae,* and *rex.*

Germānĭă, ae, *f.*     *Germany.*
Jūcundŭs, ă, ŭm.       *pleasant, delightful.*
Laudābĭlĭs, ĕ.         *praiseworthy, laudable.*
Mātūrŭs, ă, ŭm.        *ripe.*
Pōmŭm, ĭ, *n.*          *fruit.*

II. *Translate into English.*

1. Pax[1] jucunda[2] est.[3] 2. Pax jucunda erit. 3. Vita brevis est. 4. Cato bonus fuit. 5. Cives boni fuĕrunt. 6. Virtus laudabĭlis est. 7. Libri utĭles sunt. 8. Illi libri utĭles erunt. 9. Ille liber utĭlis fuĕrat. 10. Utĭlis[4] fuisti. 11. Utĭles fuistis. 12. Germania fertĭlis est. 13. Agri fertĭles fuĕrant. 14. Pomum crudum est. 15. Poma cruda sunt. 16. Poma matūra erunt. 17. Miles fortis est. 18. Milĭtes fortes sunt.

III. *Translate into Latin.*

1. The pupil is diligent.[5] 2. The pupils were diligent. 3. The boy is good. 4. He will be happy. 5. Good boys are happy. 6. You may be happy. 7. We might have been happy. 8. This soldier will be useful. 9. These soldiers have been useful. 10. Brave soldiers are useful. 11. You will be useful. 12. Let us be useful.

---

[1] *Pax* is the subject of *est*, and is therefore in the Nominative, according to Rule III.

[2] *Jucunda* is an adjective in the Nominative Singular Feminine, to agree with its noun *pax*, according to Rule XXXIII., page 32.

[3] *Est* is a verb in the *Indicative* mood, *Present* tense, *Third* person, *Singular* number, and agrees with its subject *pax*, according to Rule XXXV., page 54.

[4] *Utĭlis* agrees with the omitted subject *tu*, implied in the ending of the verb.

[5] In translating English into Latin, the pupil is expected, in the arrangement of words, to imitate the order followed in the Latin Exercises. He will observe that the subject stands first, and the verb last. But sometimes the verb precedes one or more words in the sentence. Thus the sentence, *Pax jucunda est*, might be *Pax est jucunda*.

## SUM WITH PREDICATE NOUN.

### RULE I.—Predicate Nouns.

**362.** A Predicate Noun[1] denoting the same person or thing as its subject agrees with it in CASE:

Ego sum nuntius,[1] *I am a messenger.* Liv. Servius rex est declarātus, *Servius was declared king.* Liv.

MODEL FOR PARSING PREDICATE NOUNS.

Egŏ sŭm nuntiŭs, *I am a messenger.*

*Nuntius* is a noun (31) of the Second Declension, as it has *i* in the Genitive Singular (40); STEM, *nunti.* Singular; *nuntius, nuntii, nuntio, nuntium, nuntie, nuntio.* Plural; *nuntii, nuntiōrum, nuntiis, nuntios, nuntii, nuntiis.* It is of the Masculine Gender by 45; is in the Nominative Singular, and, as a Predicate Noun, agrees in case with its subject *ego,* according to Rule I.: "A Predicate Noun denoting the same person or thing as its Subject agrees with it in CASE."

**346.** I. A DECLARATIVE SENTENCE has the form of an assertion:

Miltiădes accūsātus est, *Miltiades was accused.* Nep.

II. An INTERROGATIVE SENTENCE has the form of a question:

Quis non paupertātem extĭmescit, *Who does not fear poverty?* Cic.

1. INTERROGATIVE WORDS. — Interrogative sentences generally contain some interrogative word, — either an interrogative pronoun,

---

[1] Every sentence consists of two distinct parts, expressed or implied:
1. The SUBJECT, or that of which it speaks.
2. The PREDICATE, or that which is said of the subject.

Thus, in the first example under the Rule, *ego,* I, is the *subject,* and *sum nuntius* is the *predicate.* When the predicate thus consists of a *noun* with the verb *sum,* or of a noun with a passive verb, the noun thus used is called a *predicate noun.* Accordingly, *nuntius* in the first example, and *rex* in the second, are *predicate nouns.*

adjective, or adverb, or one of the interrogative particles, *ne, nonne, num:*

1) Questions with *ne* ask for information: *Scrībitne,* Is he writing? *Ne* is always thus appended to some other word.

2) Questions with *nonne* expect the answer *yes: Nonne scrībit,* Is he not writing?

3) Questions with *num* expect the answer *no: Num scrībit,* Is he writing?

EXERCISE XIX.

I. *Vocabulary.*

| | |
|---|---|
| Ancŭs, ī, *m.* | *Ancus,* Roman king. |
| Condĭtŏr, condĭtōrĭs, *m.* | *founder.* |
| Dēmosthĕnēs, ĭs, *m.* | *Demosthenes,* Athenian orator. |
| Ebrĭĕtās, ēbrĭĕtātĭs, *f.* | *drunkenness.* |
| Graecŭs, ă, ŭm, | *Greek, Grecian.* |
| Graecus, ī, *m.* | *Greek, a Greek.* |
| Insānĭă, ae, *f.* | *insanity, madness.* |
| Inventŏr, inventōrĭs, *m.* | *inventor.* |
| Mātĕr, mātrĭs, *f.* | *mother.* |
| Mundŭs, ī, *m.* | *world, universe.* |
| Nonnĕ, *interrog. part.* | expects answer *yes.* |
| Nŭm, *interrog. part.* | expects answer *no.* |
| Phĭlŏsŏphĭă, ae, *f.* | *philosophy.* |
| Rōmă, ae, *f.* | *Rome.* |
| Rōmānŭs, ă, ŭm, | *Roman.* |
| Rōmānŭs, ī, *m.* | *Roman, a Roman.* |
| Rōmŭlŭs, ī, *m.* | *Romulus,* the founder of Rome. |
| Scīpĭŏ, Scīpĭōnĭs, *m.* | *Scipio,* Roman general. |

II. *Translate into English.*[1]*

1. Ancus[2] fuit[3] rex[4]. 2. Nonne[5] Romŭlus rex fuĕrat? 3. Romŭlus rex fuĕrat. 4. Quis condĭtor Romae[6] fuit? 5. Romŭlus condĭtor Romae fuit. 6. Ebrĭĕtas est insania. 7. Patria[7] est parens omnium nostrum.[6] 8. Graeci[7] multā rum artium[8] inventōres erant. 9. Demosthĕnes orātor fuit.

---

\* For Notes to the references on this page, see page 61.

10. Num hic puer orātor erit? 11. Ille puer orātor sit. 12. Philosophia est mater artium. 13. Cicĕro clarissĭmus⁹ orātor fuit. 14. Cantus lusciniae jucundissĭmus⁹ est.

III. *Translate into Latin.*

1. Who¹⁰ was the king?¹¹ 2. Was not¹² Romulus king?¹¹ 3. Romulus was king. 4. Who was the leader of the Romans? 5. Was not¹² Scipio the leader of the Romans? 6. Scipio was the leader of the Romans. 7. Your brother is an orator. 8. This boy is my brother. 9. These boys will be diligent pupils. 10. These pupils will be diligent.

---

¹ In preparing the longer and more difficult sentences in this and in the subsequent exercises, it is recommended that the pupil should follow the Suggestions which are inserted in this volume, page 143, and which are intended to aid him in discerning the *process* by which he may most readily and surely reach the meaning of a Latin sentence.

² See Rule III. page 57.

³ See Rule XXXV. page 54. The verb sometimes precedes the Predicate Noun, as in this sentence; and sometimes follows it, as in several of the following sentences.

⁴ *Rex* is a *Predicate Noun*, denoting the same person as its subject *Ancus*, and is therefore in the Nominative, to agree with that subject in *case*, according to Rule I. page 59.

⁵ See 346, II. 1 above.

⁶ Genitive, according to Rule XVI. page 22.

⁷ In this sentence, before turning to the Vocabulary for the meaning of the words, notice carefully the endings of the several words in accordance with Suggestion IV. What parts of speech do you find? What cases? What mood, tense, number, and person?

In accordance with Suggestion V., what order will you follow in looking out the words in the Vocabulary?

⁸ *Artium* depends upon *inventōres*.

⁹ In accordance with Suggestion VII., for what forms will you look in the Vocabulary to find the meaning of *clarissĭmus* and *jucundissĭmus* (162)?

¹⁰ See 188.

¹¹ See Rule I.

¹² *Nonne.* See 346 II. 1.

# FIRST CONJUGATION.

### ACTIVE VOICE.

**205.** Amo, *I love.*

#### PRINCIPAL PARTS.

| Pres. Ind. | Pres. Inf. | Perf. Ind. | Supine. |
|---|---|---|---|
| ămŏ, | ămārĕ, | ămāvī, | ămātŭm. |

### INDICATIVE MOOD.

#### PRESENT TENSE.
*I love, am loving, do love.*

| SINGULAR. | | PLURAL. | |
|---|---|---|---|
| ămŏ, | I love, | ămāmŭs, | we love, |
| ămās, | thou lovest, | ămātĭs, | you love, |
| ămăt, | he loves; | ămant, | they love. |

#### IMPERFECT.
*I loved, was loving, did love.*

| ămābăm, | I was loving, | ămābāmŭs, | we were loving, |
| ămābās, | thou wast loving, | ămābātĭs, | you were loving, |
| ămābăt, | he was loving; | ămābant, | they were loving. |

#### FUTURE.
*I shall or will love.*

| ămābŏ, | I shall love, | ămābĭmŭs, | we shall love, |
| ămābĭs, | thou wilt love, | ămābĭtĭs, | you will love, |
| ămābĭt, | he will love; | ămābunt, | they will love. |

#### PERFECT.
*I loved, have loved.*

| ămāvī, | I have loved, | ămāvĭmŭs, | we have loved, |
| ămāvistī, | thou hast loved, | ămāvistĭs, | you have loved, |
| ămāvĭt, | he has loved; | ămāvērunt, ērĕ, | they have loved. |

#### PLUPERFECT.
*I had loved.*

| ămāvĕrăm, | I had loved, | ămāvĕrāmŭs, | we had loved, |
| ămāvĕrās, | thou hadst loved, | ămāvĕrātĭs, | you had loved, |
| ămāvĕrăt, | he had loved; | ămāvĕrant, | they had loved. |

#### FUTURE PERFECT.
*I shall or will have loved.*

| ămāvĕrŏ, | I shall have loved, | ămāvĕrĭmŭs, | we shall have loved, |
| ămāvĕrĭs, | thou wilt have loved, | ămāvĕrĭtĭs, | you will have loved, |
| ămāvĕrĭt, | he will have loved; | ămāvĕrint, | they will have loved. |

ETYMOLOGY.—FIRST CONJUGATION.

## Subjunctive.

### Present.
*I may or can love.*

| SINGULAR. | | PLURAL. | |
|---|---|---|---|
| ămĕm, | *I may love,* | ămēmŭs, | *we may love,* |
| ămēs, | *thou mayst love,* | ămētĭs, | *you may love,* |
| ămĕt, | *he may love;* | ămcnt, | *they may love.* |

### Imperfect.
*I might, could, would, or should love.*

| ămārĕm, | *I might love,* | ămārēmŭs, | *we might love,* |
|---|---|---|---|
| ămārēs, | *thou mightst love,* | ămārētĭs, | *you might love,* |
| ămārĕt, | *he might love;* | ămārent, | *they might love.* |

### Perfect.
*I may or can have loved.*

| ămāvĕrĭm, | *I may have loved,* | ămāvĕrĭmŭs, | *we may have loved,* |
|---|---|---|---|
| ămāvĕrĭs, | *thou mayst have loved,* | ămāvĕrĭtĭs, | *you may have loved,* |
| ămāvĕrĭt, | *he may have loved;* | ămāvĕrint, | *they may have loved.* |

### Pluperfect.
*I might, could, would, or should have loved.*

| ămāvissĕm, | *I might have loved,* | ămāvissēmŭs, | *we might have loved,* |
|---|---|---|---|
| ămāvissēs, | *thou mightst have loved,* | ămāvissētĭs, | *you might have loved,* |
| ămāvissĕt, | *he might have loved;* | ămāvissent, | *they might have loved.* |

## Imperative.

| Pres. | ămā, | *love thou;* | ămātĕ, | *love ye:* |
|---|---|---|---|---|
| Fut. | ămātŏ, | *thou shalt love,* | ămātōtĕ, | *ye shall love,* |
| | ămātŏ, | *he shall love;* | ămantŏ, | *they shall love.* |

## Infinitive.

Pres. ămārĕ, *to love.*
Perf. ămāvissĕ, *to have loved.*
Fut. ămātūrŭs[1] essĕ, *to be about to love.*

## Participle.

Pres. ămans,[2] *loving.*

Fut. ămātūrŭs,[1] *about to love.*

## Gerund.

| Gen. | ămandī, | *of loving,* |
|---|---|---|
| Dat. | ămandō, | *for loving,* |
| Acc. | ămandŭm, | *loving,* |
| Abl. | ămandō, | *by loving.* |

## Supine.

| Acc. | ămātŭm, | *to love,* |
|---|---|---|
| Abl. | ămātū, | *to love, be loved.* |

[1] Decline like *bonus*, 148.    [2] Decline like *prudens*, 153.

4

# FIRST CONJUGATION.

### PASSIVE VOICE.

**206.** Amor, *I am loved.*

#### PRINCIPAL PARTS.

| Pres. Ind. | Pres. Inf. | Perf. Ind. |
|---|---|---|
| ămŏr, | ămārī, | ămātŭs sŭm. |

## INDICATIVE MOOD.

### PRESENT TENSE.
*I am loved.*

| SINGULAR. | PLURAL. |
|---|---|
| ămŏr | ămāmŭr |
| ămārĭs, *or* rĕ | ămāmĭnī |
| ămātŭr ; | ămantŭr. |

### IMPERFECT.
*I was loved.*

| | |
|---|---|
| ămābăr | ămābāmŭr |
| ămābārĭs, *or* rĕ | ămābāmĭnī |
| ămābātŭr ; | ămābantŭr. |

### FUTURE.
*I shall* or *will be loved.*

| | |
|---|---|
| ămābŏr | ămābĭmŭr |
| ămābĕrĭs, *or* rĕ | ămābĭmĭnī |
| ămābĭtŭr ; | ămābuntŭr. |

### PERFECT.
*I have been* or *was loved.*

| | |
|---|---|
| ămātŭs sŭm [1] | ămātī sŭmŭs |
| ămātŭs ĕs | ămātī estĭs |
| ămātŭs est ; | ămātī sunt. |

### PLUPERFECT.
*I had been loved.*

| | |
|---|---|
| ămātŭs ĕrăm [1] | ămātī ĕrămŭs |
| ămātŭs ĕrās | ămātī ĕrātĭs |
| ămātŭs ĕrăt ; | ămātī ĕrant. |

### FUTURE PERFECT.
*I shall* or *will have been loved.*

| | |
|---|---|
| ămātŭs ĕrŏ [1] | ămātī ĕrĭmŭs |
| ămātŭs ĕrĭs | ămātī ĕrĭtĭs |
| ămātŭs ĕrĭt ; | ămātī ĕrunt. |

---

[1] *Fui, fuisti,* etc., are sometimes used for *sum, es,* etc.; thus *amātus fui* for *amātus sum.* So *fuĕram, fuĕras,* etc., for *ĕram, ĕras,* etc.; also *fuĕro, fuĕris,* etc., for *ĕro, ĕris,* etc.

## Subjunctive.

### Present.
*I may or can be loved.*

| Singular. | Plural. |
|---|---|
| ămĕr | ămēmŭr |
| ămērĭs, *or* rĕ | ămēmĭnī |
| ămētŭr; | ămentŭr. |

### Imperfect.
*I might, could, would, or should be loved.*

| | |
|---|---|
| ămārĕr | ămārēmŭr |
| ămārērĭs, *or* rĕ | ămārēmĭnī |
| ămārētŭr; | ămārentŭr. |

### Perfect.
*I may have been loved.*

| | |
|---|---|
| ămātŭs sĭm [1] | ămātī sīmŭs |
| ămātŭs sīs | ămātī sītĭs |
| ămātŭs sĭt; | ămātī sint. |

### Pluperfect.
*I might, could, would, or should have been loved.*

| | |
|---|---|
| ămātŭs essĕm [1] | ămātī essēmŭs |
| ămātŭs essēs | ămātī essētĭs |
| ămātŭs essĕt; | ămātī essent. |

## Imperative.

Pres. ămārĕ, *be thou loved;*     ămāmĭnī, *be ye loved.*
Fut. ămātŏr, *thou shalt be loved,*
     ămātŏr, *he shall be loved;*    ămantŏr, *they shall be loved.*

## Infinitive.

Pres. ămārī, *to be loved.*
Perf. ămātŭs essĕ, *to have been loved.*
Fut. ămātŭm īrī, *to be about to be loved.*

## Participle.

Perf. ămātŭs, *having been loved.*
Fut. ămandŭs, *to be loved.*

---

[1] *Fuĕrim, fuĕris*, etc., are sometimes used for *sim, sis*, etc. So also *fuissem, fuisses*, etc., for *essem, esses*, etc.

MODELS FOR PARSING REGULAR VERBS.

### 1. *With Subject.*

Vōs laudāvistĭs,  *You have praised.*

*Laudavistis* is a transitive verb (192, 193) of the First Conjugation (201), from *laudo;* STEM, *laud*. Principal Parts: *laudo, laudāre, laudāvi, laudātum.* Inflection of Tense: *laudāvi, laudavisti, laudāvit, laudavĭmus, laudavistis, laudavērunt,* or *laudavēre.* The form *laudavistis* is found in the *Active* voice, *Indicative* mood, *Perfect* tense, *Second* person, *Plural* number, and agrees with its subject *vos*, according to Rule XXXV.: "A Finite Verb agrees with its Subject in NUMBER and PERSON."

### 2. *Without Subject.*

Laudāvistĭs,  *You have praised.*

This is parsed like *laudavistis*, above, except that it agrees with *vos*, implied in the ending *istis;* while *laudavistis*, above, agrees with *vos* expressed.

### FIRST CONJUGATION — ACTIVE VOICE.

#### EXERCISE XX.

#### I. *Vocabulary.*

Vĭtŭpĕrŏ, āre, āvī, ātŭm,    *to blame.*
Laudŏ, āre, āvī, ātŭm,    *to praise.*

#### II. *Translate into English.*

1. Amo, amābam, amābo.[1]  2. Amas, amābas, amābis.
3. Amat, amant.[1]  4. Amābat, amābant.  5. Amābit, amā-

---

[1] The pupil should carefully compare the forms grouped together under the several numerals, and observe in what they are *alike,* and in what they are *unlike.* Thus *amo, amābam, amābo,* have the letters *am*

ETYMOLOGY.—FIRST CONJUGATION.

bunt.¹ 6. Amāmus, amabāmus, amabĭmus. 7. Amāvi, amavĕram, amavĕro. 8. Amāvit, amavĕrat, amavĕrit. 9. Amāvi, amavīmus. 10. Amavĕram, amāverāmus. 11. Amavĕro, amaverĭmus. 12. Amem, amārem, amavĕrim, amavissem. 13. Amēmus, amarēmus, amaverĭmus, amāvissēmus. 14. Amet, ament. 15. Amāret, amārent. 16. Amavĕrit, amavĕrint. 17. Amavisset, amavissent. 18. Ama, amāte, amatōte. 19. Amāto, amanto.

III. *Translate into Latin.*

1. I praise, I was praising, I will praise. 2. He praises, they praise. 3. He will praise, they will praise. 4. He was praising, they were praising. 5. You were praising, you will praise, you praise. 6. He has loved, he had loved, he will have loved. 7. I have praised, I had praised, I shall have praised. 8. He may love, they may love. 9. Let him praise, let them praise. 10. He would blame, they would blame. 11. I should have praised, we should have praised. 12. Praise thou, praise ye.

FIRST CONJUGATION — Passive Voice.

Exercise XXI.

I. *Translate into English.*

1. Amor, amābar, amābor. 2. Amāris, amabāris, amabĕris. 3. Amātur, amantur. 4. Amabātur, amabantur.

---

(the stem, 203) in common; but they differ from each other in the endings,—*o, ābam, ābo*. In the forms *amat, amant*, there is a still closer resemblance: not only is the stem *am* common to both, but the endings have the letters *at* in common; or, in other words, the plural ending *ant* differs from the singular ending *at* only in inserting *n*: AT, ANT.

¹ Here the pupil will observe that the plural ending *ābunt* differs from the singular ending *ābit*, not only in inserting *n* before *t*, but also in changing *i* into *u*: ABIT, ABUNT.

5. Amabĭtur, amabuntur. 6. Amāmur, amabāmur, amabĭmur. 7. Amātus[1] sum, amātus eram, amātus ero. 8. Amātus es, amātus eras, amātus eris. 9. Amātus est, amāti[1] sunt. 10. Amātus erat, amāti erant. 11. Amātus erit, amāti erunt. 12. Amer, amārer, amātus sim, amātus essem. 13. Amēmur, amarēmur, amāti simus, amāti essēmus. 14. Amētur, amentur. 15. Amarētur, amarentur. 16. Amātus sit, amāti sint. 17. Amātus esset, amāti essent. 18. Amātor, amantor.

II. *Translate into Latin.*

1. He is praised, they are praised. 2. He was praised, they were praised. 3. He will be praised, they will be praised. 4. I am blamed, I was blamed, I shall be blamed. 5. You are loved, you are praised. 6. You were loved, you were praised. 7. You will be loved, you will be praised. 8. I have been blamed, you have been praised. 9. I had been blamed, you had been praised. 10. I shall have been blamed, you will have been praised. 11. You may be blamed, you might be blamed. 12. He would have been blamed, they would have been praised. 13. Let him be praised, let them be praised. 14. Be thou praised, be ye praised.

---

[1] The learner will observe, that, when the verb and the subject (expressed or implied) are in the Singular, the participle (*amātus*), which forms one element of the verb, is also in the Singular; and that, when the verb and the subject are in the Plural, the participle (*amāti*) is also in the Plural.

The form of the participle also varies with the *gender* of the subject, as well as with its *number*. Thus, if the subject is Masculine, the participle will be *amātus* in the Singular, and *amāti* in the Plural; if Feminine, *amāta* in the Singular, and *amātae* in the Plural; and, if Neuter, *amātum* in the Singular, and *amāta* in the Plural. Thus the participle in the compound tenses (i.e., in those which are made up of the participle and the auxiliary *sum*) agrees with the subject in *gender*, *number*, and *case*, like an adjective, according to Rule XXXV. 1, note.

# FIRST CONJUGATION — Both Voices.

## Exercise XXII.

### I. *Translate into English.*

1. Laudo, laudor.[1]  2. Laudābo, laudābor.[2]  3. Laudābam, laudābar.[2]  4. Laudem, lauder.  5. Laudārem, laudārer.[2]  6. Laudat, laudatur.[1]  7. Amābat, amabātur.  8. Amābit, amabĭtur.  9. Amet, amētur.  10. Amāret, amarētur.  11. Laudārent, laudarentur.  12. Ament, amentur.  13. Laudant, laudantur.  14. Amābant, amabantur.  15. Laudābunt, laudabuntur.  16. Amāvit, amātus est.  17. Laudavĕrat, laudātus erat.  18. Amavĕrit, amātus erit.  19. Lauda, laudāre.  20. Amāto, amātor.  21. Laudanto, laudantor.

### II. *Translate into Latin.*

1. He blames, he is blamed.  2. I was praising, I was praised.  3. You will praise, you will be praised.  4. He

---

[1] In this Exercise, the pupil should carefully compare the corresponding forms in the two Voices, — the Active and the Passive, — and observe the difference between them. The Passive *laudor* differs from the Active *laudo* only in adding *r;* the Passive *laudābar* differs from the Active *laudābam* only in taking *r* in place of *m*. Thus we find, that, in the Indicative and in the Subjunctive, the first person of the Passive is formed from the first person of the Active by simply adding *r;* or, if the Active ends in *m*, by substituting *r* for *m*. Again: the Passive *laudātur* differs from the Active *laudat* only in adding *ur*. Thus we find, that, in the Indicative and in the Subjunctive, the third person of the Passive is formed from the third person of the Active by simply adding *ur*.

[2] Where must we look to find the meaning of these endings, — in the Vocabulary, or in the Grammar? and where to find the general meaning of the verb? See Suggestion II. To find the meaning of the verb to which *laudābor* belongs, for what form must we look in the Vocabulary? See Suggestion VII.

will blame, he will be blamed. 5. They will praise, they will be praised. 6. We blame, we are blamed. 7. He has praised, he has been praised. 8. They have blamed, they have been blamed. 9. He had praised, he had been praised. 10. They had blamed, they had been blamed. 11. He may praise, he may be praised. 12. He would blame, he would be blamed. 13. They may praise, they may be praised.

### FIRST CONJUGATION — First and Second Declensions.[1]
### Direct Object.

### RULE V. — Direct Object.

**379.** The Direct Object[2] of an action is put in the Accusative.

Deus mundum aedĭfĭcāvit, *God made the world*.[3] Cic. Lībĕra rem publĭcam, *Free the republic*. Cic. Pŏpŭli Rōmāni sălūtem dēfendĭte, *Defend the safety of the Roman people*. Cic.

---

[1] It is thought advisable that the pupil should now commence a review of the grammatical forms which he has already learned. Accordingly, this Exercise will involve nouns of the First and of the Second Declension. The pupil should therefore carefully review those Declensions (42, 45). In connection with the subsequent Exercises, it is expected that the other Declensions and the other Grammatical forms will be reviewed in order, as will be indicated in the respective headings which precede the several Exercises.

[2] The *Direct Object* of an action is generally the *object*, person, or thing, on which the action is *directly* exerted; as, *salūtem*, safety, in the third example; *defend* (what?) *the safety*. But the *Direct Object* is sometimes the *effect* of the action, i.e. the object produced by it; as, *mundum*, world, in the first example, — *made the world*.

[3] In English, the object follows the verb; thus, in this example, *world* follows *made;* but in Latin the object usually precedes the verb: thus *mundum* precedes *aedificāvit*. So also, in the third example, *salūtem* precedes *defendĭte;* but sometimes the object follows the verb: thus in the second example, *rem publĭcam* follows *lībĕra*.

## MODEL FOR PARSING DIRECT OBJECTS.

Dĕus mundŭm aedĭfĭcāvĭt, *God made the world.*

*Mundum* is a noun (31) of the Second Declension, as it has *i* in the Genitive Singular ·(40); STEM, mund. Singular: *mundus, mundi, mundo, mundum, munde, mundo.* Plural: *mundi, mundōrum, mundis, mundos, mundi, mundis.* It is of the Masculine gender, by 45; is in the Accusative Singular; and is the Direct Object of the transitive verb *aedificāvit,* according to Rule V.: "The Direct Object of an action is put in the Accusative."

### EXERCISE XXIII.

#### I. *Vocabulary.*

| | |
|---|---|
| Aedĭfĭcŏ, āre, āvī, ātŭm, | *to build.* |
| Arŏ, āre, āvī, ātŭm, | *to plough.* |
| Cantŏ, āre, avī, ātŭm, | *to sing.* |
| Ităliă, ae, *f.* | *Italy.* |
| Lĭbĕrŏ, āre, āvī,·ātŭm, | *to liberate.* |
| Rĕnŏvŏ, āre, āvī, ātŭm, | *to renew.* |
| Spērŏ, āre, āvī, ātŭm, | *to hope.* |
| Tarquĭnĭŭs, iī, *m.* | *Tarquinius,* Roman king. |
| Thĕmistŏclēs, ĭs, *m.* | *Themistocles,* Athenian commander. |

#### II. *Translate into English.*

1. Lusciniam laudo.[1] 2. Lusciniam laudāmus. 3. Luscinias laudat. 4. Luscinias laudant. 5. Luscinia laudātur. 6. Lusciniae laudantur. ·7. Patriam amāmus. 8. Pro patriā[2] pugnabĭmus. 9. Nonne[3] Themistŏcles patriam liberāvit? 10. Patriam liberāvit. 11: Italiam liberāvērunt. 12. Italia liberāta[4] est. 13. Tarquinius templum aedifica-

---

[1] *Lusciniam* is the *Direct Object* of *laudo,* according to Rule V.
[2] See Rule XXXII. page 24.
[3] See 346, II. 1, page 59.
[4] For agreement ·of participle with subject, see Rule XXXV. 460, 1, page 54.

vit. 14. Templum aedĭfĭcābat. 15. Templa aedĭfĭcavĕrant. 16. Templa aedĭfĭcāta erant. 17. Templum aedĭfĭcātum erit. 18. Puĕrum laudabāmus. 19. Puĕri laudāti sunt. 20. Nonne[1] bellum renovātum est?

### III. *Translate into Latin.*

1. The nightingale is singing. 2. The nightingales are singing. 3. The nightingales will sing. 4. The boys have been praised. 5. Did you not[1] praise the boys?[2] 6. We praised the boys. 7. The boys will be praised. 8. Have we not[1] liberated Italy? 9. You have liberated Italy. 10. We will liberate the country. 11. We were ploughing the field. 12. Will you plough the field? 13. The field will be ploughed.

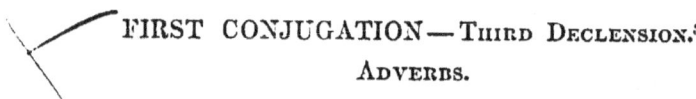

FIRST CONJUGATION — Third Declension.[3]

ADVERBS.

### RULE LI.—Use of Adverbs.

582. Adverbs[4] qualify VERBS, ADJECTIVES, and other ADVERBS:

Săpientes fēlĭcĭter[4] vīvunt, *The wise live happily.* Cic. Făcĭle[4] doctissĭmus, *unquestionably the most learned.* Cic. Haud[4] ălĭter, *not otherwise.* Virg.

---

[1] See 346, II. 1, page 59.

[2] The Latin word for *boys* in this sentence will be in the Accusative, according to Rule V., and will precede the verb.

[3] The pupil should now review the Third Declension (48–54).

[4] The Adverb is, therefore, the part of speech which is used to qualify verbs, adjectives, and other adverbs. *Felicĭter,* happily, is an adverb qualifying the verb *vivunt,* live (live *happily*). *Facile,* easily, unquestionably, is an adverb qualifying the adjective *doctissĭmus,* the most learned (*easily,* i.e. *unquestionably* the most learned). *Haud,* not, is an adverb qualifying the adverb *alĭter,* otherwise (*not otherwise*). The adverb in Latin usually stands directly before the word which it qualifies, as in these examples.

ETYMOLOGY. — FIRST CONJUGATION. 73

MODEL FOR PARSING ADVERBS.

Săpĭentēs fēlīcĭtĕr vīvunt,    *The wise live happily.*

*Felicĭter* is an adverb, and qualifies *vīvunt*, according to Rule LI.: "Adverbs qualify VERBS, ADJECTIVES, and other ADVERBS."

## EXERCISE XXIV.

### I. *Vocabulary.*

| | |
|---|---|
| Elŏquentĭă, ae, *f.* | *eloquence.* |
| Expugnŏ, āre, āvī, ātŭm, | *to take, take by storm.* |
| Fortĭtĕr, *adv.* | *bravely.* |
| Jŭventūs, jŭventūtĭs, *f.* | *youth.* |
| Ornŏ, āre, āvī, ātŭm, | *to adorn, be an ornament to.* |
| Pĭĕtās, pĭĕtātĭs, *f.* | *filial affection, piety, duty.* |
| Pugnŏ, āre, āvī, ātŭm, | *to fight.* |
| Servŏ, āre, āvī, ātŭm, | *to preserve, keep, save.* |
| Vŏlŏ, āre, āvī, ātŭm, | *to fly.* |

### II. *Translate into English.*

1. Avis volat. 2. Aves volant. 3. Nonne[1] avis cantābat? 4. Aves cantābant. 5. Rex urbem[2] aedĭfĭcāvit. 6. Urbs aedĭfĭcāta[3] est. 7. Urbes aedĭfĭcātae[3] erunt. 8. Mīlĭtes fortĭter[4] pugnavērunt. 9. Scipio[5] mīlĭtes laudāvit. 10. Scipio[5] mīlĭtum virtūtem laudābat. 11. Scipiōnem laudāmus. 12. Scipio patrem servāvit. 13. Scipio urbem expugnāvit. 14. Urbs expugnāta est. 15. Mīlĭtes patriam amant. 16. Mīlĭtes[5] pro patriā pugnābant. 17. Pĭĕtas pueros ornat. 18. Virtūtes civitātem ornant.

---

[1] See 346, II. 1, page 59.

[2] *Urbem*, direct object of *aedĭfĭcāvit*, according to Rule V.

[3] Why *aedĭfĭcāta* in one case, and *aedĭfĭcātae* in the other? Why not *aedĭfĭcātus* in both? See Rule XXXV. 460, 1, page 54.

[4] *Fortĭter*, an Adverb qualifying *pugnavērunt*, according to Rule LI.

[5] In what order will you look out the words in this sentence? See Suggestion V.

### III. *Translate into Latin.*

1. The birds are singing. 2. Do you not[1] love birds?[2] 3. We love birds.[2] 4. This bird will fly. 5. Did you not[1] save the city? 6. The soldiers saved the city. 7. Shepherds love the mountains. 8. We love virtue. 9. Is not virtue loved? 10. It is loved. 11. Do not the citizens praise the king? 12. They praise the king. 13. The king will be praised. 14. The virtue of the king is praised.

## FIRST CONJUGATION — FOURTH AND FIFTH DECLENSIONS.[3]

### EXERCISE XXV.

#### I. *Vocabulary.*

| | |
|---|---|
| Convŏcŏ, āre, āvī, ātŭm, | to assemble, call together. |
| Duplĭcŏ, āre, āvī, ātŭm, | to double, increase. |
| Dux, dŭcĭs, *m.* | general, leader. |
| Fĭdēs, fĭdĕī, *f.* | faith, fidelity, word,[4] promise. |
| Fŭgŏ, āre, āvī, ātŭm, | to rout. |
| Hŏmŏ, hŏmĭnĭs, *m.* | man. |
| Sĕnātŭs, ūs, *m.* | senate. |
| Stĭmŭlŏ, āre, āvī, ātŭm, | to stimulate. |

#### II. *Translate into English.*

1. Hŏmĭnes[5] cantum lusciniae[6] laudant. 2. Cantus lusciniae laudātur. 3. Rŏmŭlus excercĭtum fugat. 4. Nonne

---

[1] See 346, II. 1, page 59.

[2] Remember that the *object* in Latin usually precedes the verb.

[3] The pupil should now review these Declensions (116, 119).

[4] To keep one's word, *fidem servāre:* I keep my word, *fidem meam servo,* or *fidem servo,* as the Latin possessives, *meus,* my, *tuus,* your, etc., when not emphatic, are often omitted; when expressed, they usually follow their nouns.

[5] In this sentence, what order will you follow, in accordance with Suggestion V., in looking out the words in the Vocabulary? In accordance with Suggestion VII., for what forms will you look in the Vocabulary to find the meaning of *homĭnes* (51, II.), *milĭtes* (50, II.), *stimulāvit* (205)?

[6] See Rule XVI. page 22.

## ETYMOLOGY. — FIRST CONJUGATION.

exercĭtum fŭgavĭmus? 5. Exercĭtus fugātus est. 6. Exercĭtus fugātus erit. 7. Consul senātum convocāvit. 8. Senātus convocātus est. 9. Senātus consŭlem laudāvit. 10. Spes victoriae milĭtes stimulāvĭt. 11. Numĕrum diērum duplicāvi. 12. Numĕrus diērum duplicātus est.

### III. *Translate into Latin.*

1. The boy has kept his word.¹ 2. Will you not keep your word? 3. We will keep our word. 4. The consul praised the fidelity of the citizens. 5. Will not the fidelity of the citizens be praised? 6. Will not the citizens praise the fidelity of the army? 7. They have praised the fidelity of the army. 8. Did not the general praise the army? 9. He praised the army. 10. The army will be praised.

## FIRST CONJUGATION — Adjectives.²

### Exercise XXVI.

#### I. *Vocabulary.*

| | |
|---|---|
| Amplĭŏ, āre, āvī, ātŭm, | *to enlarge.* |
| Condemnŏ, āre, āvī, ātŭm, | *to condemn.* |
| Hannĭbăl, Hannĭbălis, *m.* | *Hannibal,* Carthaginian general. |
| Innŏcens, innŏcentĭs, | *innocent.* |
| Nōbĭlis, ĕ, | *noble.* |
| Nŏvŭs, ă, ŭm, | *new.* |
| Occŭpŏ, āre, āvī, ātŭm, | *to occupy.* |
| Pūnĭcŭs, ă, ŭm, | *Carthaginian, Punic.* |

---

¹ See note 4, preceding page.
² The pupil should now review Adjectives (146–162).

## II. Translate into English.

1. Rex urbem novam[1] ampliābat. 2. Urbem novam ampliābunt. 3. Rex urbem pulchram[1] ampliăvĕrat. 4. Urbs pulchra servāta[2] est. 5. Hannĭbal multas civitātes occupāvit. 6. Judĭces homĭnem innocentissĭmum[3] condemnavērunt. 7. Num Punĭcum bellum renovātum est? 8. Nonne Punĭcum bellum renovātum est? 9. Punĭcum bellum renovātum est. 10. Romāni nobilissĭmas[3] urbes expugnavērunt.

## III. Translate into Latin.

1. Will not the brave soldiers save the city? 2. The brave soldiers will save the beautiful city. 3. The noble city will be saved. 4. We praise good boys. 5. Good boys will be praised. 6. Do you not praise diligent pupils? 7. Diligent pupils are praised. 8. The citizens praise the brave soldiers.

### FIRST CONJUGATION — Pronouns.[4]

### Exercise XXVII.

#### I. Vocabulary.

| | |
|---|---|
| Alĭquis, ălĭquă, ălĭquid *or* ălĭquŏd, | *some one, somebody.* |
| Dēlectŏ, ārĕ, āvī, ātŭm, | *to delight.* |
| Dilĭgentiă, ae, *f.* | *diligence.* |
| Nōn, *adv.* | *not.* |
| Sălūtŏ, ārĕ, āvī, ātŭm, | *to salute.* |
| Suŭs, ă, ŭm, | *his, her, its, their.* |

---

[1] See Rule XXXIII. p. 32.
[2] Why *servāta* rather than *servātus*? See Rule XXXV. 460, 1, p. 54.
[3] In accordance with Suggestion VII., for what form will you look in the Vocabulary? See 162.
[4] The pupil should now review Pronouns (182–191).

## II. Translate into English.

1. Quis hanc[1] urbem servābit? 2. Hanc urbem pulchram servabĭmus. 3. Quis te[2] salutāvit? 4. Pater meus[1] te salūtat. 5. Haec[1] vita te delectat. 6. Philosophia nos[2] delectat. 7. Omnia animalia se[2] amant. 8. Fratres tui[1] laudantur. 9. Fratres mei laudāti sunt. 10. Puer parentes suos[3] amat. 11. Puĕri boni parentes suos[3] amant. 12. Parentes nostros amāmus.

## III. Translate into Latin.

1. Do you blame me? 2. We do not[4] blame you. 3. Whom do you blame? 4. We blame your brother. 5. This book delights me. 6. These books delighted us. 7. Did not[5] your father praise you? 8. He praised us. 9. Did not[5] some one praise your diligence? 10. Our parents praised our diligence. 11. Did your brother blame you? 12. He did not[4] blame me. 13. He blamed himself. 14. He will be blamed.

---

[1] These Pronouns are all used as adjectives, and agree with their nouns like any other adjectives, according to Rule XXXIII. p. 32. Pronouns thus used as adjectives generally precede their nouns; but the Possessive Pronouns, *meus, tuus*, etc. (185), generally follow their nouns, as in this Exercise.

[2] Personal Pronouns, it will be remembered, are used as substantives (184). They are accordingly governed like any other substantives. See Rule V. p. 70. Observe that the object precedes the verb.

[3] The pupil will observe that *suos* in the tenth sentence must be rendered *his*, while in the eleventh it must be rendered *their*. Thus the meaning of the Possessive *suus* depends in part upon the *number* of the word to which it refers. It must be rendered *his* (*her, its*) when that word, as *puer* in the tenth sentence, is in the *Singular;* but it must be rendered *their* when that word, as *puĕri* in the eleventh sentence, is in the *Plural*.

[4] When a verb with a direct object has also an adverb qualifying it, the usual order is *Object, Adverb, Verb;* but the adverb *non*, not, may stand either *before* or *after* the object.

[5] Nonne.

## SECOND CONJUGATION.

### ACTIVE VOICE.

**207. Moneo,** *I advise.*

#### PRINCIPAL PARTS.

| Pres. Ind. | Pres. Inf. | Perf. Ind. | Supine. |
|---|---|---|---|
| mŏneŏ, | mŏnērĕ, | mŏnŭī, | mŏnĭtŭm. |

### INDICATIVE MOOD.

**PRESENT TENSE.**
*I advise.*

| SINGULAR. | PLURAL. |
|---|---|
| mŏneŏ | mŏnēmŭs |
| mŏnēs | mŏnētĭs |
| mŏnĕt ; | mŏnent. |

**IMPERFECT.**
*I was advising.*

| | |
|---|---|
| mŏnēbăm | mŏnēbāmŭs |
| mŏnēbās | mŏnēbātĭs |
| mŏnēbăt ; | mŏnēbant. |

**FUTURE.**
*I shall* or *will advise.*

| | |
|---|---|
| mŏnēbŏ | mŏnēbĭmŭs |
| mŏnēbĭs | mŏnēbĭtĭs |
| mŏnēbĭt ; | mŏnēbunt. |

**PERFECT.**
*I advised* or *have advised.*

| | |
|---|---|
| mŏnŭī | mŏnŭĭmŭs |
| mŏnŭistī | mŏnŭistĭs |
| mŏnŭĭt ; | mŏnŭērunt, *or* ērĕ. |

**PLUPERFECT.**
*I had advised.*

| | |
|---|---|
| mŏnŭĕrăm | mŏnŭĕrāmŭs |
| mŏnŭĕrās | mŏnŭĕrātĭs |
| mŏnŭĕrăt ; | mŏnŭĕrant. |

**FUTURE PERFECT.**
*I shall* or *will have advised.*

| | |
|---|---|
| mŏnŭĕrŏ | mŏnŭĕrĭmŭs |
| mŏnŭĕrĭs | mŏnŭĕrĭtĭs |
| mŏnŭĕrĭt ; | mŏnŭĕrint. |

ETYMOLOGY.—SECOND CONJUGATION. 79

## SUBJUNCTIVE.

### PRESENT.
*I may or can advise.*

| SINGULAR. | PLURAL. |
|---|---|
| mŏneăm | mŏneāmŭs |
| mŏneās | mŏneātĭs |
| mŏneăt; | mŏneant. |

### IMPERFECT.
*I might, could, would, or should advise.*

| mŏnērĕm | mŏnērēmŭs |
|---|---|
| mŏnērēs | mŏnērētĭs |
| mŏnērĕt; | mŏnērent. |

### PERFECT.
*I may have advised.*

| mŏnuĕrĭm | mŏnuĕrĭmŭs |
|---|---|
| mŏnuĕrĭs | mŏnuĕrĭtĭs |
| mŏnuĕrĭt; | mŏnuĕrint. |

### PLUPERFECT.
*I might, could, would, or should have advised.*

| mŏnuissĕm | mŏnuissēmŭs |
|---|---|
| mŏnuissēs | mŏnuissētĭs |
| mŏnuissĕt; | mŏnuissent. |

## IMPERATIVE.

PRES. mŏnē, *advise thou;*    mŏnētĕ, *advise ye.*
FUT. mŏnētō, *thou shalt advise,*    mŏnētōtĕ, *ye shall advise,*
      mŏnētō, *he shall advise;*    mŏnentō, *they shall advise*

### INFINITIVE.   PARTICIPLE.

PRES. mŏnērĕ, *to advise.*    PRES. mŏnens, *advising.*
PERF. mŏnuissĕ, *to have advised.*
FUT. mŏnĭtūrŭs essĕ, *to be*    FUT. mŏnĭtūrŭs, *about to advise.*
     *about to advise.*

### GERUND.   SUPINE.

*Gen.* mŏnendī, *of advising,*
*Dat.* mŏnendō, *for advising,*
*Acc.* mŏnendŭm, *advising,*    *Acc.* mŏnĭtŭm, *to advise,*
*Abl.* mŏnendō, *by advising.*    *Abl.* mŏnĭtū, *to advise, be advised.*

## SECOND CONJUGATION.

### PASSIVE VOICE.

**208.** Moneor, *I am advised.*

#### PRINCIPAL PARTS.

| Pres. Ind. | Pres. Inf. | Perf. Ind. |
|---|---|---|
| mŏneŏr, | mŏnērī, | mŏnĭtŭs sŭm. |

### INDICATIVE MOOD.

#### PRESENT TENSE.
*I am advised.*

| SINGULAR. | PLURAL. |
|---|---|
| mŏneŏr | mŏnēmŭr |
| mŏnērĭs, *or* rĕ | mŏnēmĭnī |
| mŏnētŭr; | mŏnentŭr. |

#### IMPERFECT.
*I was advised.*

| mŏnēbăr | mŏnēbămŭr |
|---|---|
| mŏnēbărĭs, *or* rĕ | mŏnēbămĭnī |
| mŏnēbătŭr; | mŏnēbantŭr. |

#### FUTURE.
*I shall or will be advised.*

| mŏnēbŏr | mŏnēbĭmŭr |
|---|---|
| mŏnēbĕrĭs, *or* rĕ | mŏnēbĭmĭnī |
| mŏnēbĭtŭr; | mŏnēbuntŭr. |

#### PERFECT.
*I have been or was advised.*

| mŏnĭtŭs sŭm[1] | mŏnĭtī sŭmŭs |
|---|---|
| mŏnĭtŭs ĕs | mŏnĭtī estĭs |
| mŏnĭtŭs est; | mŏnĭtī sunt. |

#### PLUPERFECT.
*I had been advised.*

| mŏnĭtŭs ĕrăm[1] | mŏnĭtī ĕrămŭs |
|---|---|
| mŏnĭtŭs ĕrās | mŏnĭtī ĕrātĭs |
| mŏnĭtŭs ĕrăt; | mŏnĭtī ĕrant. |

#### FUTURE PERFECT.
*I shall or will have been advised.*

| mŏnĭtŭs ĕrŏ[1] | mŏnĭtī ĕrĭmŭs |
|---|---|
| mŏnĭtŭs ĕrĭs | mŏnĭtī ĕrĭtĭs |
| mŏnĭtŭs ĕrĭt; | mŏnĭtī ĕrunt. |

---

[1] See 206, foot-notes.

## SUBJUNCTIVE.

### PRESENT.
*I may or can be advised.*

| SINGULAR. | PLURAL. |
|---|---|
| mŏneăr | mŏneāmŭr |
| mŏneārĭs, *or* rĕ | mŏneāmĭnĭ |
| mŏneātŭr; | mŏneantŭr. |

### IMPERFECT.
*I might, could, would, or should be advised.*

| | |
|---|---|
| mŏnērĕr | mŏnērēmŭr |
| mŏnērērĭs, *or* rĕ | mŏnērēmĭnĭ |
| mŏnērētŭr; | mŏnērentŭr. |

### PERFECT.
*I may have been advised.*

| | |
|---|---|
| mŏnĭtŭs sĭm [1] | mŏnĭtĭ sīmŭs |
| mŏnĭtŭs sīs | mŏnĭtĭ sītĭs |
| mŏnĭtŭs sĭt; | mŏnĭtĭ sint. |

### PLUPERFECT.
*I might, could, would, or should have been advised.*

| | |
|---|---|
| mŏnĭtŭs essĕm [1] | mŏnĭtĭ essēmŭs |
| mŏnĭtŭs essēs | mŏnĭtĭ essētĭs |
| mŏnĭtŭs essĕt; | mŏnĭtĭ essent. |

## IMPERATIVE.

PRES. mŏnērĕ, *be thou advised;* | mŏnēmĭnĭ, *be ye advised.*

FUT. mŏnētŏr, *thou shalt be advised,*
mŏnētŏr, *he shall be advised;* | mŏnentŏr, *they shall be advised.*

## INFINITIVE.

PRES. mŏnērĭ, *to be advised,*
PERF. mŏnĭtŭs essĕ, *to have been advised,*
FUT. mŏnĭtŭm ĭrĭ, *to be about to be advised.*

## PARTICIPLE.

PERF. mŏnĭtŭs, *advised,*

FUT. mŏnendŭs, *to be advised.*

---

[1] See 206, foot-notes.

## SECOND CONJUGATION — Active Voice.

### Exercise XXVIII.

#### I. *Vocabulary.*

Mŏnĕŏ, mŏnērĕ, mŏnui, mŏnĭtŭm,　　*to advise.*
Pārĕŏ, pārērĕ, pāruī, pārĭtŭm,　　*to obey.*

#### II. *Translate into English.*

1. Moneo, monēbam, monēbo.[1] 2. Mones, monētis. 3. Monet, monent. 4. Monēmus, monebāmus, monebĭmus. 5. Monēbant, monēbunt. 6. Monui, monuĕram, monuĕro. 7. Monuĭmus, monuerāmus, monuerĭmus. 8. Monuit, monuĕrunt. 9. Monuĕrat, monuĕrant. 10. Monuĕrit, monuĕrint. 11. Moneam, monērem, monuĕrim, monuissem. 12. Moneat, moneant. 13. Monēret, monērent. 14. Monuĕrit, monuĕrint. 15. Monuisset, monuissent.

#### III. *Translate into Latin.*

1. You advise, you were advising, you will advise. 2. He obeys, they obey. 3. He was obeying, they were obeying. 4. He will advise, they will advise. 5. He has obeyed, he had obeyed, he will have obeyed. 6. They have advised, they had advised, they will have advised. 7. I have advised, we have advised. 8. I had advised, I had obeyed. 9. He may advise, he may obey.

---

[1] The pupil should carefully compare the forms grouped together under the several numerals, and observe wherein they differ from each other

## FIRST AND SECOND CONJUGATIONS — Active Voice.

### Exercise XXIX.

#### I. *Vocabulary.*

Cantŏ, āre̅, āvī, ātŭm,   *to sing.*
Spēro̅, āre̅, āvī. ātŭm,   *to hope.*

#### II. *Translate into English.*

1. Sperat, paret.[1] 2. Sperant, parent. 3. Sperāmus, parēmus. 4. Sperābat, parēbat. 5. Sperābant, parēbant. 6. Sperābam, parēbam. 7. Sperabāmus, parebāmus. 8. Sperabĭmus, parebĭmus. 9. Sperābo, parēbo. 10. Sperāvi, parui. 11. Speravĕram, paruĕram. 12. Speravĕro, paruĕro. 13. Speravĭmus, paruĭmus. 14. Speravĕrat, paruĕrat. 15. Speravĕrint, paruĕrint. 16. Sperāte, parēte.

#### III. *Translate into Latin.*

1. I sing, I advise. 2. I was singing, I was advising. 3. I will sing, I will advise. 4. He will hope, he will obey. 5. They will hope, they will obey. 6. They were singing, they were advising. 7. They sing, they advise. 8. He has hoped, he has obeyed. 9. They have hoped, they have obeyed. 10. He had sung, he had obeyed. 11. They had sung, they had obeyed. 12. We had hoped, we had advised. 13. We would sing, we would obey.

---

[1] In this Exercise, the pupil should carefully compare the corresponding forms in the two Conjugations, — the First and the Second, — and should carefully observe the difference between them.

## SECOND CONJUGATION — Active Voice.
### Other Parts of Speech.

### Exercise XXX.

#### I. *Vocabulary.*

| | |
|---|---|
| Aurŭm, ī, *n.* | *gold.* |
| Flōs, flōrĭs, *m.* | *flower.* |
| Hăbeŏ, hăbērĕ, hăbuī, hăbĭtŭm, | *to have, hold.* |
| Mĕreŏ, mĕrērĕ, mĕruī, mĕrĭtŭm, | *to deserve, merit.* |
| Phĭlŏsŏphŭs, ī, *m.* | *philosopher.* |
| Pondŭs, pondĕrĭs, *n.* | *weight, mass.* |
| Praebeŏ, praebērĕ, praebuī, praebĭtŭm, | *to furnish, give.* |
| Praemĭŭm, iī, *n.* | *reward.* |
| Tăceŏ, tăcērĕ, tăcuī, tăcĭtŭm, | *to be silent.* |
| Terreŏ, terrērĕ, terruī, terrĭtŭm, | *to frighten, terrify.* |

#### II. *Translate into English.*

1. Puer librum habet. 2. Puĕri libros habent. 3. Libros utĭles[1] habēmus. 4. Librum utĭlem habuisti. 5. Nonne bonum[1] amīcum habēbis? 6. Bonum amīcum habēbo. 7. Bonos amīcos habuĭmus. 8. Rex amīcos habēbat. 9. Rex aurum habēbat. 10. Rex[2] magnum auri pondus[3] habuĕrat. 11. Gloriam veram habebĭtis. 12. Ver praebet flores. 13. Ver praebēbit flores. 14. Philosŏphus tacēbat. 15. Discipŭlus praemium meret.

---

[1] Observe that the Latin adjective may either precede or follow its noun; though it seems more frequently to follow, unless it is emphatic.

[2] In this sentence, endeavor, in accordance with Suggestion IV., to discover the *subject, verb,* and *object,* before looking out the words in the Vocabulary. In what order will you look out the words in accordance with Suggestion V.?

[3] When a noun is qualified by both an adjective and a genitive, as *pondus* by *magnum* and *auri,* the adjective usually precedes both nouns, and is followed by the genitive, as in this example: *magnum auri pondus.*

III. *Translate into Latin.*

1. Who has my book? 2. I have your book. 3. Which book have you? 4. I have three[1] books. 5. My brother has ten books. 6. The king had a golden crown. 7. Did he not have many friends? 8. He had many friends. 9. You will have true friends. 10. The pupils are silent.[2] 11. Will you not be silent? 12. We will be silent.

## SECOND CONJUGATION—Passive Voice.

### Exercise XXXI.

I. *Translate into English.*

1. Moneor, monēbar, monēbor. 2. Monēmur, monebāmur, monebīmur. 3. Moneātur, moneantur. 4. Monerētur, monerentur. 5. Monĭtus est, monĭti sunt. 6. Monĭtus erat, monĭti erant. 7. Monĭtus erit, monĭti erunt. 8. Monētor, monentor. 9. Monet, monētur. 10. Monent, monentur. 11. Monēbat, Monebātur. 12. Monēbant, monebantur. 13. Monēbit, monebītur. 14. Monēbunt, monebuntur. 15. Monēmus, monēmur. 16. Monebāmus, Monebāmur. 17. Monebĭmus, monebĭmur.

II. *Translate into Latin.*

1. He is advised, they are advised. 2. I was terrified, we were terrified. 3. He will be advised, they will be advised. 4. You have been terrified, I have been terrified. 5. He had been advised, he had been terrified. 6. I shall have been advised, I shall have been terrified. 7. I advise, I am advised. 8. I was advising, I was advised. 9. I shall advise, I shall be advised. 10. They terrify, they are terrified. 11. They were terrifying, they were terrified. 12. They will terrify, they will be terrified.

---

[1] Place the Numeral *before* the noun.
[2] *Are silent* is to be rendered by the Latin verb *taceo.*

## FIRST AND SECOND CONJUGATIONS — Passive Voice.

### Exercise XXXII.

#### I. *Vocabulary.*

| | |
|---|---|
| Admŏnĕŏ, admŏnēre, admŏnuī, admŏnĭtum, | *to admonish.* |
| Amŏ, āre, āvī, ātum, | *to love.* |
| Invītŏ, āre, āvī, ātum, | *to invite.* |
| Laudŏ, āre, āvī, ātum, | *to praise.* |
| Terreŏ, terrēre, terruī, terrĭtum, | *to terrify.* |
| Vĭtŭpĕrŏ, āre, āvī, ātum, | *to blame.* |

#### II. *Translate into English.*

1. Invītātur, terrētur. 2. Invītantur, terrentur. 3. Invītāmur, terrēmur. 4. Invītabāmur, terrebāmur. 5. Invītabātur, terrebātur. 6. Invītabantur, terrebantur. 7. Invītabuntur, terrebuntur. 8. Invītabĭtur, terrebĭtur. 9. Invītābor, terrēbor. 10. Invītātus sum, terrĭtus sum. 11. Invītāti sumus, terrĭti sumus. 12. Invītātus est, terrĭtus est. 13. Invītāti sunt, terrĭti sunt. 14. Invītāti erant, terrĭti erant. 15. Invītātus erat, terrĭtus erat.

#### III. *Translate into Latin.*

1. I am invited, I am admonished. 2. You are invited, you are admonished. 3. He was praised, he was advised. 4. They were praised, they were advised. 5. You will be invited, you will be admonished. 6. He has been blamed, he has been terrified. 7. They had been loved, they had been admonished. 8. They will have been invited, they

will have been admonished. 9. I may be invited, I may be admonished. 10. I should be invited, I should be admonished.

## SECOND CONJUGATION — Passive Voice.
### Other Parts of Speech.

### Exercise XXXIII.

#### I. *Vocabulary.*

| | |
|---|---|
| Apŭd, *prep. with acc.* | *near, before, among.* |
| Exerceŏ, exercērĕ, exercuī, exercĭtŭm, | *to exercise, train.* |
| Frāter, frātrĭs, *m.* | *brother.* |
| Măgistĕr, măgistrī, *m.* | *master, teacher.* |
| Mĕmŏriă, ae, *f.* | *memory.* |
| Pŭĕr, pŭĕrī, *m.* | *boy.* |
| Quĭs, quae, quĭd,[1] | *who, which, what?* |
| Rectē, *adv.* | *rightly.* |
| Tuŭs, ă, ŭm, | *your, yours.* |

#### II. *Translate into English.*

1. Quis monētur? 2. Nonne puer monētur? 3. Puer recte monētur. 4. Puĕri recte monentur. 5. Discĭpŭli recte monĭti sunt. 6. Discĭpŭlus recte monĭtus est. 7. Frater tuus recte admonĭtus erit. 8. Fratres tui recte admonĭti erunt. 9. Nonne admonĭti sumus? 10. Recte admonĭti sumus. 11. Memoria exercētur. 12. Memoria

---

[1] For the declension of the Interrogative Pronoun *quis*, see 188.

exerceātur.¹ 13. Memoria exercebĭtur. 14. Discipŭli apud magistros exercentur.

### III. *Translate into Latin.*

1. Were not the boys terrified? 2. They were terrified. 3. Let² the pupils be admonished. 4. They have been admonished. 5. Who will be advised? 6. These boys will be advised. 7. Has your memory been exercised? 8. My memory has been exercised. 9. Was not the general terrified? 10. The general himself³ was not terrified. 11. The soldiers were terrified.

## FIRST AND SECOND CONJUGATIONS—Miscellaneous Examples.

### Exercise XXXIV.

#### I. *Vocabulary.*

| | |
|---|---|
| Cămillŭs, i, *m.* | *Camillus*, Roman general. |
| Exspectŏ, ārĕ, āvī, ātŭm, | *to await, expect.* |
| Hostĭs, is, *m.* and *f.* | *enemy.* |
| Ingens, ingentĭs, | *huge, large, great.* |
| Lĕgĭŏ, lĕgĭōnĭs, *f.* | *legion, body of soldiers.* |
| Nōn, *adv.* | *not.* |
| Nŭmĕrŭs, i, *m.* | *number.* |
| Optŏ, ārĕ, āvī, ātŭm, | *to wish for, desire.* |
| Pĕcūnĭă, ae, *f.* | *money.* |

---

¹ *Exerceātur;* the Subjunctive is sometimes best rendered by *let.* See 196. I 2.

² *Let be admonished* is to be rendered into Latin by a single verb in the Subjunctive. See 196, I. 2.

³ *Himself* = ipse. See 186.

Philŏsŏphŭs, ī, m. — philosopher.
Praeceptŏr, praeceptōrĭs, m. — teacher.
Proeliŭm, iī, n. — battle.
Rōmānŭs, ī, m. — Roman, a Roman.
Sŭpĕrŏ, ārĕ, āvī, ātŭm, — to conquer.
Vĕrēcundiŭ, ae, f. — modesty.

## II. Translate into English.

1. Camillus hostes superāvit. 2. Hostes superāti sunt. 3. Omnes discipŭli paruĕrant.[1] 4. Romāni hostem exspectābant. 5. Romāni[2] ingentem hostium numĕrum[3] exspectavĕrant.[1] 6. Hostes proelium exspectābant. 7. Praeceptor tacēbat. 8. Discipŭli tacēbant. 9. Verecundia juventūtem ornat. 10. Philosŏphus pecuniam non habet. 11. Philosŏphi pecuniam non optant.

## III. Translate into Latin.

1. Are you expecting me? 2. We are expecting you. 3. Did you not await the enemy?[4] 4. We awaited the enemy. 5. Have you not a good memory? 6. I have a good memory. 7. Will the soldiers obey? 8. The brave soldiers will obey. 9. Camillus had an army. 10. He praised the army. 11. Did you advise the boy? 12. We advised the boys. 13. Were not the enemy put to flight?[5] 14. They were put to flight.

---

[1] In accordance with Suggestion VII. 3, for what form will you look in the Vocabulary? See 205, 207.

[2] Apply to this sentence Suggestions IV. and V.

[3] *Ingentem hostium numĕrum*, for arrangement see note on *pondus*, Exercise XXX.

[4] Put the Latin word in the plural.

[5] *Put to flight* is to be rendered by a single Latin verb.

## THIRD CONJUGATION.

### ACTIVE VOICE.

**209.** Rego, *I rule.*

#### PRINCIPAL PARTS.

| Pres. Ind. | Pres. Inf. | Perf. Ind. | Supine. |
|---|---|---|---|
| rĕgŏ, | rĕgĕrĕ, | rexī, | rectŭm. |

### INDICATIVE MOOD.

#### PRESENT TENSE.
*I rule.*

| SINGULAR. | PLURAL. |
|---|---|
| rĕgŏ | rĕgĭmŭs |
| rĕgĭs | rĕgĭtĭs |
| rĕgĭt ; | rĕgunt. |

#### IMPERFECT.
*I was ruling.*

| | |
|---|---|
| rĕgēbăm | rĕgēbămŭs |
| rĕgēbās | rĕgēbātĭs |
| rĕgēbăt ; | rĕgēbant. |

#### FUTURE.
*I shall or will rule.*

| | |
|---|---|
| rĕgăm | rĕgēmŭs |
| rĕgēs | rĕgētĭs |
| rĕgĕt ; | rĕgent. |

#### PERFECT.
*I ruled or have ruled.*

| | |
|---|---|
| rexī | reximŭs |
| rexistī | rexistĭs |
| rexĭt ; | rexērunt, *or* ērĕ. |

#### PLUPERFECT.
*I had ruled.*

| | |
|---|---|
| rexĕrăm | rexĕrāmŭs |
| rexĕrās | rexĕrātĭs |
| rexĕrăt ; | rexĕrant. |

#### FUTURE PERFECT.
*I shall or will have ruled.*

| | |
|---|---|
| rexĕrŏ | rexĕrĭmŭs |
| rexĕrĭs | rexĕrĭtĭs |
| rexĕrĭt ; | rexĕrint. |

ETYMOLOGY.—THIRD CONJUGATION.

SUBJUNCTIVE.

PRESENT.
*I may or can rule.*

| SINGULAR. | PLURAL. |
|---|---|
| rĕgăm | rĕgāmŭs |
| rĕgās | rĕgātĭs |
| rĕgăt; | rĕgant. |

IMPERFECT.
*I might, could, would, or should rule.*

| rĕgĕrĕm | rĕgĕrēmŭs |
| rĕgĕrēs | rĕgĕrētĭs |
| rĕgĕret; | rĕgĕrent. |

PERFECT.
*I may have ruled.*

| rexĕrĭm | rexĕrĭmŭs |
| rexĕrĭs | rexĕrĭtĭs |
| rexĕrĭt; | rexĕrint. |

PLUPERFECT.
*I might, could, would, or should have ruled.*

| rexissĕm | rexissēmŭs |
| rexissēs | rexissētĭs |
| rexissĕt; | rexissent. |

IMPERATIVE.

PRES. rĕgĕ, *rule thou;* | rĕgĭtĕ, *rule ye.*
FUT. rĕgĭtŏ, *thou shalt rule,* | rĕgĭtōtĕ, *ye shall rule,*
rĕgĭtŏ, *he shall rule;* | rĕguntŏ, *they shall rule.*

INFINITIVE.

PRES. rĕgĕrĕ, *to rule.*
PERF. rexissĕ, *to have ruled.*
FUT. rectūrŭs essĕ, *to be about to rule.*

PARTICIPLE.

PRES. rĕgens, *ruling.*
FUT. rectūrŭs, *about to rule.*

GERUND.

Gen. rĕgendī, *of ruling,*
Dat. rĕgendŏ, *for ruling,*
Acc. rĕgendŭm, *ruling,*
Abl. rĕgendŏ, *by ruling.*

SUPINE.

Acc. rectŭm, *to rule,*
Abl. rectū, *to rule, be ruled.*

## THIRD CONJUGATION.

### PASSIVE VOICE.

**210. Regor,** *I am ruled.*

#### PRINCIPAL PARTS.

| Pres. Ind. | Pres. Inf. | Perf. Ind. |
|---|---|---|
| rĕgŏr, | rĕgī, | rectŭs sŭm. |

### INDICATIVE MOOD.

#### PRESENT TENSE.
*I am ruled.*

| SINGULAR. | PLURAL. |
|---|---|
| rĕgŏr | rĕgĭmŭr |
| rĕgĕrĭs, *or* rĕ | rĕgĭmĭnī |
| rĕgĭtŭr ; | rĕguntŭr. |

#### IMPERFECT.
*I was ruled.*

| | |
|---|---|
| rĕgēbăr | rĕgēbāmŭr |
| rĕgēbārĭs, *or* rĕ | rĕgēbāmĭnī |
| rĕgēbātŭr ; | rĕgēbantŭr. |

#### FUTURE.
*I shall* or *will be ruled.*

| | |
|---|---|
| rĕgăr | rĕgēmŭr |
| rĕgērĭs, *or* rĕ | rĕgēmĭnī |
| rĕgētŭr ; | rĕgentŭr. |

#### PERFECT.
*I have been* or *was ruled.*

| | |
|---|---|
| rectŭs sŭm [1] | rectī sŭmŭs |
| rectŭs ĕs | rectī estĭs |
| rectŭs est ; | rectī sunt. |

#### PLUPERFECT.
*I had been ruled.*

| | |
|---|---|
| rectŭs ĕrăm [1] | rectī ĕrămŭs |
| rectŭs ĕrās | rectī ĕrātĭs |
| rectŭs ĕrăt ; | rectī ĕrant. |

#### FUTURE PERFECT.
*I shall* or *will have been ruled.*

| | |
|---|---|
| rectŭs ĕrō [1] | rectī ĕrĭmŭs |
| rectŭs ĕrĭs | rectī ĕrĭtĭs |
| rectŭs ĕrĭt ; | rectī ĕrunt. |

[1] See 206, foot-notes.

## ETYMOLOGY. — THIRD CONJUGATION.

### SUBJUNCTIVE.

#### PRESENT.
*I may or can be ruled.*

| SINGULAR. | PLURAL. |
|---|---|
| rĕgăr | rĕgāmŭr |
| rĕgāris, *or* rĕ | rĕgāmĭnĭ |
| rĕgātŭr; | rĕgantŭr. |

#### IMPERFECT.
*I might, could, would,* or *should be ruled.*

| | |
|---|---|
| rĕgĕrĕr | rĕgĕrēmŭr |
| rĕgĕrēris, *or* rĕ | rĕgĕrēmĭnĭ |
| rĕgĕrētŭr; | rĕgĕrentŭr. |

#### PERFECT.
*I may have been ruled.*

| | |
|---|---|
| rectŭs sĭm [1] | rectī sĭmŭs |
| rectŭs sīs | rectī sītĭs |
| rectŭs sĭt; | rectī sĭnt. |

#### PLUPERFECT.
*I might, could, would,* or *should have been ruled.*

| | |
|---|---|
| rectŭs essĕm [1] | rectī essēmŭs |
| rectŭs essēs | rectī essētĭs |
| rectŭs essĕt; | rectī essent. |

### IMPERATIVE.

PRES. rĕgĕrĕ, *be thou ruled;* | rĕgĭmĭnĭ, *be ye ruled.*

FUT. rĕgĭtŏr, *thou shalt be ruled,*
rĕgĭtŏr, *he shall be ruled;* | rĕguntŏr, *ye shall be ruled.*

### INFINITIVE.

PRES. rĕgī, *to be ruled.*
PERF. rectŭs essĕ, *to have been ruled.*
FUT. rectŭm īrī, *to be about to be ruled.*

### PARTICIPLE.

PERF. rectŭs,     *ruled.*
FUT. rĕgendŭs, *to be ruled.*

---

[1] See 206, foot-notes.

## THIRD CONJUGATION—Active Voice.

### Exercise XXXV.

#### I. *Vocabulary.*

Dūcŏ, ĕrĕ, duxī, ductŭm,   to lead.
Rĕgŏ, ĕrĕ, rexī, rectŭm,   to rule, govern.

#### II. *Translate into English.*

1. Rego, regēbam, regam. 2. Regĭmus, regebāmus, regēmus. 3. Regĭtis, regis. 4. Regēbas, regebātis. 5. Regēbant, regēbat. 6. Reget, regent. 7. Rexērunt, rexit. 8. Rexi, rexĕram, rexĕro. 9. Rexĭmus, rexerāmus, rexerĭmus. 10. Regas, regĕres, rexĕris, rexisses. 11. Regātis, regerētis, rexerĭtis, rexissētis. 12. Regam, regāmus. 13. Regerēmus, regĕrem. 14. Rexĕrit, rexĕrint. 15. Rexissent, rexisset. 16. Rege, regĭte.

#### III. *Translate into Latin.*

1. He leads, he was leading, he will lead. 2. He rules, he was ruling, he will rule. 3. They lead, they rule. 4. They were leading, they were ruling. 5. They will lead, they will rule. 6. You have led, you have ruled. 7. He had led, he had ruled. 8. They had led, they had ruled. 9. He will have led, he will have ruled. 10. They may lead, they may rule. 11. He would lead, he would rule. 12. They would lead, they would rule. 13. We should have led, we should have ruled.

## FIRST, SECOND, AND THIRD CONJUGATIONS — Active Voice.

### Exercise XXXVI.

#### I. *Vocabulary.*

Dīcŏ, dīcĕrĕ, dixī, dictŭm,    *to say, tell, speak.*
Vŏcŏ, ārĕ, āvī, ātŭm,    *to call.*

#### II. *Translate into English.*

1. Vocat, tacet, dicit.[1] 2. Vocant, tacent, dicunt. 3. Vocābant, tacēbant, dicēbant. 4. Vocābo, tacēbo, dicam. 5. Vocavĭmus, tacuĭmus, dixĭmus. 6. Vocāvi, tacui, dixi. 7. Vocavērunt, tacuērunt, dixērunt. 8. Vocavĕrat, tacuĕrat, dixĕrat. 9. Vocavĕrint, tacuĕrint, dixĕrint. 10. Vocem, taceam, dicam. 11. Vocārent, tacērent, dicĕrent. 12. Vocāte, tacēte, dicĭte.

#### III. *Translate into Latin.*

1. I invite, I admonish, I lead. 2. We call, we are silent, we speak. 3. We were inviting, we were admonishing, we were leading. 4. I shall call, I shall be silent, I shall speak. 5. He has invited, he has been silent, he has led. 6. He had praised, he had obeyed, he had ruled. 7. They had blamed, they had advised, they had spoken. 8. He may call, he may admonish, he may rule.

---

[1] In this Exercise, the pupil should carefully compare the corresponding forms in the three Conjugations here represented, — the First, the Second, and the Third, — and should carefully observe the difference between them. The advantages of such a course are twofold: first, it teaches the pupil to distinguish the several Conjugations from each other, which is one of the most important lessons to be learned in the study of the language; and, secondly, it tends to form in him, thus early, the habit of close and accurate observation, the habit of marking differences and of tracing resemblances in kindred forms, which is of vital importance in the whole course of classical study.

## THIRD CONJUGATION — Active Voice.
### Other Parts of Speech.

### Exercise XXXVII.

#### I. Vocabulary.

| | |
|---|---|
| Anĭmŭs, ī, *m.* | mind, passion. |
| Bĕnĕ, *adv.* | well. |
| Dēfectĭŏ, dēfectiōnĭs, *f.* | eclipse. |
| Dīsertē, *adv.* | clearly, eloquently. |
| Edūcŏ, ēdūcĕrĕ, ēduxī, ēductŭm, | to lead forth. |
| Indīcŏ, indīcĕrĕ, indixī, indictŭm, | to declare. |
| Lătīnē, *adv.* | in Latin. |
| Praedīcŏ, praedīcĕrĕ, praedixī, praedictŭm, | to predict, foretell. |
| Săpientĕr, *adv.* | wisely. |
| Thălēs, ĭs, *m.* | Thales, a philosopher. |
| Tullŭs, ī, *m.* | Tullus, a Roman name. |
| Vērŭm, ī, *n.* | truth. |

#### II. *Translate into English.*

1. Bene dixisti. 2. Nonne Cicĕro in senātu dixĕrat? 3. Cicĕro diserte dicēbat. 4. Oratōres diserte dicent. 5. Philosŏphus sapienter dixit. 6. Philosŏphi sapienter dixĕrant. 7. Oratōres Latīne dixērunt. 8. Caesar legiōnes eduxit. 9. Hannĭbal exercĭtum in Italiam duxit. 10. Quis bellum indixit? 11. Tullus bellum indixit. 12. Thales defectiōnem solis praedixit.

#### III. *Translate into Latin.*

1. Who will speak the truth? 2. Have we not spoken the truth? 3. You have spoken the truth. 4. Will not the general lead forth the army? 5. He has led forth the army. 6. Do you not govern your mind? 7. We govern our minds. 8. Did you predict this war? 9. We did not predict the war. 10. Who has declared war? 11. The Romans have declared war.

## THIRD CONJUGATION — Passive Voice.

### Exercise XXXVIII.

#### I. *Translate into English.*

1. Regor, regēbar, regar. 2. Regĭmur, regebāmur, regē-mur. 3. Regar, regāmur. 4. Regerētur, regerentur. 5. Rectus est, rectus erat, rectus erit. 6. Recti sunt, recti erant, recti erunt. 7. Regit, regĭtur. 8. Regunt, reguntur. 9. Regēbat, regebātur. 10. Regēbant, regebantur. 11. Reget, regētur. 12. Regent, regentur. 13. Regĭmus, regĭmur. 14. Regebāmus, regebāmur. 15. Regēmus, regēmur.

#### II. *Translate into Latin.*

1. He is ruled, they are ruled. 2. I am ruled, I am led. 3. We are ruled, we are led. 4. He was ruled, they were ruled. 5. He will be ruled, they will be ruled. 6. We have been ruled, we have been led. 7. I lead, I am led. 8. We lead, we are led. 9. We were ruling, we were ruled. 10. He was leading, he was led. 11. They may rule, they may be ruled.

## FIRST, SECOND, AND THIRD CONJUGATIONS — Passive Voice.

### Exercise XXXIX.

#### I. *Translate into English.*

1. Vocor, moneor, ducor. 2. Vocāmur, monēmur, ducĭmur. 3. Vocātur, monētur, ducĭtur. 4. Vocabātur, monebātur, ducebātur. 5. Vocabantur, monebantur, ducebantur. 6. Vocabuntur, monebuntur, ducentur. 7. Vocā-

tus es, monĭtus es, ductus es.  8. Vocāti estis, monĭti estis, ducti estis.  9. Vocātus eram, monĭtus eram, ductus eram.  10. Vocātus erit, monĭtus erit, ductus erit.

## II.  *Translate into Latin.*

1. He is invited, he is admonished, he is led.  2. We were called, we were advised, we were ruled.  3. He will be called, he will be advised, he will be ruled.  4. He may be invited, he may be admonished, he may be led.  5. He has been called, he has been advised, he has been led.  6. They have been called, they have been advised, they have been led.

### THIRD CONJUGATION — Passive Voice.
#### Other Parts of Speech.

### Exercise XL.

#### I.  *Vocabulary.*

| | |
|---|---|
| Mundŭs, i, *m.* | *world.* |
| Semper, *adv.* | *always, ever.* |
| Vērŭm, i, *n.* | *truth.* |

## II.  *Translate into English.*

1. Mundus regĭtur.  2. Omnis hic mundus semper rectus est.  3. Hic mundus semper regētur.  4. Haec civĭtas bene regĭtur.  5. Hae civitātes bene reguntur.  6. Civitātes rectae sunt.  7. Anĭmus regātur.  8. Exercĭtus in Italiam ductus est.  9. Multi exercĭtus in Italiam ducti erant.  10. Bellum indictum[1] erat.  11. Multa bella indicta[1] sunt.

## III.  *Translate into Latin.*

1. Was not the army led forth?  2. The army was led forth.  3. Has not this state been well governed?  4. This

---

[1] Why *indictum* in one example, and *indicta* in the other?  Why not rather *indictus* in both?  See Rule XXXV. 1, page 54.

state has been well governed. 5. Will not the truth be spoken? 6. The truth has been spoken. 7. Let[1] the truth always be spoken. 8. Would not war have been declared? 9. War would have been declared.

## FIRST, SECOND, AND THIRD CONJUGATIONS —
### Miscellaneous Examples.

#### Exercise XLI.

##### I. *Vocabulary.*

| | |
|---|---|
| Gallŭs, ī, *m.* | *Gallus*, a proper name. |
| Hĭrundŏ, hĭrundĭnĭs, *f.* | *swallow.* |
| Lūnă, ae, *f.* | *moon.* |
| Nuntĭŏ, ārĕ, āvī, ātŭm, | *to proclaim, announce.* |
| Sensŭs, ūs, *m.* | *feeling, perception.* |
| Supplĭcĭŭm, ĭī, *n.* | *punishment.* |

##### II. *Translate into English.*

1. Hirundĭnes adventum veris nuntiant. 2. Hirundĭnes adventum veris nuntiavĕrant. 3. Discĭpŭli laudabuntur. 4. Gallus defectiōnes solis praedixit. 5. Defectiōnes lunae praedixit. 6. Defectiōnes lunae praedicuntur. 7. Omne anĭmal sensus habet. 8. Puĕri tacēbant.

##### III. *Translate into Latin.*

1. This boy has not observed the law. 2. Good citizens will observe the laws. 3. Let the laws be observed. 4. Who has your book? 5. That boy has my book. 6. You shall have my book. 7. What did you say? 8. I spoke the truth. 9. The truth would have been spoken.

---

[1] *Let be spoken*, render by the Latin Subjunctive. See 196, I. 2.

## FOURTH CONJUGATION.

### ACTIVE VOICE.

**211. Audio,** *I hear.*

#### PRINCIPAL PARTS.

| Pres. Ind. | Pres. Inf. | Perf. Ind. | Supine. |
|---|---|---|---|
| audiŏ, | audīrĕ, | audīvī, | audītŭm. |

### INDICATIVE MOOD.

**PRESENT TENSE.**
*I hear.*

| SINGULAR. | PLURAL. |
|---|---|
| audiŏ | audīmŭs |
| audīs | audītīs |
| audĭt ; | audiunt. |

**IMPERFECT.**
*I was hearing.*

| | |
|---|---|
| audiēbăm | audiēbāmŭs |
| audiēbās | audiēbātīs |
| audiēbăt ; | audiēbant. |

**FUTURE.**
*I shall or will hear.*

| | |
|---|---|
| audiăm | audiēmŭs |
| audiēs | audiētīs |
| audiĕt ; | audient. |

**PERFECT.**
*I heard or have heard.*

| | |
|---|---|
| audīvī | audīvīmŭs |
| audīvistī | audīvistīs |
| audīvĭt ; | audīvērunt, *or* ērĕ. |

**PLUPERFECT.**
*I had heard.*

| | |
|---|---|
| audīvĕrăm | audīvĕrāmŭs |
| audīvĕrās | audīvĕrātīs |
| audīverăt ; | audīvĕrant. |

**FUTURE PERFECT.**
*I shall or will have heard.*

| | |
|---|---|
| audīvĕrŏ | audīvĕrīmŭs |
| audīvĕrīs | audīvĕrītīs |
| audīvĕrĭt ; | audīvĕrint. |

## SUBJUNCTIVE.

### PRESENT.
*I may or can hear.*

| SINGULAR. | PLURAL. |
|---|---|
| audiăm | audiāmŭs |
| audiās | audiātĭs |
| audiăt ; | audiant. |

### IMPERFECT.
*I might, could, would, or should hear.*

| | |
|---|---|
| audīrĕm | audīrēmŭs |
| audīrēs | audīrētĭs |
| audīrĕt ; | audīrent. |

### PERFECT.
*I may have heard.*

| | |
|---|---|
| audīvĕrĭm | audīvĕrĭmŭs |
| audīvĕrĭs | audīvĕrĭtĭs |
| audīvĕrĭt ; | audīvĕrint. |

### PLUPERFECT.
*I might, could, would, or should have heard.*

| | |
|---|---|
| audīvissĕm | audīvissēmŭs |
| audīvissēs | audīvissētĭs |
| audīvissĕt ; | audīvissent. |

## IMPERATIVE.

| PRES. | audī, | *hear thou ;* | audītĕ, | *hear ye.* |
|---|---|---|---|---|
| FUT. | audītō, | *thou shalt hear,* | audītōtĕ, | *ye shall hear,* |
| | audītō, | *he shall hear ;* | audiuntō, | *they shall hear.* |

## INFINITIVE.

PRES. audīrĕ, *to hear.*
PERF. audīvissĕ, *to have heard.*
FUT. audītūrŭs essĕ, *to be about to hear.*

## PARTICIPLE.

PRES. audiens, *hearing.*
FUT. audītūrŭs, *about to hear.*

## GERUND.

| Gen. | audiendī, | *of hearing.* |
| Dat. | audiendō, | *for hearing.* |
| Acc. | audiendŭm, | *hearing.* |
| Abl. | audiendō, | *by hearing.* |

## SUPINE.

| Acc. | audītŭm, | *to hear.* |
| Abl. | audītū, | *to hear, be heard.* |

## FOURTH CONJUGATION.

**PASSIVE VOICE.**

**212.** Audior, *I am heard.*

PRINCIPAL PARTS.

| Pres. Ind. | Pres. Inf. | Perf. Ind. |
|---|---|---|
| audĭŏr, | audīrī, | audītŭs sŭm. |

### INDICATIVE MOOD.

**PRESENT TENSE.**
*I am heard.*

| SINGULAR. | PLURAL. |
|---|---|
| audĭŏr | audīmŭr |
| audīrĭs, *or* rĕ | audīmĭnī |
| audītŭr ; | audiuntŭr. |

**IMPERFECT.**
*I was heard.*

| | |
|---|---|
| audiēbăr | audiēbămŭr |
| audiēbărĭs, *or* rĕ | audiēbămĭnī |
| audiēbātŭr ; | audiēbantŭr. |

**FUTURE.**
*I shall or will be heard.*

| | |
|---|---|
| audiăr | audiēmŭr |
| audiērĭs, *or* rĕ | audiēmĭnī |
| audiētŭr ; | audientŭr. |

**PERFECT.**
*I have been heard.*

| | |
|---|---|
| audītŭs sŭm [1] | audītī sŭmŭs |
| audītŭs ĕs | audītī estĭs |
| audītŭs est ; | audītī sunt. |

**PLUPERFECT.**
*I had been heard.*

| | |
|---|---|
| audītŭs ĕrăm [1] | audītī ĕrămŭs |
| audītŭs ĕrās | audītī ĕrātĭs |
| audītŭs ĕrăt ; | audītī ĕrant. |

**FUTURE PERFECT.**
*I shall or will have been heard.*

| | |
|---|---|
| audītŭs ĕrō [1] | audītī ĕrĭmŭs |
| audītŭs ĕrĭs | audītī ĕrĭtĭs |
| audītŭs ĕrĭt ; | audītī ĕrunt. |

---

[1] See 206, foot-notes.

## SUBJUNCTIVE.

### PRESENT.

*I may or can be heard.*

| SINGULAR. | PLURAL. |
|---|---|
| audi**ăr** | audi**āmŭr** |
| audi**ārĭs**, *or* **rĕ** | audi**āmĭnī** |
| audi**ātŭr**; | audi**antŭr**. |

### IMPERFECT.

*I might, could, would, or should be heard.*

| | |
|---|---|
| aud**īrĕr** | aud**īrēmŭr** |
| aud**īrērĭs**, *or* **rĕ** | aud**īrēmĭnī** |
| aud**īrētŭr**; | aud**īrentŭr**. |

### PERFECT.

*I may have been heard.*

| | |
|---|---|
| audītŭs **sĭm** [1] | audītī **sĭmŭs** |
| audītŭs **sīs** | audītī **sītĭs** |
| audītŭs **sĭt**; | audītī **sint**. |

### PLUPERFECT.

*I might, could, would, or should have been heard.*

| | |
|---|---|
| audītŭs **essĕm** [1] | audītī **essēmŭs** |
| audītŭs **essēs** | audītī **essētĭs** |
| audītŭs **essĕt**; | audītī **essent**. |

## IMPERATIVE.

| | | | |
|---|---|---|---|
| PRES. | aud**īrĕ**, *be thou heard*; | aud**īmĭnī**, | *be ye heard.* |
| FUT. | aud**ītŏr**, *thou shalt be heard,* | | |
| | aud**ītŏr**, *he shall be heard*; | aud**iuntŏr**, | *they shall be heard.* |

## INFINITIVE.  PARTICIPLE.

| | | | | |
|---|---|---|---|---|
| PRES. | aud**īrī**, *to be heard.* | | | |
| PERF. | audītŭs **essĕ**, *to have been heard.* | PERF. | audītŭs, | *heard.* |
| FUT. | audīt**um īrī**, *to be about to be heard.* | FUT. | aud**iendŭs**, | *to be heard.* |

---

[1] See 206, foot-notes.

## FOURTH CONJUGATION.—Active Voice.

### Exercise XLII.

#### I. *Vocabulary.*

Custōdiŏ, īrĕ, īvī, ītŭm,   to guard.
Dormiŏ, īrĕ, īvī, ītŭm,   to sleep.
Erŭdiŏ, īrĕ, īvī, ītŭm,   to instruct, refine, educate.

#### II. *Translate into English.*

1. Audis, audiēbas, audies. 2. Audītis, audiebātis, audiētis. 3. Audio, audīmus. 4. Audiēbam, audiebāmus. 5. Audiam, audiēmus. 6. Audivīmus, audiverāmus, audiverĭmus. 7. Audīvi, audivĕram, audivĕro. 8. Audīvit, audivērunt. 9. Audiam, audīrem, audivĕrim, audivissem. 10. Audiāmus, audirēmus, audiverĭmus, audivissēmus. 11. Audīto, auditōte.

#### III. *Translate into Latin.*

1. I hear, I guard. 2. We hear, we guard. 3. He was hearing, they were sleeping. 4. He was sleeping, they were hearing. 5. He will hear, they will hear. 6. We have slept, you have heard. 7. I had heard, I had guarded. 8. He may hear, they may sleep. 9. They may hear, he may sleep. 10. He might hear, they might sleep. 11. He might sleep, they might hear.

## FIRST, SECOND, THIRD, AND FOURTH CONJUGATIONS.—Active Voice.

### Exercise XLIII.

#### I. *Translate into English.*

1. Invītat, admŏnet, ducit, custōdit. 2. Invītant, admŏnent, ducunt, custodiunt. 3. Invitābant, admonēbant, du-

cēbant, custodiēbant. 4. Invitābat, admonēbat, ducēbat, custodiēbat. 5. Invitavĕram, admonuĕram, duxĕram, audivĕram. 6. Invitaverāmus, admonuerāmus, duxerāmus, audiverāmus. 7. Invitavĕrim, admonuĕrim, duxĕrim, custodivĕrim. 8. Invitavērunt, admonuērunt, duxērunt, audivērunt.

## II. *Translate into Latin.*

1. We invite, we admonish, we lead, we instruct. 2. I was inviting, I was admonishing, I was leading, I was instructing. 3. We were praising, we were obeying, we were speaking, we were instructing. 4. He will blame, he will advise, he will speak, he will instruct. 5. I have invited, you have obeyed, he has led, they have guarded.

## FOURTH CONJUGATION. — ACTIVE VOICE.
### OTHER PARTS OF SPEECH.

### EXERCISE XLIV.

#### I. *Vocabulary.*

| | |
|---|---|
| Arctē, *adv.* | *closely, soundly.* |
| Mūniŏ, īrĕ, īvī, ītŭm, | *to fortify.* |
| Sermŏ, sermōnĭs, *m.* | *discourse, conversation.* |
| Thrăsўbūlŭs, ī, *m.* | *Thrasybulus,* Athenian general. |

#### II. *Translate into English.*

1. Cives urbem custodiēbant. 2. Urbem custodiēmus. 3. Milītes templum custodiunt. 4. Verum audītis. 5. Verum audīte. 6. Verum audiverāmus. 7. Verba tua audīmus. 8. Verba mea audivīsti. 9. Oratiōnem tuam audīvi. 10. Sermōnem audiēbam. 11. Puĕri arcte dormiunt. 12. Puĕri cantum lusciniae audiēbant. 13. Thrasybūlus urbem munīvit.

### III. *Translate into Latin.*

1. Do you not hear us? 2. We hear you. 3. Who heard the oration? 4. We heard the oration. 5. The pupils heard the conversation. 6. They did not hear your oration. 7. The citizens are fortifying the city. 8. Who will guard this beautiful city? 9. The brave soldiers will guard the city. 10. Will you guard the temple? 11. We will guard the temple.

## FOURTH CONJUGATION. — Passive Voice.

### Exercise XLV.

#### I. *Translate into English.*

1. Audīmur, audiebāmur, audiēmur. 2. Audiātur, audiantur. 3. Audīrer, audirēmur. 4. Audītus sum, audīti sumus. 5. Audīti erāmus, audītus eram. 6. Audītus erit, audīti erunt. 7. Audit, audītur. 8. Audiunt, audiuntur. 9. Audiet, audiētur. 10. Audīrem, audīrer. 11. Audiēbam, audiēbar. 12. Audiēbat, audiebātur. 13. Audīvit, audītus est. 14. Audivĕrat, audītus erat.

#### II. *Translate into Latin.*

1. I am instructed, we are instructed. 2. He will be instructed, they will be instructed. 3. They have been heard, they have been instructed. 4. They had been heard, he had been instructed. 5. He was instructing, he was instructed. 6. They are instructing, they are instructed. 7. We have heard, you have been heard. 8. You have instructed, we have been instructed. 9. I have heard, you have been heard.

## FIRST, SECOND, THIRD, AND FOURTH CONJUGATIONS.—Passive Voice.

### Exercise XLVI.

I. *Translate into English.*

1. Invitāris, admonēris, educĕris, custodīris. 2. Invitantur, admonentur, educuntur, custodiuntur. 3. Invitātur, admonētur, educĭtur, custodītur. 4. Invitabĭtur, admonebĭtur, educētur, custodiĕtur. 5. Invitabātur, admonebātur, educebātur, custodiebātur. 6. Invitātus sum, admonĭtus sum, eductus sum, custodītus sum. 7. Invitāti erant, admonĭti erant, educti erant, custodīti erant. 8. Invitāti essēmus, educti essēmus. 9. Admonĭtus esses, custodītus esses.

II. *Translate into Latin.*

1. He is called, he is terrified, he is led forth, he is guarded. 2. They are called, they are terrified, they are led forth, they are guarded. 3. They will be loved, they will be advised, they will be led, they will be heard. 4. I have been blamed, I have been admonished, you had been ruled, you had been guarded. 5. You had been blamed, I had been admonished. 6. You have been ruled, I have been guarded.

## FOURTH CONJUGATION.—Passive Voice.
### Other Parts of Speech.

### Exercise XLVII.

I. *Vocabulary.*

| | |
|---|---|
| Bellŭm, ī, *n.* | *war.* |
| Bĕnignē, *adv.* | *kindly.* |
| Civīlĭs, ĕ. | *civil.* |

| | |
|---|---|
| Egrĕgiē, *adv.* | *excellently.* |
| Fīlĭŭs, ĭi, *m.* | *son.* |
| Fīnĭŏ, īrĕ, īvī, ītŭm, | *to finish, bring to a close.* |
| Lēgātĭŏ, lēgātĭŏnĭs, *f.* | *embassy.* |
| Vox, vōcĭs, *f.* | *voice.* |

## II. *Translate into English.*

1. Vox audīta¹ est. 2. Voces audiuntur. 3. Cantus lusciniae audītur. 4. Cantus lusciniārum audiētur. 5. Urbs munīta erat. 6. Urbes munientur. 7. Templum custodiētur. 8. Templa custodiuntur. 9. Legatio benigne audīta est. 10. Haec legatio benigne audiētur. 11. Verba tua benigne audientur. 12. Filii regis egregie erudiuntur. 13. Bellum civīle finītum¹ est.

## III. *Translate into Latin.*

1. Was not the orator heard? 2. The renowned orator was kindly heard. 3. Let the city be fortified.² 4. Let the temples be guarded. 5. The city has been fortified. 6. The temples will be guarded. 7. Let the war be brought to a close. 8. Let the boys be instructed. 9. Let the words of the instructor be heard.

## FIRST, SECOND, THIRD, AND FOURTH CONJUGATIONS. — MISCELLANEOUS EXAMPLES.

### EXERCISE XLVIII.

#### I. *Vocabulary.*

| | |
|---|---|
| Athēniensĭs, ĭs, *m.* and *f.* | *an Athenian.* |
| Cănĭs, cănĭs, *m.* and *f.* | *dog.* |
| Cŏlŏ, cŏlĕrĕ, cŏluī, cultŭm, | *to practise, cultivate.* |
| Cŭm, *prep. with abl.* | *with.* |

---

[1] Why *audīta* and *finītum*, instead of *audītus* and *finītus?* See Rule XXXV. 1, p. 54.

[2] *Let be fortified* is to be rendered into Latin by a single verb in the Subjunctive. See 196, I. 2.

| | |
|---|---|
| Firmŏ, ārĕ, āvī, ātŭm, | to strengthen. |
| Grex, grĕgĭs, m. | herd, flock. |
| Illustrŏ, ārĕ, āvī, ātŭm, | to illumine. |
| Jungŏ, jungĕrĕ, junxī, junctŭm, | to join. |
| Lăbŏr, lăbŏrĭs, m. | labor. |
| Mŏdestiă, ae, f. | modesty. |
| Ovĭs, ŏvĭs, f. | sheep. |
| Portŭs, ūs, m. | port, harbor. |
| Prūdentiă, ae, f. | prudence. |
| Terră, ae, f. | earth. |
| Vălētūdŏ, vălētūdĭnĭs, f. | health. |
| Vărĭĕtās, vărĭĕtātĭs, f. | variety. |
| Vĭŏlŏ, ārĕ, āvī, ātŭm, | violate. |

## II. Translate into English.

1. Sol terram illustrat. 2. Modestia puĕros ornat. 3. Discipŭli memoriam exercent. 4. Discipŭli tui memoriam exercēbant. 5. Canes gregem custodiēbant. 6. Greges ovium custodiuntur. 7. Praeceptōres juventūtem erudient. 8. Labor valetudĭnem tuam firmābit. 9. Variĕtas nos delectat. 10. Athenienses portum munivērunt. 11. Philosophia nos erudīvit.

## III. Translate into Latin.

1. Good men love virtue. 2. Virtue will always[1] be loved. 3. Let virtue be always practised. 4. We will always practise virtue. 5. The soldiers are violating the laws of the state. 6. They will be punished. 7. Will you instruct these boys? 8. We will instruct good boys. 9. Who[2] led this army into Italy? 10. Hannibal led the army into Italy.

---

[1] For the syntax of adverbs, and for their place in the Latin sentence, see Rule LI. and note 4, p. 72.

[2] Which form of the Interrogative should be used, *quĭs* or *quī*? See 188.

## VERBS IN IO OF THE THIRD CONJUGATION.

**213.** *Verbs in io* are generally of the fourth conjugation; and even the few which are of the third are inflected with the endings of the fourth wherever those endings have two successive vowels, as follows:

### ACTIVE VOICE.
### 214. Capio, *I take.*

#### PRINCIPAL PARTS.

| Pres. Ind. | Pres. Inf. | Perf. Ind. | Supine. |
|---|---|---|---|
| căpĭŏ, | căpĕrĕ, | cēpī, | captŭm. |

### INDICATIVE MOOD.
#### PRESENT TENSE.

SINGULAR. — PLURAL.
căpĭŏ, căpĭs, căpĭt; | căpĭmŭs, căpĭtĭs, căpiunt.

IMPERFECT.
căpiēbăm, -iēbās, -iēbăt; | căpiēbāmŭs, -iēbātĭs, -iēbant.

FUTURE.
căpiăm, -iēs, -iĕt; | căpiēmŭs, -iētĭs, -ient.

PERFECT.
cēpī, -istī, -ĭt; | cēpĭmŭs, -istĭs, -ērunt, *or* ērĕ.

PLUPERFECT.
cēpĕrăm, -ĕrās, -ĕrăt; | cēpĕrāmŭs, -ĕrātĭs, -ĕrant.

FUTURE PERFECT.
cēpĕrŏ, -ĕrĭs, -ĕrĭt; | cēpĕrĭmŭs, -ĕrĭtĭs, -ĕrint.

### SUBJUNCTIVE.
#### PRESENT.

căpiăm, -iās, -iăt; | căpiāmŭs, -iātĭs, -iant.

IMPERFECT.
căpĕrĕm, -ĕrēs, -ĕrĕt; | căpĕrēmŭs, -ĕrētĭs, -ĕrent.

PERFECT.
cēpĕrĭm, -ĕrĭs, -ĕrĭt; | cēpĕrĭmŭs, -ĕrĭtĭs, -ĕrint.

PLUPERFECT.
cēpissĕm, -issēs, -issĕt; | cēpissēmŭs, -issētĭs, -issent.

## IMPERATIVE.

| SINGULAR. | PLURAL. |
|---|---|
| Pres. căpĕ; | căpĭtĕ. |
| Fut. căpĭtŏ, | căpĭtōte, |
| căpĭtŏ; | căpiuntŏ. |

| INFINITIVE. | PARTICIPLE. |
|---|---|
| Pres. căpĕrĕ. | Pres. căpiens. |
| Perf. cēpissĕ. | |
| Fut. captūrŭs essĕ. | Fut. captūrŭs. |

| GERUND. | SUPINE. |
|---|---|
| *Gen.* căpiendī. | |
| *Dat.* căpiendŏ. | |
| *Acc.* căpiendŭm. | *Acc.* captŭm. |
| *Abl.* căpiendŏ. | *Abl.* captū. |

### PASSIVE VOICE.

215. Capior, *I am taken.*

#### PRINCIPAL PARTS.

| Pres. Ind. | Pres. Inf. | Perf. Ind. |
|---|---|---|
| căpiŏr, | căpī, | captŭs sŭm. |

### INDICATIVE MOOD.

#### PRESENT TENSE.

| SINGULAR. | PLURAL. |
|---|---|
| căpiŏr, căpĕrĭs, căpĭtŭr; | căpĭmŭr, căpĭmĭnī, căpiuntŭr. |

IMPERFECT.

căpiēbăr, -iēbārĭs, -iēbātŭr; | căpiēbāmŭr, -iēbāmĭnī, -iēbantŭr.

FUTURE.

căpiăr, -iērĭs, -iētŭr; | căpiēmŭr, -iēmĭnī, -ientur.

PERFECT.

captŭs sŭm, ĕs, est; | captī sŭmŭs, estĭs, sunt.

PLUPERFECT.

captŭs ĕrăm, ĕrās, ĕrăt; | captī ĕrāmŭs, ĕrātĭs, ĕrant.

FUTURE PERFECT.

captŭs ĕrŏ, ĕrĭs, ĕrĭt; | captī ĕrĭmŭs, ĕrĭtĭs, ĕrunt.

## Subjunctive.

### Present.

| Singular. | Plural. |
|---|---|
| căpiăr, -iăris, -iātŭr; | căpiāmŭr, -iāmĭnī, -iantŭr. |

### Imperfect.
| | |
|---|---|
| căpĕrĕr, -ĕrĕris, -ĕrētŭr; | căpĕrēmŭr, -ĕrēmĭnī, -ĕrentŭr. |

### Perfect.
| | |
|---|---|
| captŭs sīm, sīs, sīt; | captī sīmŭs, sītĭs, sint. |

### Pluperfect.
| | |
|---|---|
| captŭs essĕm, essēs, essĕt; | captī essēmŭs, essētĭs, essent. |

## Imperative.

| | |
|---|---|
| Pres. căpĕrĕ; | căpĭmĭnī. |
| Fut. căpĭtŏr, căpĭtŏr; | căpiuntŏr. |

## Infinitive. | Participle.

| | |
|---|---|
| Pres. căpī. | |
| Perf. captŭs essĕ. | Perf. captŭs. |
| Fut. captŭm īrī. | Fut. căpiendŭs.¹ |

## Exercise XLIX.

### I. *Vocabulary.*

| | |
|---|---|
| A, ăb, *prep. with abl.* | *from, by.* |
| Accĭpĭŏ, accĭpĕrĕ, accēpī, acceptŭm, | *to receive.* |
| Bellŭm, ī, *n.* | *war.* |
| Căpĭŏ, căpĕrĕ, cēpī, captŭm, | *to take, capture.* |
| Carthāgŏ, Carthāgĭnĭs, *f.* | *Carthage*, city in Africa. |
| Cornēlĭŭs, iī, *m.* | *Cornelius*, a proper name. |
| Gallŭs, ī, *m.* | *Gaul, a Gaul.*² |

---

¹ The pupil will observe that the conjugation of *Capio* is somewhat peculiar, combining certain characteristics of the *Fourth Conjugation* with others of the *Third.* He should now carefully compare it with the conjugation of *Rego* and with that of *Audio*, and note with accuracy both the differences and the resemblances.

² The Gauls were a people inhabiting the country of ancient Gaul, embracing modern France.

Jăcĭŏ, jăcĕrĕ, jēcī, jactŭm,   to cast, throw, hurl.
Lăpĭs, lăpĭdĭs, m.   stone.
Lux, lūcĭs, f.   light.
Mūrŭs, ī, m.   wall.
Publĭŭs, iī, m.   Publius, a proper name.
Rēgŭlŭs, ī, m.   Regulus, Roman general.
Tēlŭm, ī, n.   javelin.
Trōjă, ae, f.   Troy, city in Asia Minor.

II. *Translate into English.*

1. Graeci Trojam capiēbant. 2. Trojam cepērunt. 3. Troja capta[1] est. 4. Troja capta erat. 5. Regŭlus ipse captus est. 6. Belli duces capientur. 7. Haec urbs capiĕtur. 8. Illam urbem capiĕmus. 9. Roma a Gallis[2] capta erat. 10. Galli Romam cepĕrant. 11. Scipio multas civitātes cepit. 12. Luna lucem a sole accĭpit. 13. Lucem a sole accipĭmus. 14. Tuam[3] epistŏlam accēpi. 15. Milĭtes tela jaciēbant.

III. *Translate into Latin.*

1. We were taking the city. 2. The city will be taken. 3. The city has been taken. 4. The cities will be taken. 5. The cities have been taken. 6. Who[4] took Carthage? 7. Publius Cornelius Scipio took Carthage. 8. Have you not[5] received my letter? 9. I have received your letter. 10. Have you not received five letters? 11. We have received ten letters.

---

[1] For the agreement of the participle in the compound tenses with the subject, see Rule XXXV. 1, page 54.

[2] See Rule XXXII., page 24.

[3] What is the usual place of the Possessive Pronoun? See page 77, note 1. In this sentence, *tuam* precedes its noun because it is emphatic.

[4] Which form of the Interrogative Pronoun should be used, *quis* or *qui?* See 188.

[5] Which Interrogative Particle should be used? See 346, II. 1, page 59.

# PART THIRD.

# SYNTAX.

## CHAPTER I.

### SYNTAX OF SENTENCES.

#### SECTION I.

*CLASSIFICATION OF SENTENCES.*

**343.** SYNTAX treats of the construction of sentences.

**344.** A sentence is thought expressed in language.

**345.** In their STRUCTURE, sentences are either *Simple, Complex*, or *Compound:*

I. A SIMPLE SENTENCE expresses but a single thought:

Deus mundum aedĭfĭcāvit, *God made the world.* Cic.

II. A COMPLEX SENTENCE expresses two (or more) thoughts, so related that one is dependent upon the other:

Dōnec ĕris fēlix, multos nŭmĕrābis ămīcos; *So long as you are prosperous, you will number many friends.* Ovid.

1. CLAUSES.—In this example, two simple sentences, (1) "*You will be prosperous,*" and (2) "*You will number many friends,*" are so united that the first only specifies the *time* of the second: *You will number many friends,* (when?) *so long as you are prosperous.* The parts thus united are called *Clauses* or *Members.*

III. A COMPOUND SENTENCE expresses two or more independent thoughts:

Sol ruit, et montes umbrantur, *The sun descends, and the mountains are shaded.* Virg.

**346.** In their USE, sentences are either *Declarative, Interrogative, Imperative,* or *Exclamatory.*

I. A Declarative Sentence has the form of an assertion:

Miltiădes accūsātus est, *Miltiades was accused.* Nep.

II. An Interrogative Sentence has the form of a question:

Quis non paupertātem extĭmescit, *Who does not fear poverty?* Cic.

1. Interrogative Words. — Interrogative sentences generally contain some interrogative word, — either an interrogative pronoun, adjective, or adverb, or one of the interrogative particles, *ne, nonne, num:*

1) Questions with *ne* ask for information: *Scrībitne,* Is he writing? *Ne* is always thus appended to some other word.

2) Questions with *nonne* expect the answer *yes: Nonne scribit,* Is he not writing?

3) Questions with *num* expect the answer *no : Num scribit,* Is he writing?

III. An Imperative Sentence has the form of a command, exhortation, or entreaty:

Justĭtiam cŏle, *Cultivate justice.* Cic.

IV. An Exclamatory Sentence has the form of an exclamation:

Rĕlĭquit quos vĭros, *What heroes he has left!* Cic.

## SECTION II.

### *SIMPLE SENTENCES.*

### Elements of Sentences.

347. The simple sentence in its *most simple form* consists of two distinct parts, expressed or implied:

1. The Subject, or that of which it speaks.
2. The Predicate, or that which is said of the subject:

Cluilius mŏrĭtur, *Cluilius dies.* Liv.

Here *Cluilius* is the subject, and *morĭtur* the predicate.

348. The simple sentence in its *most expanded form* consists only of these same parts with their various modifiers:

In his castris Cluilius, Albānus rex, morĭtur; *Cluilius, the Alban king, dies in this camp.* Liv.

Here *Cluilius, Albānus rex,* is the subject in its enlarged or modified form, and *in his castris morĭtur* is the predicate in its enlarged or modified form.

**349. Principal and Subordinate.** — The subject and predicate, being essential to the structure of every sentence, are called the *Principal* or *Essential* elements; but their modifiers, being subordinate to these, are called the *Subordinate* elements.

**350. Simple and Complex.** — The elements, whether principal or subordinate, may be either simple or complex:

1. *Simple,* when not modified by other words.
2. *Complex,* when thus modified.[1]

### Simple Subject.

**351.** The subject of a sentence must be a noun, or some word or words used as a noun:

*Rex*[2] dēcrēvit, *The king decreed.* Nep. *Ego*[2] ad te scrībo, *I write to you.* Cic.

### Simple Predicate.

**353.** The simple predicate must be either a verb or the copula *sum* with a noun or adjective:

Miltiădes est accūsātus,[3] *Miltiades was accused.* Nep. Tu es testis, *You are a witness.* Cic. Fortūna caeca est, *Fortune is blind.* Cic.

1. Like *Sum,* several other verbs sometimes unite with a noun or adjective to form the predicate. A noun or adjective thus used is called a *Predicate Noun* or *Predicate Adjective.*[4]

---

[1] Thus, in the example given above, the simple subject is *Cluilius;* the complex, *Cluilius, Albānus rex;* the simple predicate, *morĭtur;* the complex, *in his castris morĭtur.*

[2] In these examples, the noun *rex* and the pronoun *ego,* used as a noun, are the subjects.

[3] In the first of these examples, the predicate is the verb, *est accusātus;* in the second, the noun and copula, *est testis;* and in the third, the adjective and copula, *caeca est.*

[4] Thus *testis,* in the second example, is a *Predicate Noun,* and *caeca,* in the third, is a *Predicate Adjective.*

## CHAPTER II.
## SYNTAX OF NOUNS.

### SECTION I.
*AGREEMENT OF NOUNS.*

#### RULE I.—Predicate Nouns.[1]

**362.** A Predicate Noun[2] denoting the same person or thing as its Subject agrees with it in CASE:

Ego sum nuntius,[2] *I am a messenger.* Liv.  Servius rex est dēclārātus, *Servius was declared king.* Liv.

### Exercise L.
#### I. *Vocabulary.*

| | |
|---|---|
| Amnĭs, amnĭs, *m.* | *river.* |
| Creŏ, āre, āvi, ātŭm, | *to create, make, elect.* |
| Graeciă, ae, *f.* | *Greece.* |
| Impĕrātŏr, impĕrātōrĭs, *m.* | *commander.* |
| Lătīnŭs, ī, *m.* | *Latinus,* Italian king. |
| Lāviniă, ae, *f.* | *Lavinia,* a proper name. |
| Mălŭm, ī, *n.* | *evil.* |
| Nōmĭnŏ, āre, āvi, ātŭm, | *to call, name.* |
| Nŭmă, ae, *m.* | *Numa,* Roman king. |
| Rhēnŭs, ī, *m.* | *the Rhine,* river in Europe. |
| Serviŭs, iī, *m.* | *Servius,* Roman king. |
| Stultĭtiă, ae, *f.* | *folly.* |
| Tŭm, *adv.* | *then, at that time.* |

---

[1] In illustrating in the subsequent pages the leading principles of the Latin Syntax, we shall take up the most common Rules in the order in which they stand in the Grammar. In doing so, we shall repeat in their proper places those Rules which we have had occasion to anticipate in the previous Exercises.

[2] See 353, 1; also Rule I. note, p. 59.

II. *Translate into English.*

1. Cicĕro *consul*¹ fuit.² 2. Cicĕro *orātor* fuit. 3. Cicĕro tum³ erat² *orātor* clarissĭmus.⁴ 4. Puer *orātor* erit. 5. Numa erat rex. 6. Numa rex¹ creātus est. 7. Cato imperātor fuit. 8. Cato magnus imperātor fuit. 9. Scipio consul creātus est. 10. Scipio consul fuĕrat. 11. Stultitia est malum. 12. Gloria est fructus virtūtis. 13. Graecia artium⁵ mater nominātur.

III. *Translate into Latin.*

1. The Rhine is a large *river*. 2. Rome was a beautiful *city*. 3. Cato was a wise *man*. 4. Your father is a wise man. 5. Lavinia was the daughter of the king. 6. Latinus was king. 7. Lavinia was the daughter of Latinus. 8. Tullia was the daughter of Servius.

APPOSITIVES.

**RULE II.—Appositives.**

363. An Appositive⁶ agrees with its Subject in CASE:

Cluilius rex⁶ mŏrĭtur, *Cluilius the king dies.* Liv. Urbes Carthāgo⁶ atque Nŭmantia, *the cities Carthage and Numantia.* Cic.

---

¹ Predicate Noun. See Rule I. For Model for parsing Predicate Nouns, see p. 59.

² For the *place* of the verb with Predicate Nouns, see note on *fuit* under Exercise XIX.

³ Adverb qualifying *erat*. See Rule LI. p. 72.

⁴ See 162; also Rule XXXIII. p. 32.

⁵ *Artium* depends upon *mater*. See Rule XVI. p. 22.

⁶ See 363, note, p. 15; also Model, p. 16. *Rex, Carthāgo,* and *Numantia* are all Predicate Nouns.

## Exercise LI.

### I. Vocabulary.

| | |
|---|---|
| Alexandĕr, Alexandrī, *m.* | *Alexander*, the Great. |
| Conjux, conjŭgĭs, *m.* and *f.* | *wife, husband.* |
| Epīrŭs, ī, *f.* | *Epirus,* country in Greece. |
| Erŭdītŭs, ă, ŭm, | *learned, instructed in.* |
| Hannŏ, Hannōnĭs, *m.* | *Hanno,* Carthaginian general. |
| Justŭs, ă, ŭm, | *just, upright.* |
| Măcĕdŏniă, ae, *f.* | *Macedonia, Macedon.* |
| Nĕpōs, nĕpōtĭs, *m.* | *grandson.* |
| Paulŭs, ī, *m.* | *Paulus,* Roman consul. |
| Phĭlippŭs, ī, *m.* | *Philip,* king of Macedon. |
| Pyrrhŭs, ī, *m.* | *Phyrrhus,* king of Epirus. |
| Vulnĕrŏ, ārĕ, āvī, ātŭm, | *to wound.* |

### II. Translate into English.

1. Cicĕro, eruditissĭmus *homo,*[1] consul[2] fuit. 2. Numa, justissĭmus *vir,* erat rex. 3. Ancus, Numae *nepos,*[1] rex fuit. 4. Hanno *dux* captus est.[3] 5. Pyrrhus, Epīri rex, vulnerātus est. 6. Philippus, rex Macedoniae, Athenienses superāvit. 7. Paulus consul[1] regem superāvit. 8. Philosophia, mater bonārum artium, nos erŭdit.

### III. Translate into Latin.

1. Tullia, *the daughter*[1] of Servius, was the wife[2] of Tarquin. 2. Servius, *the father* of Tullia, was a king. 3. Scipio, *the leader* of the Romans, took Carthage. 4. Scipio the general was praised. 5. Philip, king of Macedonia, was the father of Alexander. 6. Alexander, the son of Philip, was king of Macedonia.

---

[1] Appositive. See Rule II. For Model for parsing Appositives, see p. 16.
[2] Predicate Noun. See Rule I.
[3] See 214.

## SECTION II.

### NOMINATIVE.

**364. Cases.** — Nouns have different forms or cases to mark the various relations in which they are used. These cases, in accordance with their general force, may be arranged and characterized as follows:

I. Nominative,    Case of the Subject.
II. Vocative,    Case of Address.
III. Accusative,    Case of Direct Object.
IV. Dative,    Case of Indirect Object.
V. Genitive,    Case of Adjective Relations.
VI. Ablative,    Case of Adverbial Relations.[1]

**RULE III.—Subject Nominative.**

**367.** The Subject of a Finite verb is put in the Nominative:

Servius regnāvit, *Servius reigned.* Liv. Pătent portae, *The gates are open.* Cic. Rex vīcit, *The king conquered.* Liv.

1. The Subject is always a substantive, a pronoun, or some word or clause used substantively:

Ego rēges ejēci, *I have banished kings.* Cic.

2. Subject Omitted. — See 460, 2, p. 54.

### Exercise LII.

#### I. *Vocabulary.*

| | |
|---|---|
| Lībertās, lībertātis, *f.* | *liberty.* |
| Opŭlentŭs, ă, ŭm, | *rich, opulent.* |
| Quŏtĭdĭē, *adv.* | *daily.* |
| Vĭtĭŭm, iĭ, *n.* | *fault, vice.* |
| Oppĭdum, ī, *n.* | *town, city.* |

---

[1] This arrangement is adopted in the discussion of the cases, because it is thought it will best present the force of the several cases, and their relation to each other.

## SYNTAX. — VOCATIVE.

II. *Translate into English.*

1. Italia[1] liberāta[2] est. 2. Urbs Roma liberāta erat. 3. Haec urbs clarissĭma liberabĭtur. 4. Haec urbs opulentissĭma est capta. 5. Virtus quotidie laudātur. 6. Virtūtes semper laudabuntur. 7. Sapientia semper est laudāta. 8. Libertas semper laudabĭtur. 9. Omnia hostium oppĭda expugnāta sunt.

III. *Translate into Latin.*

1. Was not *Philip* wounded? 2. *Philip*, king of Macedonia, was wounded. 3. Many *soldiers* were wounded. 4. Did not the soldiers fight bravely? 5. The soldiers fought bravely. 6. Will not the laws be observed? 7. The laws have been observed. 8. They will be observed.

### SECTION III.

*VOCATIVE.*

#### RULE IV.—Case of Address.

**369.** The Name of the person or thing addressed is put in the Vocative:

Perge, Laeli,[3] *Proceed, Laelius.* Cic. Quid est, Catilīna,[3] *Why is it, Catiline?* Cic. Tuum est, Servi,[3] regnum. *The kingdom is yours, Servius.* Liv.

### Exercise LIII.

#### I. *Vocabulary.*

| | |
|---|---|
| Auditŏr, auditōris, *m.* | *hearer, auditor.* |
| Cārŭs, ă, ŭm, | *dear.* |
| Jŭvĕnĭs, ĭs, *m.* and *f.* | *a youth, young man.* |
| Lēgātŭs, ī, *m.* | *ambassador.* |
| Sălūtŏ, ārĕ, āvī, ātŭm, | *to salute.* |

---

[1] Subject of *liberāta est.* See Rule III. For Model for parsing Subjects, see p. 57.

[2] Why *liberāta* rather than *liberātus?* See Rule XXXV. 1, p. 54.

[3] *Laeli, Catilīna,* and *Servi* are all in the Vocative by this Rule. *Laeli* is for *Laelie;* and *Servi,* for *Servie.*

## II. *Translate into English.*

1. Te, *Scipio*,[1] salutāmus. 2. Vos, *amīci*[1] carissĭmi,[2] salūto. 3. Vos, *audītōres* omnes, salutāmus. 4. Verba mea, *judĭces*, audīte. 5. Haec verba, legāti, audīte. 6. Vos, milĭtes, hanc urbem clarissĭmam custodīte. 7. Milĭtes[1] fortissĭmi, patriam vestram liberāte. 8. Vestram virtūtem, juvĕnes, laudāmus.

## III. *Translate into Latin.*

1. *Boys*,[1] hear the words of your father. 2. *Judges*, you shall hear the truth. 3. *Father*, have we not spoken the truth? 4. You, boys, have spoken the truth. 5. Soldiers, you have fought bravely. 6. You, brave soldiers, have saved your country. 7. Pupils, I praise your diligence.

### SECTION IV.

*ACCUSATIVE.*

**RULE V.—Direct Object.**

371. The Direct Object[3] of an action is put in the Accusative:

Deus mundum aedĭfĭcāvit, *God made the world.*[4] Cic. Libĕram rem publĭcam, *Free the republic.* Cic. Popŭli Rōmāni salūtem dēfendīte, *Defend the safety of the Roman people.* Cic.

---

[1] In the Vocative, according to Rule IV. No special Model for parsing is deemed necessary, as all nouns are parsed substantially in the same way; though different Rules are, of course, assigned for different cases. See Directions for Parsing, p. 15; also Model, p. 16.

The Vocative is not often the first word in the sentence, though it is sometimes thus placed, as in the seventh sentence in this Exercise.

[2] See 162.

[3] See *note* on Direct Object, p. 70.

[4] See *note* on the position of the Object in the Latin sentence, p. 70.

## Exercise LIV.

### I. Vocabulary.

| | |
|---|---|
| Flāmĭnĭŭs, ĭi, *m.* | *Flaminius*, Roman general. |
| Marcellŭs, ī, *m.* | *Marcellus*, Roman general. |
| Poenŭs, ă, ŭm, | *Carthaginian.* |
| Poenus, ī, *m.* | *a Carthaginian.* |
| Sanctŭs, ă, ŭm, | *holy, sacred.* |
| Sĭcĭlĭă, ae, *f.* | *Sicily*, the island of. |
| Spŏlĭŏ, āre, āvi, ātŭm, | *to rob, spoil, despoil.* |
| Sўrācūsae, ārŭm, *f. plur.* | *Syracuse*, city in Sicily. |

### II. Translate into English.

1. Alexander multas *urbes*[1] expugnāvit. 2. Italia pulchras *urbes* habuit. 3. Hostes *templa* spoliābant. 4. *Templa* sanctissĭma spoliavērunt. 5. Hannĭbal Flaminium[1] consŭlem[2] superāvit. 6. Poeni Siciliam occupavĕrant. 7. Marcellus[3] magnam hujus insŭlae[4] partem cepit. 8. Marcellus Syracūsas,[1] nobilissĭmam urbem,[2] expugnāvit.

### III. Translate into Latin.

1. Do you not[5] love your *parents?*[1] 2. We love our *parents.* 3. You practise *virtue.* 4. Our pupils will practise virtue. 5. Did not Rome have beautiful temples? 6. Rome had beautiful temples. 7. Have not the enemy[6] taken the city? 8. They have taken the beautiful city. 9. They will plunder all the temples.

---

[1] Direct Object, in the Accusative, according to Rule V. For Model for parsing, see p. 71.

[2] Appositive. See Rule II. 363.

[3] Apply to this sentence Suggestions IV. and V.

[4] *Hujus insŭlae*, of this island; i.e., of Sicily. Observe the position of the Genitive between the adjective *magnam* and its noun *partem.* See note on *pondus*, Exercise XXX. II. 10.

[5] See 346, II. 1.

[6] The Latin word must be in the plural.

## ACCUSATIVE OF TIME AND SPACE.

**RULE VIII.—Accusative of Time and Space.**

**378. DURATION OF TIME**, and **EXTENT OF SPACE**, are expressed by the Accusative:

Rōmŭlus septem et trīginta regnāvit annos,[1] *Romulus reigned thirty-seven years.* Liv. Quinque millia passuum ambŭlāre, *To walk five miles.* Cic. Pĕdes octōginta distāre, *To be eighty feet distant.* Caes. Nix quattuor pĕdes[1] alta, *Snow four feet deep.* Liv.

### EXERCISE LV.

#### I. *Vocabulary.*

| | |
|---|---|
| Aggĕr, aggĕris, *m.* | *mound, rampart.* |
| Ambŭlō, āre, āvī, ātŭm, | *to walk.* |
| Centŭm, | *hundred.* |
| Glădiŭs, iī, *m.* | *sword.* |
| Lăcĕdaemŏniŭs, iī, *m.* | *a Lacedaemonian, Spartan.* |
| Lātŭs, ă, ŭm, | *broad, wide.* |
| Longŭs, ă, ŭm, | *long.* |
| Mensĭs, mensĭs, *m.* | *month.* |
| Nox, noctĭs, *f.* | *night.* |
| Octōgintā, | *eighty.* |
| Pēs, pĕdis, *m.* | *foot.* |
| Quinquāgintā, | *fifty.* |
| Regnō, āre, āvī, ātŭm, | *to reign.* |
| Vĭgĭlō, āre, āvī, ātŭm, | *to watch, be awake.* |

#### II. *Translate into English.*

1. Lacedaemonii pacem sex *annos*[2] servavērunt. 2. Magnam noctis *partem*[2] vigilavĕram. 3. Puer octo *horas*

---

[1] *Annos* denotes *Duration of Time*, while *millia* and *pedes* denote *Extent of Space*. They are all in the Accusative by this Rule.

[2] In the Accusative denoting Duration of Time. See Rule VIII. No special Model for parsing is necessary. The pupil will be guided by previous directions and Models.

dormīvit. 4. Latīnus multos *annos* regnāvit. 5. In Italiā sex menses fuĭmus. 6. In illā urbe decem dies fuĭmus. 7. Agger octoginta pedes[1] latus fuit. 8. Hic gladius sex pedes longus est.

### III. *Translate into Latin.*

1. Did you not walk two *hours?* 2. We walked three *hours.* 3. Did you not sleep six *hours?* 4. We slept eight hours. 5. The soldiers guarded the city ten months. 6. Were you not in the city four months? 7. We were in the city five months. 8. The mound was fifty feet high.

### ACCUSATIVE OF LIMIT.

**RULE IX.—Accusative of Limit.**

**379.** The Name of a Town used as the Limit of motion is put in the Accusative:

Nuntius Rōmam rĕdit, *The messenger returns to Rome.* Liv. Plāto Tărentum[2] vēnit, *Plato came to Tarentum.* Cic. Fūgit Tarquĭnios,[2] *He fled to Tarquinii.* Cic.

### Exercise LVI.

#### I. *Vocabulary.*

| | |
|---|---|
| Athēnae, ārŭm, *f. plur.* | *Athens*, capital of Attica. |
| Fŭgĭŏ, fŭgĕrĕ, fūgī, fŭgĭtŭm, | *to flee, fly, run away.* |
| Lȳsandĕr, Lȳsandrī, *m.* | *Lysander*, Spartan general. |
| Miltĭădēs, ĭs, *m.* | *Miltiades*, Athenian general. |
| Nāvĭgŏ, ārĕ, āvī, ātŭm, | *to sail, sail to.* |

---

[1] In the Accusative, denoting *Extent of Space.*

[2] *Romam, Tarentum,* and *Tarquinios* are all names of towns used as the *Limit of Motion;* i.e., the motion is represented as ending in those towns. They are in the Accusative, according to Rule IX.

Rĕdūcŏ, rĕdūcĕrĕ, rĕdūxī, rĕductŭm,   to lead back.
Rĕvŏcŏ, ārĕ, āvī, ātŭm,   to recall.
Spartă, ae, f.   Sparta, capital of Laconia.
Tărentŭm, ī, n.   Tarentum, Italian town.
Thēbānŭs, ă, ŭm,   Theban.
Thēbānŭs, ī, m.   a Theban.

II. *Translate into English.*

1. Cicĕro *Romam*[1] revocātus est. 2. Consŭles *Romam* revocāti sunt. 3. Hannĭbal *Carthaginem*[1] revocātus erat. 4. Lysander *Athēnas*[1] navigāvit. 5. Pyrrhus Tarentum fugātus est. 6. Consul regem Tarentum fugāvit. 7. Thebāni exercĭtum Spartam ducunt. 8. Miltiădes exercĭtum Athēnas reduxit.

III. *Translate into Latin.*

1. Who fled *to Carthage?*[2] 2. Did not the enemy flee *to Carthage?* 3. They fled *to Carthage.* 4. Will not the army be led back to Rome?[2] 5. The army has been led back to Rome. 6. The commander led the army to Athens.

## SECTION V.

### DATIVE.

382. The Dative is the Case of the Indirect Object, and is used,

I. With Verbs.
II. With Adjectives.
III. With their Derivatives, — Adverbs and Substantives.

### DATIVE WITH VERBS.

383. INDIRECT OBJECT. — A verb is often attended by a noun designating the object indirectly affected by the

---

[1] In the Accusative, according to Rule IX.

[2] The Latin word will be in the Accusative, in accordance with Rule IX.

action, — that TO or FOR which something is or is done. A noun thus used is called an Indirect Object.

### RULE XII. — Dative with Verbs.

384. The INDIRECT OBJECT is put in the Dative:

I. With INTRANSITIVE and PASSIVE Verbs:

Tempŏri[1] cēdit, *He yields to the time.* Cic.   Sĭbi tĭmuĕrant, *They had feared for themselves.* Caes.   Lăbōri stŭdent, *They devote themselves to labor.* Caes.   Nōbis[1] vīta dăta est, *Life has been granted to us.* Cic.   Nŭmĭtōri dēdĭtur, *He is delivered to Numitor.* Liv.

II. With TRANSITIVE Verbs, in connection with the ACCUSATIVE:

Pons ĭter hostĭbus[2] dĕdit, *The bridge gave a passage to the enemy.* Liv.   Lēges cīvĭtātĭbus suis scripsērunt, *They prepared laws for their states.* Cic.

### EXERCISE LVII.

#### I. *Vocabulary.*

| | |
|---|---|
| Carthāgĭniensĭs, ĕ, | *Carthaginian.* |
| Carthāgĭniensĭs, ĭs, *m.* and *f.* | *a Carthaginian.* |
| Cŏnŏn, Cŏnōnĭs, *m.* | *Conon,* Athenian gen'l. |
| Dēbeŏ, dēbērĕ, dēbuī, dēbĭtum, | *to owe.* |
| Displĭceŏ, displĭcērĕ, displĭcuī, displĭcĭtum, | *to displease.* |
| Dōnŏ, ārĕ, āvī, ātum, | *to give.* |
| Gens, gentĭs, *f.* | *race.* |
| Grātiă, ae, *f.* | *favor, gratitude, thanks.* |
| Lăbōrŏ, ārĕ, āvī, ātum, | *to strive for.* |

---

[1] *Tempŏri, sibi,* and *labōri* are in the Dative with the Intransitive verbs *cedit, timuĕrant* (intransitive here), and *student;* while *nobis* and *Numitōri* are in the Dative with the Passive verbs *data est* and *dedĭtur.*

[2] *Hostĭbus* is in the Dative, in connection with the Accusative *iter,* with the Transitive verb *dedit.* In the same way, *civitatĭbus* is in the Dative, in connection with the Accusative *leges,* with the Transitive verb *scripsērunt.*

Monstrŏ, āre, āvī, ātŭm,   to show, point out.
Plăceŏ, plăcērĕ, plăcuī, plăcĭtŭm,   to please.
Sĕnectūs, sĕncctūtĭs, f.   old age.
Sententĭă, ae, f.   opinion.
Servĭŏ, servīrĕ, servīvī, servītŭm,   to serve.
Vĭă, ae, f.   way, road.

## II. *Translate into English.*

1. Cives *legĭbus*[1] parent. 2. Multae Italiae civitātes *Romānis* parēbant. 3. Haec sententia *Caesări*[1] placuit. 4. Illa sententia *Caesări* displicuit. 5. Milītes gloriae labōrant. 6. Hoc consilium Caesări nuntiātum est. 7. Nostra consilia hostĭbus nuntiāta sunt. 8. *Tibi*[2] magnam *gratiam* habēmus. 9. Habeo *senectūti* magnam *gratiam*. 10. Conon pecuniam civĭbus donāvit. 11. Pastor puĕro viam monstrāvit. 12. Tibi viam monstrābo. 13. Romāni Carthaginiensĭbus bellum indixērunt.

## III. *Translate into Latin.*

1. Did I not obey my[3] *father?*[1] 2. You obeyed your *father.* 3. We will obey *the laws* of the state. 4. Do not the citizens serve *the king?* 5. They have served the king. 6. Will you not serve the state? 7. We will serve the state. 8. Will you not tell *me* (to me[4]) *the truth?*[5] 9. I have told *you* (to you) *the truth.* 10. Will you show

---

[1] Indirect Object, in the Dative, according to Rule XII. I.

[2] Indirect Object, in the Dative, in connection with the Accusative *gratiam* with the Transitive verb *habēmus*, according to Rule XII. II.

In the arrangement of Objects, the *Indirect* generally precedes the *Direct*, as in this sentence; though the order is sometimes reversed, as in the tenth sentence in this Exercise.

[3] In examples like this, the Possessive pronoun may either be expressed or omitted, as it is often omitted in Latin when not emphatic.

[4] Dative. See Rule XII. II.

[5] Accusative. See Rule XII. II.

me (to me) the way? 11. We will show you the way. 12. Did they declare war against the Romans? 13. They had declared war against the Romans.

## DATIVE WITH ADJECTIVES.

### RULE XIV.—Dative.

391. With Adjectives, the OBJECT TO WHICH the quality is directed is put in the Dative :

Patriae sŏlum omnĭbus[1] cārum est, *The soil of their country is dear to all.* Cic. Id aptum est tempŏri, *This is adapted to the time.* Cic. Omni aetāti mors est commūnis, *Death is common to every age.* Cic. Cănis sĭmĭlis lŭpo est, *A dog is similar to a wolf.* Cic. Nātūrae accommŏdātum, *Adapted to nature.* Cic. Graeciae ūtĭle, *Useful to Greece.* Nep.

1. ADJECTIVES WITH DATIVE. — The most common are those signifying :

*Agreeable, easy, friendly, like, near, necessary, suitable, subject, useful,* together with others of a similar or opposite meaning, and verbals in *bilis*.

### EXERCISE LVIII.

#### I. *Vocabulary.*

| | |
|---|---|
| Amīcŭs, a, ŭm, | *friendly.* |
| Hispāniă, ae, *f.* | *Spain.* |
| Multĭtūdŏ, multĭtūdĭnĭs, *f.* | *multitude.* |
| Săguntŭm, ī, *n.* | *Saguntum,* city in Spain. |
| Sĭmĭlĭs, ĕ, | *like.* |
| Sŏlŭm, ī, *n.* | *soil.* |
| Vērĭtās, vērĭtātĭs, *f.* | *verity, truth.* |

---

[1] Dative, showing *to whom* the soil is *dear,* — *dear* TO ALL. In the same way in these examples, *tempŏri* is used with *aptum,* *aetāti* with *commūnis,* *lupo* with *sĭmĭlis,* *natūrae* with *accommŏdātum,* and *Graeciae* with *utĭle.*

## II. *Translate into English.*

1. Parentes *nobis*[1] cari sunt. 2. Patria *nobis* cara est. 3. Patria *tibi*[1] erit carissima. 4. Patriae solum *nobis* carum est. 5. Hannĭbal exercitui carus fuit. 6. Victoria Romānis grata fuit. 7. Libertas multitudĭni grata est. 8. Verĭtas nobis gratissĭma est. 9. Jucunda mihi oratio fuit. 10. Saguntum Romānis amīcum fuit. 11. Hannĭbal Saguntum,[2] Hispaniae civitātem[3] Romānis[4] amīcam,[5] expugnāvit.

## III. *Translate into Latin.*

1. Will not these books be useful *to you?* 2. They are useful *to us.* 3. They will be useful *to you.* 4. This law has been useful to the state. 5. Will not this book be acceptable to you? 6. That book will be acceptable to me. 7. This book will be most acceptable[6] to my brother.

### SECTION VI.
#### GENITIVE.

393. The Genitive in its primary meaning denotes *source* or *cause;* but, in its general use, it corresponds to the English Objective with *of,* and expresses various adjective relations.

#### GENITIVE WITH NOUNS.

**RULE XVI.—Genitive.**

395. Any Noun, not an Appositive, qualifying the meaning of another noun, is put in the Genitive:

---

[1] Dative, according to Rule XIV.
[2] Accusative. See Rule V.
[3] Appositive, in agreement with Saguntum. See Rule II.
[4] Dative with *amīcam.* See Rule XIV.
[5] *Amīcam* agrees with *civitātem.* See Rule XXXIII. p. 32.
[6] See 162.

Cătōnis[1] ōrātiōnes, *Cato's orations.* Cic. Castra hostium, *The camp of the enemy.* Liv. Mors Hămilcăris, *The death of Hamilcar.* Liv. See 363.

## Exercise LIX.

### I. *Vocabulary.*

| | |
|---|---|
| Commūnĭs, ĕ, | *common.* |
| Conscientiă, ae, *f.* | *consciousness.* |
| Dulcĭs, ĕ, | *sweet, pleasant.* |
| Hŏnŏr, hŏnōrĭs, *m.* | *honor.* |
| Orbĭs, orbĭs, *m.* | *circle, world.* |
| Orbĭs terrārŭm,[2] | *the world.* |
| Parvŭs, ă, ŭm, | *small.* |
| Princĭpĭŭm, iī, *n.* | *beginning.* |
| Rectŭm, ī, *n.* | *rectitude, right.* |
| Sōcrătēs, ĭs, *m.* | *Socrates,* Athenian philosopher. |

### II. *Translate into English.*

1. Justitia *virtūtum*[3] regīna est. 2. Sapientia est mater omnium bonārum *artium.* 3. Socrătes parens *philosophiae* fuit. 4. Virtus veri *honōris*[4] mater est. 5. Patria commūnis[5] est omnium nostrum[6] parens. 6. Roma orbis[7] terrārum caput fuit. 7. Omnium rerum principia parva sunt. 8. Conscientia recti est praemium virtūtis dulcissĭmum.

---

[1] *Catōnis* qualifies *oratiōnes,* and is in the Genitive, in accordance with the Rule.

[2] Literally *the circle of lands.*

[3] Genitive, depending upon *regīna.* Rule XVI.

[4] Genitive, depending upon *mater.*

[5] *Commūnis* agrees with *parens.* See Rule XXXIII. p. 32.

[6] Genitive, depending upon *parens.*

[7] *Orbis* depends upon *caput,* and *terrārum* upon *orbis.*

### III. *Translate into Latin.*

1. The orations *of Cicero* are praised. 2. The courage *of the soldiers* saved the city. 3. The crown *of the king* was golden. 4. The sword of the general was beautiful. 5. The son of the consul violated the laws of the state. 6. The citizens will observe the laws of the state.

## GENITIVE WITH ADJECTIVES.
### RULE XVII.—Genitive.

**399.** Many Adjectives take a Genitive to complete their meaning:

Avĭdus laudis,[1] *Desirous of praise.* Cic. Otii cŭpĭdus, *Desirous of leisure.* Liv. Amans sui virtus, *Virtue fond of itself.* Cic. Effĭciens vŏluptātis, *Productive of pleasure.* Cic. Glōriae mĕmor, *Mindful of glory.* Liv.

1. FORCE OF THIS GENITIVE.—The genitive here retains its usual force,—*of, in respect of,*—and may be used after adjectives which admit this relation.

2. ADJECTIVES WITH THE GENITIVE.—The most common are

1) Verbals in **ax**, and participles in **ans** and **ens** used adjectively.

2) Adjectives denoting *desire, knowledge, skill, recollection, participation, mastery, fulness,* and their contraries.

### EXERCISE LX.
#### I. *Vocabulary.*

| | |
|---|---|
| Amans, ămantĭs, | *loving, fond of.* |
| Avĭdŭs, ă, ŭm, | *desirous of, eager for.* |

---

[1] *Laudis* completes the meaning of *avĭdus; desirous* (of what?) *of praise.* It is in the Genitive, by this Rule. In the same way, *otii* completes the meaning of *cupĭdus; sui,* of *amans; voluptātis,* of *efficiens;* and *gloriae,* of *memor.*

| | |
|---|---|
| Certāmĕn, certāmĭnĭs, *n.* | *contest, strife, battle.* |
| Cŭpĭdŭs, ă, ŭm, | *desirous of.* |
| Fons, fontĭs, *m.* | *fountain.* |
| Laus, laudĭs, *f.* | *praise.* |
| Nŏvĭtās, nŏvĭtātĭs, *f.* | *novelty.* |
| Pĕrītŭs, ă, ŭm, | *skilled in.* |
| Piscĭs, piscĭs, *m.* | *fish.* |
| Plēnŭs, ă, ŭm, | *full.* |
| Vŏluptās, vŏluptātĭs, *f.* | *pleasure.* |

II. *Translate into English.*

1. Romāni avĭdi *gloriae*[1] fuērunt. 2. Homĭnes *novitātis* avĭdi sunt. 3. Numa *pacis*[1] erat amantissĭmus.[2] 4. *Patriae* amantissĭmi sumus. 5. Consul gloriae cupĭdus erat. 6. Cicĕro gloriae cupidissĭmus[2] fuit. 7. Milĭtes erant avidissĭmi certamĭnis. 8. Fons piscium plenissĭmus est. 9. Athenienses belli navālis peritissĭmi fuērunt.

III. *Translate into Latin.*

1. Boys are fond *of praise*. 2. Are you not fond *of praise?* 3. We are fond *of praise*. 4. Were not the Athenians fond of pleasure? 5. They were always fond of pleasure. 6. They are desirous of glory. 7. Are you not desirous of a victory? 8. We are desirous of a victory.

## SECTION VII.
### ABLATIVE.

412. The Ablative in its primary meaning is closely related to the Genitive; but, in its general use, it corresponds to the English Objective with *from, by, in, with,* and expresses various adverbial relations. It is accordingly used with Verbs and Adjectives; while the Genitive, as the case of adjective relations, is most common with Nouns. See 393.

---

[1] Genitive, completing the meaning of the adjective. See Rule XVII.
[2] See 162.

## ABLATIVE OF CAUSE, MANNER, MEANS.

### RULE XXI.—Cause, Manner, Means.

**414.** Cause, Manner, and Means[1] are denoted by the Ablative:

Ars ūtilĭtāte laudātur, *An art is praised because of its usefulness.* Cic. Glōriā dūcĭtur, *He is led by glory.* Cic. Duōbus mŏdis fit, *It is done in two ways.* Cic. Sol omnia lūce collustrat, *The sun illumines all things with its light.* Cic. Apri dentĭbus se tūtantur, *Boars defend themselves with their tusks.* Cic. Aeger ĕrat vulnĕrĭbus, *He was ill in consequence of his wounds.* Nep. Laetus sorte tua, *Pleased with your lot.* Hor.

1. APPLICATION OF RULE.—This Ablative is of very frequent occurrence, and is used both with verbs and adjectives.

2. ABLATIVE OF CAUSE.—This designates that *by which, by reason of which, because of which, in accordance with which,* any thing is or is done.

3. ABLATIVE OF MANNER.—This Ablative is regularly accompanied by some modifier, or by the preposition *cum;* but a few ablatives, chiefly those signifying *manner,* — *mōre, ordĭne, rătiōne,* etc., — occur without such accompaniment:

Vi summa, *With the greatest violence.* Nep. Mōre Persārum, *In the manner of the Persians.* Nep. Cum silentio audīre, *To hear in silence.* Liv. Id ordĭne fŭcĕre, *To do it in order,* or *properly.* Cic.

---

[1] It is not always possible to distinguish between *Cause, Manner,* and *Means.* Sometimes the same Ablative may involve both *Cause* and *Means,* or both *Means* and *Manner.* Still the pupil should be taught to determine in each instance, as far as possible, what is the real force of the Ablative. Thus in the examples, *utilĭtāte* denotes cause, because of its usefulness; *gloriā,* means, with perhaps the accessory notion of cause; *modis,* manner; *luce,* means; *dentĭbus,* means; *vulnerĭbus,* cause, with perhaps the accessory notion of means; and *sorte,* cause and means.

SYNTAX. — ABLATIVE.   135

4. ABLATIVE OF MEANS. — This includes the *Instrument* and all other *Means* employed.

5. ABLATIVE OF AGENT. — This designates the Person by whom any thing is done as a voluntary agent, and takes the preposition *a* or *ab:*

Occīsus est a Thēbānis, *He was slain by the Thebans.*[1] Nep.

### EXERCISE LXI.

#### I. *Vocabulary.*

| | |
|---|---|
| Mūnŭs, mūnĕrĭs, *n.* | reward, gift. |
| Nātūră, ae, *f.* | nature. |
| Pellĭs, pellĭs, *f.* | skin, hide. |
| Quŏtĭdiānŭs, ă, ŭm, | daily. |
| Scy̆thae, ārum, *m. plur.* | Scythians. |
| Triumphŏ, ārĕ, āvī, ātŭm, | to triumph. |
| Usŭs, ūs, *m.* | use. |
| Vestĭŏ, īrĕ, īvī, ītŭm, | to clothe. |

#### II. *Translate into English.*

1. Consul *virtūte*[2] laudātus est. 2. Urbs *natūrā*[3] munīta erat. 3. Haec urbs *arte* munĭctur. 4. *Munerĭbus*[3] delectāmur. 5. Roma Camilli virtūte est servāta. 6. Camillus hostes magno proelio superāvit. 7. Scipio patrem singulāri virtūte servāvit. 8. Scipio ingenti gloriā[4] triumphāvit.[5] 9. Scythae corpŏra pellĭbus vestiēbant.

---

[1] By comparing this example with those under the Rule, the second for instance, it will be seen that the Latin construction distinguishes the *person by whom* any thing is done from the *means by which* it is done, designating the former by the Ablative with *a* or *ab* (*a Thebānis*, by the Thebans), and the latter by the Ablative without a preposition ; *gloriā*, by glory.

[2] Ablative of Cause, according to Rule XXI.

[3] Ablative of Means.

[4] Ablative of Manner.

[5] The privilege of entering Rome in grand triumphal procession was sometimes awarded to eminent Roman generals as they returned from victory. *Triumphāvit* here refers to such a triumph.

### III. Translate into Latin.

1. Are not the fields adorned *with flowers*?[1] 2. The fields are adorned *with* beautiful *flowers*. 3. Have you not strengthened your memory *by use*? 4. I have strengthened my memory by daily use. 5. You will be praised for (because of) your diligence.[2] 6. Our pupils have been praised for their diligence. 7. The general saved the city by his valor. 8. Rome was saved by the valor of the Roman soldiers.

### ABLATIVES WITH COMPARATIVES.

**RULE XXIII.— Ablative with Comparatives.**

417. Comparatives without QUAM are followed by the Ablative:

Nihil est ămābĭlius virtūte,[3] *Nothing is more lovely than virtue.* Cic. Quid est mĕlius bŏnĭtāte,[3] *What is better than goodness?* Cic.

1. COMPARATIVES WITH QUAM[4] are followed by the Nominative, or by the case of the corresponding noun before them:

Hībernia mĭnor quam Brĭtannia existĭmātur, *Hibernia is considered smaller than Britannia.* Caes. Agris quam urbi[5] terrĭbĭlior, *More terrible to the country than to the city.* Liv.

---

[1] Ablative of Means. Rule XXI.
[2] Ablative of Cause.
[3] *Virtūte* and *bonitāte* are both in the Ablative, by this Rule; the former after the comparative *amabilius*, and the latter after the comparative *melius*.
[4] *Quam* is a conjunction, meaning *than*. Conjunctions are mere connectives, used to connect words or clauses.
[5] *Agris* and *urbi*, the one *before* and the other *after* quam, are both in the same construction, in the Dative, depending upon *terribilior* according to Rule XIV. 391.

## Exercise LXII.

### I. Vocabulary.

| | |
|---|---|
| Argentŭm, ī. *n.* | silver. |
| Avārĭtĭă ac. *f.* | avarice. |
| Bŏnĭtās, bŏnĭtātĭs, *f.* | goodness, excellence. |
| Elŏquens, ēlŏquentĭs, | eloquent. |
| Ferrŭm, ī, *n.* | iron. |
| Foedŭs, ă, ŭm, | detestable. |
| Prĕtĭōsŭs, ă, ŭm, | valuable. |
| Quŭm, *conj.* | than. |
| Scientĭă, ae, *f.* | knowledge. |
| Turrĭs, turrĭs, *f.* | tower. |

### II. Translate into English.

1. Virtus mihi[1] *glorĭā*[2] est carior. 2. Patria mihi *vĭtā*[2] meā est carior. 3. Quid est jucundius *amīcĭtĭā?* 4. Quid foedius est *avarĭtĭā?* 5. Aurum argento pretiosius est. 6. Anĭmus corpŏre est nobilior. 7. Turris altior erat quam murus.[3] 8. Quid multitudĭni[1] gratius quam libertas est? 9. Pater tuus est sapientior quam tu.[4] 10. Quis eloquentior fuit quam Demosthĕnes?

### III. Translate into Latin.

1. Silver is more valuable than *iron.*[2] 2. Virtue is more valuable than *gold.* 3. Wisdom is more valuable than *money.* 4. Will not wisdom be more useful to you than gold? 5. Wisdom will be more useful to me than gold. 6. Goodness is more valuable than[5] knowledge. 7. Good-

---

[1] See Rule XIV. 391.

[2] Ablative, depending upon the comparative without *quam*, according to Rule XXIII.

[3] In the same case as *turris*, the corresponding noun before *quam*. It is the subject of *erat* understood.

[4] Subject of *es* understood.

[5] In this and the following examples use *quam*, according to 417, 1.

ness is dearer to us than glory. 8. The Romans were braver than the Gauls. 9. The soldiers were braver than the general.

### ABLATIVE OF PLACE.

**420.** This Ablative designates

I. The PLACE IN WHICH any thing is or is done:

II. The PLACE FROM WHICH any thing proceeds, including *Source* and *Separation*.

### RULE XXVI.—Ablative of Place.

**421.** I. The PLACE IN WHICH and the PLACE FROM WHICH are generally denoted by the Ablative with a Preposition. But

II. NAMES OF TOWNS drop the Preposition, and in the Singular of the First and Second declensions designate the PLACE IN WHICH by the Genitive:

I. Hannĭbal in Italiā[1] fuit, *Hannibal was in Italy*. Nep. In nostris castris, *In our camps*. Caes. In Appiā viā, *On the Appian Way*. Cic. Ab urbe profĭciscĭtur, *He departs from the city*. Caes. Ex Afrĭcā, *From Africa*. Liv.

II. Athēnis[2] fuit, *He was at Athens*. Cic. Bābȳlōne mortuus est, *He died at Babylon*. Cic. Fūgit Cŏrintho, *He fled from Corinth*. Cic. Rōmae[2] fuit, *He was at Rome*. Cic.

### EXERCISE LXIII.

#### I. *Vocabulary*.

A, ăb, *prep. with abl.*     *from, by*.
Bābȳlōn, Bābȳlōnĭs, *f.*     *Babylon, the city of*.

---

[1] *In Italiā, in castris*, and *in viā* designate the PLACE IN WHICH; while *ab urbe* and *ex Afrĭcā* designate the PLACE FROM WHICH. They are in the Ablative with a preposition.

[2] *Athēnis, Babylōne*, and *Corintho*, being names of towns, omit the preposition; while *Romae*, also the name of a town, is in the Genitive, as it is in the Singular of the First declension.

| | |
|---|---|
| Cŏrinthŭs, ī, f. | Corinth, city in Greece. |
| Diŏnȳsĭŭs, ii, m. | Dionysius, tyrant of Syracuse. |
| Hăbĭtŏ, āre, āvī, ātŭm, | to dwell, reside. |
| Hortŭs, ī, m. | garden. |
| Laetĭtĭă, ae, f. | joy. |
| Lūcŭs, ī, m. | grove. |
| Rĕgĭŏ, rĕgĭōnĭs, f. | region, territory. |
| Sĕnātŏr, sĕnātōrĭs, m. | senator. |
| Trīgintā, | thirty. |

## II. Translate into English.

1. Hannĭbal *in Hispaniā*[1] fuit. 2. Latīnus *in Italiā* regnāvit. 3. Latīnus in illis regionĭbus regnābat. 4. Cives ab urbe[2] fugiēbant. 5. Themistŏcles e Graeciā fugit. 6. Sex menses[3] *Athēnis*[4] fui. 7. Alexander *Babylōne* erat. 8. Dionysius tyrannus Syracūsis fugit. 9. Themistŏcles Athēnis fugit. 10. Athēnis habitābat. 11. Romŭlus *Romae*[5] regnāvit. 12. *Romae* ingens laetitia fuit.

## III. Translate into Latin.

1. Is not your father *in Italy*? 2. My father is *in Greece*. 3. Were you not in Greece? 4. We resided in Greece three years. 5. Who is in the garden? 6. My brother is in the garden. 7. The pupils were walking in the fields. 8. The nightingales are singing in the groves. 9. Your father resided many years *at Athens*. 10. Did he not reside at Carthage? 11. He resided four years at Carthage. 12. Did you not receive my letter *at Rome*? 13. I received your letter at Corinth.

---

[1] Ablative of PLACE IN WHICH, with the preposition *in*. See Rule XXXII.

[2] Ablative of PLACE FROM WHICH, with the preposition *ab*.

[3] See Rule VIII.

[4] In the Ablative, without a preposition, because it is the name of a town.

[5] In the Genitive, because it is the name of a *town*, and is in the Singular of the First declension.

## ABLATIVE OF TIME.

### RULE XXVIII.—Time.

**426.** The TIME of an Action is denoted by the Ablative:

Octōgēsĭmo anno[1] est mortuus, *He died in his eightieth year.* Cic. Vēre convēnēre, *They assembled in the spring.* Liv. Nātāli die suo, *On his birth-day.* Nep. Hiĕme et aestāte, *In winter and summer.* Cic.

1. DESIGNATIONS OF TIME.—Any word so used as to involve the time of an action or event may be put in the ablative: *bello,* in the time of war; *pugnā,* in the time of battle; *lūdis,* at the time of the games; *mĕmŏriā,* in memory, i.e., in the time of one's recollection.

### EXERCISE LXIV.

#### I. *Vocabulary.*

| | |
|---|---|
| Brūtus, ī, *m.* | *Brutus,* a Roman patriot. |
| Dēflăgrŏ, ārĕ, ūvī, ūtŭm, | *to burn, be consumed.* |
| Diānă, ae, *f.* | *Diana,* a goddess. |
| Ephĕsĭus, ă, ŭm, | *Ephesian, of Ephesus.* |
| Hĭems, hĭĕmĭs, *f.* | *winter.* |
| Nātālĭs, ĕ, | *belonging to one's birth, natal.* |
| Nātālĭs dĭēs, | *birth-day.* |
| Pompēĭŭs, ĭī, *m.* | *Pompey,* Roman general. |
| Persae, ārŭm, *m. plur.* | *Persians.* |
| Scrībŏ, scrībĕrĕ, scrīpsī, scrīptŭm, | *to write.* |
| Tempŭs, tempŏrĭs, *n.* | *time.* |

#### II. *Translate into English.*

1. Nātāli *die*[2] tuo scripsisti epistŏlam. 2. Eōdem *die* epistŏlam tuam accēpi.[3] 3. Pompēius urbem tertio *mense*

---

[1] *Anno, vere, die, hĭĕme,* and *aestāte* are all in the Ablative, by this Rule.
[2] Ablative of Time, according to Rule XXVIII.
[3] From *accipio.*

cepit. 4. Eōdem *die* Persae superāti sunt. 5. Pompēius illo tempŏre miles fuit. 6. Illo anno Diānae Ephesiae templum deflagrāvit. 7. Occāsu solis hostes fugāti sunt. 8. Illo die Brutus patriam servāvit.

    III. *Translate into Latin.*

1. Were you not in Athens[1] *at* that *time?* 2. We were at Corinth[2] *at* that *time.* 3. Do you not reside in the city[1] *in winter?* 4. We reside in this beautiful city in the winter. 5. The city was taken at sunset. 6. Were you not in the city at that hour? 7. I was in the city at that time. 8. Were you not in Rome[2] on your birth-day? 9. I was in that city on my birth-day.

## SECTION VIII.
### CASES WITH PREPOSITIONS.
### RULE XXXII.—Cases with Prepositions.

432. The Accusative and Ablative may be used with Prepositions:

Ad ămīcum[3] scripsi, *I have written to a friend.* Cic. In cūriam, *Into the senate-house.* Liv. In Itălĭā, *In Italy.* Nep. Pro castris, *Before the camp.*

433. The Accusative is used with

Ad, adversus (adversum), ante, ăpud, circa, circum, circĭter, cis, citra, contra, erga, extra, infra, inter, intra, juxta, ob, pĕnes, per, pōne, post, praeter, prŏpe, propter, sĕcundum, supra, trans, ultra, versus:

Ad urbem, *To the city.* Cic. Adversus deos, *Toward the gods.* Cic.

434. The Ablative is used with

| A *or* ab (abs), | absque, | cōram, | cum, | de, |
|---|---|---|---|---|
| e *or* ex, | prae, | pro, | sĭne, | tĕnus: |

[1] Ablative of Place. See Rule XXVI.
[2] Genitive of Place. See Rule XXVI. II.
[3] The Accusative *amīcum* is here used with the preposition *ad;* curiam, with *in;* the Ablative *Italiā,* with *in.* See 435, 1.

Ab urbe, *From the city.* Caes. Cōram conventu, *In the presence of the assembly.* Nep.

**435.** The ACCUSATIVE or ABLATIVE is used with

In, sub, subter, sŭper:

In Asiam prōfūgit, *He fled into Asia.* Cic. Hannĭbal in Ităliā fuit, *Hannibal was in Italy.* Nep.

1. *In* and *Sub* take the Accusative in answer to the question *whither*, the Ablative in answer to *where:* In Asiam, (whither?) *into Asia;* In Ităliā, (where?) *in Italy.*

EXERCISE LXV.

I. *Vocabulary.*

Adversŭs, *prep. with acc.* — *against.*
Dīmĭcŏ, āre, āvī, ātŭm, — *to fight.*
Pĕr, *prep. with acc.* — *of, through.*
Prospĕrē, *adv.* — *successfully.*
Prōvŏcŏ, āre, āvī, ātŭm, — *to challenge.*

II. *Translate into English.*

1. Lacedaemonii hostes ad *proelium* provocābant. 2. Scipio contra *Hannōnem,* ducem Carthaginiensium, prospĕre pugnat. 3. Caesar adversus Pompĕium dimicāvit. 4. Verĭtas per se[1] mihi grata est. 5. Virtus per se laudabĭlis est. 6. Persae a *Graecis*[2] superāti sunt. 7. Cicĕro de *amicitiā* scripsit.

III. *Translate into Latin.*

1. Will not the army be led back to *the city?* 2. It has been led back to *the city.* 3. Will you not write to me? 4. I will write to you. 5. Friendship is valuable of itself. 6. Have you not received five letters from *me?* 7. I have received four letters from *you.* 8. I have received two letters from your brother.

---

[1] *Per se,* literally *through itself:* render *in itself* or *of itself.*
[2] *A Graecis,* by the Greeks. See 414, 5.

# SUGGESTIONS TO THE LEARNER.

I. THE preparation of a Reading Lesson in Latin involves,
1. A knowledge of the Meaning of the Latin.
2. A knowledge of the Structure of the Latin Sentences.
3. A translation into English.

MEANING OF THE LATIN.

II. Remember that almost every inflected word in a Latin sentence requires the use of both the Dictionary and the Grammar to ascertain its meaning.

The Dictionary gives the meaning of the word, without reference to its Grammatical properties of *case, number, mood, tense,* etc.; and the Grammar, the meaning of the endings which mark these properties. The Dictionary will give the meaning of *mensa,* a table, but not of *mensārum,* of tables: the Grammar alone will give the force of the ending *arum.*

III. Make yourself so familiar with all the endings of inflection, with their exact form and force, whether in declension or conjugation, that you will not only readily distinguish the different parts of speech from each other, but also the different forms of the same word, with their exact and distinctive force.

IV. In taking up a Latin sentence,
1. Notice carefully the endings of the several words, and thus determine which words are *nouns,* which *verbs,* etc.

2. Observe the force of each ending, and thus determine *case, number, voice, mood, tense,* etc.

This will be found to be a very important step toward the mastery of the sentence. By this means, you will discover not only the relation of the words to each other, but also an important part of their meaning, — that which they derive from their endings.

V. The key to the meaning of any simple sentence (345, I.) will be found in the simple subject and predicate; i.e., in the Nominative and its Verb. Hence, in looking out the sentence, observe the following order. Take

1. The Subject, or Nominative.

The ending will, in most instances, enable you to distinguish this from all other words, except the adjectives which agree with it. These may be looked out at the same time with the subject.

Sometimes the subject is not expressed, but only implied, in the ending of the verb. It may then be readily supplied, as it is always a pronoun of such person and number as the verb indicates: as, *audio*, I hear, the ending *io* showing that the subject is *ego*; *auditis*, you hear, the ending *itis* showing that the subject is *vos*.

2. The Verb, with Predicate Noun or Adjective, if any.

This will be readily known by the ending. Now, combining this with the Subject, you will have an outline of the sentence. All the other words must now be associated with these two parts.

3. The Modifiers of the Subject; i.e., adjectives agreeing with it, nominatives in apposition with it, genitives dependent upon it, etc.

But perhaps some of these have already been looked out in the attempt to ascertain the subject.

In looking out these words, bear in mind the meaning of the subject to which they belong. This will greatly aid you in selecting from the dictionary the true meaning in the passage before you.

4. The Modifiers of the Verb, i.e. (1) Oblique cases, accusatives, datives, etc., dependent upon it, and (2) Adverbs qualifying it.

Bear in mind all the while the force of the case and the meaning of the verb, that you may be able to select for each word the true meaning in the passage before you.

VI. In complex and compound sentences (345, II., III.), discover first the connectives which unite the several members, and then proceed with each member as with a simple sentence.

VII. In the use of Dictionary and Vocabulary, remember that you are not to look for the particular form which occurs in the sentence, but for the Nom. Sing. of nouns, adjectives, and pronouns, and for the First Pers. Sing. Pres. Indic. Act. of verbs. Therefore,

1. In Pronouns, make yourself so familiar with their declension, that any oblique case will at once suggest the Nom. Sing.

<small>If *vobis* occurs, you must remember that the Nom. Sing. is *tu*.</small>

2. In Nouns and Adjectives, make yourself so familiar with the case-endings, that you will be able to drop that of the given case, and substitute for it that of the Nom. Sing.

<small>Thus mens$\bar{i}$bus; stem *mens*, Nom. Sing. *mensis*, which you will find in the Vocabulary. So urb*em*, *urb*, *urbs*.</small>

3. In Verbs, change the ending of the given form into that of the First Pers. Sing. of the Pres. Indic. Act.

<small>Thus am$\bar{a}$bat; stem *am*, First Pers. Sing. Pres. Indic. Act. *amo*, which you will find in the Vocabulary. So amav$\bar{e}$runt; First Pers. Perf. am$\bar{a}$vi, Perf. stem *amav*, Verb stem *am*; *amo*.</small>

To illustrate the steps recommended in the preceding suggestions, we add the following

## Model.

VIII. Themist$\breve{o}$cles imper$\bar{a}$tor servit$\bar{u}$te totam Graeciam liber$\bar{a}$vit.

1. Without knowing the meaning of the words, you will discover from their *forms*,

1) That *Themist$\breve{o}$cles* and *imper$\bar{a}$tor* are probably nouns in the Nom. Sing.

2) That *servit$\bar{u}$te* is a noun in the Abl. Sing.

3) That *totam* and *Graeciam* are either nouns or adjectives in the Accus. Sing.

4) That *liber$\bar{a}$vit* is a verb in the Act. voice, Indic. mood, Perf. tense, Third Person, Singular number.

2. Now, turning to the Vocabulary for the meaning of the words, you will learn,

1) That *Themistŏcles* is the name of an eminent Athenian general: THEMISTOCLES.

2) That *libĕro*, for which you must look, not for *liberāvit*, means *to liberate:* LIBERATED.

  Themistocles liberated.

3) That *imperātor* means *commander:* THE COMMANDER.

  Themistocles the commander liberated.

4) That *Graeciam* is the name of a country: GREECE.

  Themistocles the commander liberated Greece.

5) That *totus* means *the whole, all:* ALL.

  Themistocles the commander liberated all Greece.

6) That *servĭtus* means *servitude:* FROM SERVITUDE.

  Themistocles the commander liberated all Greece from servitude.

## STRUCTURE OF THE LATIN SENTENCE.

IX. The structure of a sentence is best shown by *analyzing*[1] it, and by *parsing* the words which compose it.

### Parsing.

XVII.[2] In parsing a word,

1. Name the Part of Speech to which it belongs.
2. Inflect[3] it, if capable of inflection.
3. Give its gender, number, case, voice, mood, tense, person, etc.[4]
4. Give its Syntax, and the Rule for it.[5]

### TRANSLATION.

XIX. In translating, render as literally as possible without doing violence to the English.

---

[1] It has not been thought advisable to enter upon the subject of *analysis* at this early stage of the course. That will be presented in the Reader, which follows this work.

[2] These suggestions are taken, without change, from the Reader. Accordingly, the numerals are made to correspond to those in that work.

[3] Inflect; i.e., decline, compare, or conjugate.

[4] That is, such of these properties as it possesses.

[5] For Models for Parsing, see pp. 16, 22, 27, 33, 55, 57, 59, 66, 71, and 73.

# LATIN-ENGLISH VOCABULARY.

*For Explanation of Abbreviations and References, see p. ix.*

### A.

A, ăb, *prep. with abl.* *From, by.*
Accĭpĭŏ, accĭpĕrĕ, accēpī, acceptŭm. *To receive.*
Acĕr, ācrĭs, ācrĕ. *Sharp, severe, valiant.*
Aciēs, ăciēī, *f.* *Order of battle, battle-array, army.*
Ad, *prep. with acc.* *To, towards, near.*
Admĭnistrŏ, ārĕ, āvī, ātŭm. *To administer, manage.*
Admŏneŏ, admŏnērĕ, admŏnuī, admŏnĭtŭm. *To admonish.*
Adventŭs, ūs, *m.* *Arrival, approach.*
Adversŭs, *prep. with acc.* *Against.*
Aedĭfĭcŏ, ārĕ, āvī, ātŭm. *To build.*
Aestās, aestātĭs, *f.* *Summer.*
Agĕr, ăgrī, *m.* *Field, land.*
Aggĕr, aggĕrĭs, *m.* *Mound, rampart.*
Agĭs, Agĭdĭs, *m.* *Agis, a king of Sparta.*
Albānŭs, ă, ŭm. *Alban.*
Alexandĕr, Alexandrī, *m.* *Alexander,* the Great.
Alĭquĭs, ălĭquă, ălĭquĭd or ălĭquŏd. *Some, some one.* See 191.
Altŭs, ă, ŭm. *High, lofty.*
Amans, ămantĭs. *Loving, fond of.*

Ambŭlŏ, ārĕ, āvī, ātŭm. *To walk.*
Amīcĭtĭă, ae, *f.* *Friendship.*
Amīcŭs, ă, ŭm. *Friendly.*
Amīcŭs, ī, *m.* *Friend.*
Amnĭs, amnĭs, *m.* *River.*
Amŏ, ārĕ, āvī, ātŭm. *To love.*
Amŏr, amŏrĭs, *m.* *Love.*
Amplĭŏ, ārĕ, āvī, ātŭm. *To enlarge.*
Ancŭs, ī, *m.* *Ancus,* a Roman king.
Anĭmăl, ănĭmālĭs, *n.* *Animal.*
Anĭmŭs, ī, *m.* *Soul, mind, passion, disposition.*
Annŭlŭs, ī, *m.* *Ring.*
Annŭs, ī, *m.* *Year.*
Antĕ, *prep. with acc.* *Before.*
Antīquŭs, ă, ŭm. *Ancient.*
Apĭs, ăpĭs, *f.* *Bee.*
Appellŏ, ārĕ, āvī, ātŭm. *To call.*
Appĕtens, appĕtentĭs. *Desiring, striving for.*
Apŭd, *prep. with acc.* *In the presence of, near, before, among.*
Apūlĭă, ae, *f.* *Apulia,* a country in Italy.
Arabs, Arăbĭs, *m* and *f.* *Arab, an Arab.*
Arctē, *adv.* *Closely, soundly.*
Argentŭm, ī, *n.* *Silver.*
Arŏ, ărārĕ, ărāvī, ărātŭm. *To plough.*

147

Arrŏgantiă, ae, *f.* *Arrogance.*
Ars, artĭs, *f.* *Art, skill.*
Artăxerxēs, ĭs, *m.* *Artaxerxes,* a Persian king.
Arx, arcĭs, *f.* *Citadel, fortress.*
Athēnae, ārŭm, *f. plur.* *Athens,* the capital of Attica.
Athēnĭensĭs, ĕ. *Athenian.*
Athēniensĭs, ĭs, *m.* and *f.* *Athenian,* *an Athenian.*
Attĭcŭs, ī, *m.* *Atticus,* a Roman name.
Audĭŏ, īrĕ, īvī, ītŭm. *To hear.*
Audītŏr, audītŏrĭs, *m.* *Hearer, auditor.*
Aureŭs, ă, ŭm. *Golden.*
Aurŭm, ī, n. *Gold.*
Avārĭtĭă, ae, *f.* *Avarice.*
Avĭdŭs, ă, ŭm. *Desirous of, eager for.*
Avĭs, ăvĭs, *f.* *Bird.*

## B.

Băbўlōn, Băbўlōnĭs, *f.* *Babylon,* the celebrated capital of the Assyrian Empire, on the banks of the Euphrates.
Beātŭs, ă, ŭm. *Happy, blessed.*
Bellŭm, ī, *n.* *War, warfare.*
Běně, *adv.* *Well.*
Běnignē, *adv.* *Kindly.*
Bŏnĭtās, bŏnĭtātĭs, *f.* *Goodness, excellence.*
Bŏnŭs, ă, ŭm. *Good.*
Brěvĭs, ĕ. *Short, brief.*
Brūtŭs, ī, *m.* *Brutus,* a celebrated Roman patriot.

## C.

Caesăr, Caesărĭs, *m.* *Cæsar,* a celebrated Roman commander.
Cāiŭs, iī, *m.* *Caius,* a proper name.

Cămillŭs, ī, *m.* *Camillus,* a Roman general.
Campŭs, ī, *m.* *Plain.*
Cănĭs, cănĭs, *m.* and *f.* *Dog.*
Cantŏ, ārĕ, āvī, ātŭm. *To sing.*
Cantŭs, ūs, *m.* *Singing, song.*
Căpĭŏ, căpĕrĕ, cēpī, captŭm. *To take, capture.*
Căpŭt, căpĭtĭs, *n.* *Head, capital.*
Carmĕn, carmĭnĭs, *n.* *Song, poem, verse.*
Carthāgĭniensĭs, ĕ. *Carthaginian.*
Carthāgĭniensĭs, ĭs, *m.* and *f.* *A Carthaginian.*
Carthāgŏ, Carthāgĭnĭs, *f.* *Carthage,* a city of Northern Africa.
Carthāgŏ Nŏvă. *New Carthage,* *Carthagena,* a city of Spain.
Cărŭs, ă, ŭm. *Dear.*
Cătŏ, Cătŏnĭs, *m.* *Cato,* a distinguished Roman.
Centŭm. *One hundred.* See 175, 2.
Certāmĕn, certāmĭnĭs, *n.* *Contest, strife, battle.*
Cĭbŭs, ī, *m.* *Food.*
Cĭcĕrŏ, Cĭcĕrōnĭs, *m.* *Cicero,* the celebrated Roman orator.
Cīvīlĭs, ĕ. *Civil.*
Cīvĭs, cīvĭs, *m.* and *f.* *Citizen.*
Cīvĭtās, cīvĭtātĭs, *f.* *State, city.*
Clārŭs, ă, ŭm. *Renowned, distinguished, illustrious.*
Classĭs, classĭs, *f.* *Fleet, navy.*
Coerceŏ, coercērĕ, coercuī, coercĭtŭm. *To check.*
Cŏlŏ, cŏlĕrĕ, cŏluī, cultŭm. *To practise, cultivate.*
Commūnĭs ĕ. *Common.*
Condemnŏ, ārĕ, āvī, ātŭm. *To condemn.*
Condĭtŏr, condĭtŏrĭs, *m.* *Founder.*
Conjux, conjŭgĭs, *m.* and *f.* *Wife, husband, spouse.*

Cŏnōn, Cŏnōnĭs, *m.* *Conon,* an Athenian general.
Conscientĭă, ae, *f.* *Consciousness.*
Consĭlĭum, ĭī, *n.* *Design, plan.*
Conspectŭs, ūs, *m.* *Sight, view, presence.*
Consŭl, consŭlĭs, *m.* *Consul.*
Contrā, *prep. with acc.* *Against, opposite to, contrary to.*
Convŏcŏ, ārĕ, āvī, ātŭm. *To assemble, call together.*
Cŏrinthŭs, ī, *f.* *Corinth,* city in Greece.
Cornēlĭŭs, ĭī, *m.* *Cornelius,* a Roman name.
Cŏrōnă, ae, *f.* *Crown.*
Corpŭs, corpŏrĭs, *n.* *Body, person.*
Creŏ, ārĕ, āvī, ātŭm. *To create, make, appoint, elect.*
Crūdēlĭs, ĕ. *Cruel.*
Crūdŭs, ă, ŭm. *Unripe.*
Culpŏ, ārĕ, āvī, ātŭm. *To blame.*
Cŭm, *prep. with abl.* *With.*
Cŭpĭdŭs, ă, ŭm. *Desirous of.*
Cŭrēs, Cŭrĭŭm, *m. plur.* *Cures,* a Sabine town.
Custōdĭŏ, īrĕ, īvī, ītŭm. *To guard.*
Custōs, custōdĭs, *m.* and *f.* *Keeper, guard.*

### D.

Dē, *prep. with abl.* *Concerning.*
Dēbeŏ, dēbērĕ, dēbuī, dēbĭtŭm. *To owe.*
Dĕcĕm. *Ten.* See 175.
Dĕcĭmŭs, ă, ŭm. *Tenth.*
Dēfectĭŏ, dēfectĭōnĭs, *f.* *Eclipse.*
Dēflăgrŏ, ārĕ, āvī, ātŭm. *To burn, be consumed.*
Dēlectŏ, ārĕ, āvī, ātŭm. *To delight, please.*
Dēmărătŭs, ī, *m.* *Demaratus,* a Corinthian.

Dēmosthĕnēs, ĭs, *m.* *Demosthenes,* the celebrated Athenian orator.
Dĭănă, ae, *f.* *Diana,* the goddess of the chase.
Dīcŏ, dīcĕrĕ, dixī, dictŭm. *To say, speak, tell.*
Dĭēs, diēī, *m.* *Day.* See 119, note.
Dīlĭgens, dīlĭgentĭs. *Diligent.*
Dīlĭgentĭă, ae, *f.* *Diligence.*
Dīmĭcŏ, ārĕ, āvī, ātŭm. *To fight.*
Dĭŏnȳsĭŭs, ĭī, *m.* *Dionysius,* tyrant of Syracuse.
Discĭpŭlŭs, ī, *m.* *Pupil.*
Dĭsertē, *adv.* *Clearly, eloquently.*
Displĭceŏ, displĭcērĕ, displĭcuī, displĭcĭtŭm. *To displease.*
Dīvīnŭs, ă, ŭm. *Divine.*
Dŏlŏr, dŏlōrĭs, *m.* *Pain, grief, suffering.*
Dōnŏ, ārĕ, āvī, ātŭm. *To give, present.*
Dōnŭm, ī, *n.* *Gift.*
Dormĭŏ, īrĕ, īvī, ītŭm. *To sleep.*
Drăcŏ, Drăcōnĭs, *m.* *Draco,* an Athenian lawgiver.
Dŭcentī, ae, ă. *Two hundred.*
Dūcŏ, dūcĕrĕ, duxī, ductŭm. *To lead.*
Dulcĭs, ĕ. *Sweet, pleasant.*
Dŭŏ, ae, ŏ. *Two.* See 176.
Dŭplĭcŏ, ārĕ, āvī, ātŭm. *To double, increase.*
Dux, dŭcĭs, *m.* and *f.* *Leader, general.*

### E.

E, ex, *prep. with abl.* *From.*
Ēbrĭĕtās, ēbrĭĕtātĭs, *f.* *Drunkenness.*
Ēdūcŏ, ēdūcĕrĕ, ēduxī, ēductum. *To lead forth, lead out.*
Effŭgĭŏ, effŭgĕrĕ, effŭgi, effŭgĭtŭm. *To escape.*
Ĕgŏ, meī. *I.* See 184.

Egrĕgĭus, ă, ŭm. *Distinguished.*
Egrĕgĭē, *adv. Excellently.*
Elĕphantŭs, ī, *m. Elephant.*
Elŏquens, ēlŏquentĭs. *Eloquent.*
Elŏquentĭă, ae, *f. Eloquence.*
Ephĕsĭŭs, ă, ŭm. *Ephesian, of Ephesus.*
Epīrŭs, ī, *f. Epirus,* a country in Greece.
Epistŏlă, ae, *f. Letter.*
Erŭdĭō, īrĕ, īvī, ītŭm. *To instruct, refine, educate.*
Erŭdītŭs, ă, ŭm. *Learned, instructed in.*
Ex, *prep. with abl. From.*
Exerceō, exercērĕ, exercuī, exercĭtŭm. *To exercise, train.*
Exercĭtŭs, ūs, *m. Army.*
Expugnō, ārĕ, āvī, ātŭm. *To take, take by storm.*
Exspectō, ārĕ, āvī, ātŭm. *To await, expect.*
Exsŭl, exsŭlĭs, *m.* and *f. Exile.*

**F.**

Făcĭēs, făcĭēī, *f. Face, appearance.*
Ferrŭm, ī, *n. Iron.*
Fertĭlĭs, ĕ. *Fertile.*
Fĭdēlĭtās, fĭdēlĭtātĭs, *f. Fidelity, faithfulness.*
Fĭdēs, fĭdeī, *f. Faith, fidelity.*
Fīdŭs, ă, ŭm. *Faithful.*
Fīlĭă, ae, *f. Daughter.*
Fīlĭŭs, iī, *m. Son.*
Fīnĭō, īrĕ, īvī, ītŭm. *To finish, bring to a close.*
Fīnĭs, fīnĭs, *m. Limit, territory.*
Firmō, ārĕ, āvī, ātŭm. *To strengthen, confirm.*
Flămĭnĭŭs, iī, *m. Flaminius,* a Roman general.
Flōs, flōrĭs, *m. Flower.*
Foedŭs, ă, ŭm. *Detestable.*

Fons, fontĭs, *m. Fountain.*
Fortĭs, ĕ. *Brave.*
Fortĭtĕr, *adv. Bravely.*
Fortĭtūdō, fortĭtūdĭnĭs, *f. Bravery, fortitude.*
Fossă, ae, *f. Ditch, moat.*
Frātĕr, frātrĭs, *m. Brother.*
Fructŭs, ūs, *m. Fruit, produce, income.*
Frūmentŭm, ī, *n. Corn, grain.*
Fŭgă, ae, *f. Flight.*
Fŭgĭō, fŭgĕrĕ, fūgī, fŭgĭtŭm. *To flee, fly, run away.*
Fŭgō, ārĕ, āvī, ātŭm. *To rout, drive away.*
Fūnestŭs, ă, ŭm. *Destructive.*
Fŭrŏr, fŭrōrĭs, *m. Madness, insanity.*

**G.**

Gallŭs, ī, *m. Gallus,* a proper name.
Gallŭs, ī, *m. Gaul,* a *Gaul,* an inhabitant of ancient Gaul, embracing modern France.
Gemmă, ae, *f. Gem.*
Gĕnĕr, gĕnĕrī, *m. Son-in-law.*
Gens, gentĭs, *f. Race.*
Germānĭă, ae, *f. Germany.*
Glădĭŭs, iī, *m. Sword.*
Glŏbōsŭs, ă, ŭm. *Spherical.*
Glōrĭă, ae, *f. Glory.*
Graecĭă, ae, *f. Greece.*
Graecŭs, ă, ŭm. *Grecian, Greek.*
Graecŭs, ī, *m. Greek,* a *Greek.*
Grātĭă, ae, *f. Favor, gratitude, thanks.*
Grātŭs, ă, ŭm. *Acceptable, pleasing.*
Grex, grĕgĭs, *m. Herd, flock.*

**H.**

Hăbĕō, hăbērĕ, hăbuī, hăbĭtŭm. *To have, hold.*
Hăbĭtō, ārĕ, āvī, ātŭm. *To dwell, reside.*

Hannĭbăl, Hannĭbălĭs, *m.* *Hannibal*, a celebrated Carthaginian general.
Hannŏ, Hannōnĭs, *m.* *Hanno*, a Carthaginian general.
Hastă, ae, *f.* *Spear.*
Hĭc, haec, hŏc. *This.*
Hiems, hiĕmĭs, *f.* *Winter.*
Hĭrundŏ, hĭrundĭnĭs, *f.* *Swallow.*
Hispānĭă, ae, *f.* *Spain.*
Hispānŭs, ī, *m.* *A Spaniard.*
Hŏmērŭs, ī, *m.* *Homer*, the celebrated Grecian poet.
Hŏmŏ, hŏmĭnĭs, *m.* *Man.*
Hŏnŏr, hŏnōrĭs, *m.* *Honor.*
Hōră, ae, *f.* *Hour.*
Hostĭs, hostĭs, *m.* and *f.* *Enemy.*

## I.

Idĕm, cădĕm, ĭdĕm. *Same, the same.* See 186.
Ignōrŏ, ārĕ, āvī, ātŭm. *To be ignorant of, not to know.*
Illĕ, illă, illŭd. *That, he, she, it.* See 186.
Illustrŏ, ārĕ, āvī, ātŭm. *To illustrate, illumine.*
Imāgŏ, ĭmāgĭnĭs, *f.* *Image, picture.*
Impătiens, impătientĭs. *Impatient.*
Impĕrātŏr, impĕrātŏrĭs, *m.* *Commander.*
Impĕrĭŭm, iī, *n.* *Reign, power, government.*
Impĕtŭs, ūs, *m.* *Attack.*
Imprŏbĭtās, imprŏbĭtātĭs, *f.* *Wickedness.*
In, *prep. with acc.* and *abl.* *Into, in, within.*
Incertŭs, ă, ŭm. *Uncertain.*
Indīcŏ, indīcĕrĕ, indixī, indictŭm. *To declare.*
Infestŏ, ārĕ, āvī, ātŭm. *To infest.*
Ingens, ingentĭs. *Huge, large, great.*

Innŏcens, innocentĭs. *Innocent.*
Insānĭă, ae, *f.* *Insanity.*
Insŭlă, ae, *f.* *Island.*
Intĕr, *prep. with acc.* *Between, among, in the midst of.*
Intrŏ, ārĕ, āvī, ātŭm. *To enter.*
Inventŏr, inventōrĭs, *m.* *Inventor.*
Invītŏ, ārĕ, āvī, ātŭm. *To invite.*
Ipsĕ, ipsă, ipsŭm. *Self, he, himself.* See 186.
Is, eă, ĭd. *That, he, she, it.*
Istĕ, istă, istŭd. *That, such.* See 186.
Ităliă, ae, *f.* *Italy.*

## J.

Jăciŏ, jăcĕrĕ, jēcī, jactŭm. *To cast, throw, hurl.*
Jăm, *adv.* *Now, already.*
Jūcundŭs, ă, ŭm. *Delightful, pleasant.*
Jūdex, jūdĭcĭs, *m.* and *f.* *Judge.*
Jungŏ, jungĕrĕ, junxī, junctŭm. *To join.*
Justĭtĭă, ae, *f.* *Justice.*
Justŭs, ă, ŭm. *Upright, just.*
Jŭvĕnĭs, jŭvĕnĭs, *m.* and *f.* *A youth, young man.*
Jŭventūs, jŭventūtĭs, *f.* *Youth, a youth, a young person.*

## L.

Lăbŏr, lăbōrĭs, *m.* *Labor.*
Lăbōrŏ, ārĕ, āvī, ātŭm. *To strive for, labor, work.*
Lăcĕdaemŏnĭŭs, iī, *m.* *Spartan, a Spartan*, inhabitant of Sparta in Greece.
Laetĭtĭă, ae, *f.* *Joy.*
Lăpĭs, lăpĭdĭs, *m.* *Stone.*
Lătīnē, *adv.* *In Latin.*
Lătīnŭs, ī, *m.* *Latinus*, a Latin king.
Lătŭs, ă, ŭm. *Broad.*

Laudābĭlĭs, ĕ. *Praiseworthy, laudable.*
Laudŏ, ārĕ, āvī, ātūm. *To praise.*
Laus, laudĭs, *f. Praise.*
Lāvīniă, ae, *f. Lavinia,* a proper name.
Lēgātĭŏ, lēgātiōnĭs, *f. Embassy.*
Lēgātŭs, ī, *m. Ambassador.*
Lĕgĭŏ, lĕgiōnĭs, *f. Legion,* a body of soldiers.
Lĕgŏ, lĕgĕrĕ, lēgī, lectūm. *To choose, appoint.*
Lĕŏ, leōnĭs, *m. Lion.*
Lētālĭs, ĕ. *Mortal, deadly.*
Lex, lēgĭs, *f. Law.*
Lĭbĕr, lĭbrī, *m. Book.*
Lībĕrŏ, ārĕ, āvī, ātŭm. *To liberate.*
Lĭbertās, lībertātĭs, *f. Liberty.*
Longŭs, ă, ŭm. *Long.*
Lūcŭs, ī, *m. Grove.*
Lūnă, ae, *f. Moon.*
Luscĭniă, ae, *f. Nightingale.*
Lux, lūcĭs, *f. Light.*
Luxūriă, ae, *f. Luxury.*
Lȳcurgŭs, ī, *m. Lycurgus,* a Spartan lawgiver.
Lȳsandĕr, Lȳsandrī, *m. Lysander,* a Spartan general.

*M.*

Măcĕdŏniă, ae, *f. Macedonia, Macedon,* a country of Northern Greece.
Măgistĕr, măgistrī, *m. Master, teacher.*
Magnŏpĕrĕ, *adv. Greatly.*
Magnŭs, ă, ŭm. *Great, large.*
Mălŭm, ī, *n. Evil.*
Marcellŭs, ī, *m. Marcellus,* a celebrated Roman general.
Mărĕ, mărĭs, *n. Sea.*
Mătĕr, mātrĭs, *f. Mother.*
Mātūrŭs, ă, ŭm. *Ripe.*
Mĕmŏriă, ae, *f. Memory.*

Mensă, ae, *f. Table.*
Mensis, mensĭs, *m. Month.*
Mercēs, mercēdĭs, *f. Reward.*
Mĕrĕŏ, mĕrērĕ, mĕruī, mĕrĭtŭm. *To deserve, merit.*
Mĕŭs, ă, ŭm. *My.* See 185.
Mīlĕs, mīlĭtĭs, *m. Soldier.*
Miltĭādēs, ĭs, *m. Miltiades,* an Athenian general.
Mŏdestiă, ae, *f. Modesty.*
Mŏneŏ, mŏnērĕ, mŏnuī, mŏnĭtŭm. *To advise.*
Mons, montĭs, *m. Mountain.*
Monstrŏ, ārĕ, āvī, ātŭm. *To show, point out.*
Mŏră, ae, *f. Delay.*
Mors, mortĭs, *f. Death.*
Multĭtūdŏ, multĭtūdĭnĭs, *f. Multitude.*
Multŭs, ă, ŭm. *Much, many.*
Mundŭs, ī, *m. World, universe.*
Mūniŏ, īrĕ, īvī, ītŭm. *To fortify, defend.*
Mūnŭs, mūnĕrĭs, *n. Gift, present.*
Mūrŭs, ī, *m. Wall.*
Mūtātĭŏ, mūtātiōnĭs, *f. Change, phase.*

*N.*

Nātālĭs, ĕ. *Belonging to one's birth, natal.*
Nātālĭs diēs. *Birth-day.*
Nātūră, ae, *f. Nature.*
Nāvālĭs, ĕ. *Naval.*
Nāvĭgŏ, ārĕ, āvī, ātŭm. *To sail to.*
Nāvĭs, nāvĭs, *f. Ship.*
Nĕcessāriŭs, ă, ŭm. *Necessary.*
Nĕcessĭtās, nĕcessĭtātĭs, *f. Necessity.*
Nĕpōs, nĕpōtĭs, *m. Grandson.*
Nōbĭlĭs, ĕ. *Noble.*
Nōmĕn, nōmĭnĭs, *n. Name.*
Nōmĭnŏ, ārĕ, āvī, ātŭm. *To call, name.*

# LATIN-ENGLISH VOCABULARY.

Nōn, *adv. Not.*
Nonnĕ, *interrog. part.* Expects the answer, *Yes.* See 346, II., 2.
Nostĕr, nŏstră, nŏstrŭm. *Our, our own, ours.*
Nŏvĭtās, nŏvĭtātĭs, *f. Novelty.*
Nŏvŭs, ă, ŭm. *New.*
Nox, noctĭs, *f. Night.*
Nūbēs, nūbĭs, *f. Cloud.*
Nŭm, *interrog. part.* Expects the answer, *No.* See 346, II., 1.
Nŭmă, ae, *m. Numa*, a Roman king.
Nŭmĕrŭs, ī, *m. Number, quantity.*
Nummŭs, ī, *m. Money, a piece of money, a coin.*
Nuntĭŏ, ārĕ, āvī, ātŭm. *To proclaim, announce.*

## O.

Obsĕs, obsĭdĭs, *m.* and *f. Hostage.*
Occāsŭs, ūs, *m. Setting, going down.*
Occŭpŏ, ārĕ, āvī, ātŭm. *To occupy, take possession of.*
Octāvŭs, ă, ŭm. *Eighth.*
Octŏ. *Eight.* See 175, 2.
Octōgintā. *Eighty.* See 175, 2.
Ocŭlŭs, ī, *m. Eye.*
Odiōsŭs, ă, ŭm. *Odious, hateful.*
Omnĭs, ĕ. *All, every, whole.*
Oppĭdŭm, ī, *n. Town, city.*
Oppugnŏ, ārĕ, āvī, ātŭm. *To besiege, take by storm.*
Optŏ, ārĕ, āvī, ātŭm. *To wish for, desire.*
Opŭlentŭs, ă, ŭm. *Rich, opulent.*
Opŭs, ŏpĕrĭs, *n. Work.*
Orātĭŏ, ōrātĭōnĭs, *f. Oration, speech.*
Orātŏr, ōrātŏrĭs, *m. Orator.*
Orbĭs, orbĭs, *m. Circle.*
Orbĭs terrārŭm. *The world.*
Ornŏ, ārĕ, āvī, ātŭm. *To adorn, be an ornament to.*
Ovĭs, ŏvĭs, *f. Sheep.*

## P.

Pārens, pārentĭs, *m.* and *f. Parent.*
Pārĕŏ, pārērĕ, pāruī, pārĭtŭm. *To obey.*
Pars, partĭs, *f. Part, portion.*
Parvŭs, ă, ŭm. *Small.*
Passĕr, passĕrĭs, *m. Sparrow.*
Pastŏr, pastōrĭs, *m. Shepherd.*
Pătĕr, pătrĭs, *m. Father.*
Pătrĭă, ae, *f. Native country, country.*
Paulŭs, ī, *m. Paulus*, a Roman consul.
Pax, pācĭs, *f. Peace.*
Pĕcūnĭă, ae, *f. Money.*
Pellĭs, pellĭs, *f. Skin, hide.*
Pĕr, *prep. with acc. Of, through.*
Pĕrăgrŏ, ārĕ, āvī, ātŭm. *To wander through.*
Pĕrītŭs, ă, ŭm. *Skilled in.*
Persă, ae, *m. A Persian.*
Pēs, pĕdĭs, *m. Foot.*
Phĭlippŭs, ī, *m. Philip*, king of Macedon.
Phĭlŏsŏphĭă, ae, *f. Philosophy.*
Phĭlŏsŏphŭs, ī, *m. Philosopher.*
Pĭĕtās, pĭĕtātĭs, *f. Filial affection, piety, duty.*
Pīrātă, ae, *m. Pirate.*
Piscĭs, piscĭs, *m. Fish.*
Pīsistrătŭs, ī, *m. Pisistratus*, tyrant of Athens.
Plăcĕŏ, plăcērĕ, plăcuī, plăcĭtŭm. *To please.*
Plēnŭs, ă, ŭm. *Full.*
Poenŭs, ă, ŭm. *Carthaginian.*
Poenus, ī, *m. A Carthaginian.*
Pōmŭm, ī, *n. Fruit.*
Pompĭliŭs, iī, *m. Pompilius*, a Roman name.
Pompēiŭs, iī, *m. Pompey*, a celebrated Roman general.
Pondŭs, pondĕrĭs, *n. Weight, mass.*

Portŭs, ūs, m. *Port, harbor.*
Post, *prep. with acc. After.*
Pŏtens, pŏtentĭs. *Powerful, able.*
Praebĕŏ, praebērĕ, praebuī, praebĭ-
tŭm. *To show, furnish, give.*
Praeceptŏr, praeceptōrĭs, m. *Teacher, instructor.*
Praeceptŭm, ī, n. *Rule, precept.*
Praeclārŭs, ă, ŭm. *Renowned, distinguished.*
Praedīcŏ, praedīcĕrĕ, praedixī, praedictŭm. *To predict, foretell.*
Praemiŭm, iī, n. *Reward.*
Prātŭm, ī, n. *Meadow.*
Prĕtiōsŭs, ă, ŭm. *Valuable.*
Prīmŭs, ă, ŭm. *First.*
Princĭpiŭm, iī, n. *Beginning.*
Prō, *prep. with abl. In behalf of, for.*
Proeliŭm, iī, n. *Battle.*
Prospĕrē, *adv. Successfully.*
Prŭvŏcŏ, ārĕ, āvī, ātŭm. *To challenge.*
Prūdentiă, ae, f. *Prudence.*
Publiŭs, iī, m. *Publius, a Roman name.*
Puellă, ae, f. *Girl.*
Puĕr, puĕrī, m. *Boy.*
Pugnă, ae, f. *Battle.*
Pugnŏ, ārĕ, āvī, ātŭm. *To fight.*
Pulchĕr, pulchră, pulchrŭm. *Beautiful.*
Pūnĭcŭs, ă, ŭm. *Carthaginian, Punic.*
Pyrrhŭs, ī, m. *Pyrrhus, a king of Epirus.*

### Q.

Quăm, *conj. Than.*
Quartŭs, ă, ŭm. *Fourth.*
Quattuŏr. *Four.* See 175, 2.
Quī, quae, quŏd, *rel. pronoun. Who, which, what.* See 187.

Quinquāgintā. *Fifty.* See 175, 2.
Quinquĕ. *Five.* See 175, 2.
Quintŭs, ă, ŭm. *Fifth.*
Quĭs, quae, quĭd? *interrog. pronoun. Who, which, what?* See 188.
Quīvīs, quaevīs, quodvīs, or quidvīs, *indef. pronoun. Whoever, whatever.* See 191.
Quŏtĭdiānŭs, ă, ŭm. *Daily.*
Quŏtĭdiē, *adv. Daily.*

### R.

Rāmŭs, ī, m. *Branch.*
Rătiŏ, rătiōnĭs, f. *Reason.*
Rectē, *adv. Rightly.*
Rectŭm, ī, n. *Right, rectitude.*
Rĕdūcŏ, rĕdūcĕrĕ, rĕduxī, rĕductŭm. *To lead back.*
Rēgīnă, ae, f. *Queen.*
Rĕgĭŏ, rĕgiōnĭs, f. *Region, territory.*
Rēgŭlŭs, ī, m. *Regulus, a Roman general.*
Regnŏ, ārĕ, āvī, ātŭm. *To reign.*
Regnŭm, ī, n. *Kingdom, royal authority.*
Rĕgŏ, rĕgĕrĕ, rexī, rectŭm. *To rule.*
Rĕnŏvŏ, ārĕ, āvī, ātŭm. *To renew.*
Rēs, reī, f. *Thing, affair.*
Rēs pūblĭcă. *Republic.*
Rĕvŏcŏ, ārĕ, āvī, ātŭm. *To recall.*
Rex, rēgĭs, m. *King.*
Rhēnŭs, ī, m. *Rhine.*
Rōmă, ae, f. *Rome.*
Rōmānŭs, ă, ŭm. *Roman.*
Rōmānŭs, ī, m. *Roman, a Roman.*
Rōmŭlŭs, ī, m. *Romulus, the founder of Rome.*

### S.

Săguntŭm, ī, n. *Saguntum, a town in Spain.*

Sălūs, sălūtĭs, f. Safety.
Sălūtārĭs, ĕ. Beneficial, salutary, advantageous.
Sălūtŏ, ārĕ, āvī, ātŭm. To salute.
Sanctŭs, ă, ŭm. Holy, sacred.
Săpiens, săpientĭs. Wise.
Săpientĕr, adv. Wisely.
Săpientiă, ae, f. Wisdom.
Schŏlă, ae, f. School.
Scientiă, ae, f. Knowledge.
Scīpiŏ, Scīpiōnĭs, m. Scipio, a distinguished Roman.
Scrībŏ, scrībĕrĕ, scripsī, scriptŭm. To write.
Scȳthae, ārŭm, m. plur. The Scythians.
Sĕcundŭs, ă, ŭm. Second, favorable.
Sempĕr, adv. Always, ever.
Sĕnātŏr, sĕnātōrĭs, m. Senator.
Sĕnātŭs, ūs, m. Senate.
Sĕnectūs, sĕnectūtĭs, f. Old age.
Sensŭs, ūs, m. Feeling, perception, sense.
Sententiă, ae, f. Opinion.
Sermŏ, sermōnĭs, m. Discourse, conversation.
Serviŏ, īrĕ, īvī, ītŭm. To serve.
Serviŭs, ii, m. Servius, a Roman proper name.
Servŏ, ārĕ, āvī, ātŭm. To preserve, keep, save.
Servŭs, ī, m. Slave.
Sex. Six. See 175, 2.
Sĭcĭliă, ae, f. Sicily.
Sĭlentiŭm, iī, n. Silence.
Sĭmĭlĭs, ĕ. Like.
Singŭlārĭs, ĕ. Remarkable, singular.
Sŏcĕr, sŏcĕrī, m. Father-in-law.
Sŏciŭs, iī, m. Ally, associate.
Sōcrătēs, ĭs, m. Socrates, the celebrated Athenian philosopher.
Sōl, sōlĭs, m. Sun.

Sŏlōn, Sŏlōnĭs, m. Solon, an Athenian legislator.
Sŏlŭm, ī, n. Soil.
Spartă, ae, f. Sparta, capital of Laconia.
Spĕciēs, spĕciēī, f. Appearance.
Spērŏ, ārĕ, āvī, ātŭm. To hope.
Spēs, spĕī, f. Hope.
Spŏliŏ, ārĕ, āvī, ātŭm. To rob, spoil, despoil.
Stĭmŭlŏ, ārĕ, āvī, ātŭm. To stimulate.
Stultĭtiă, ae, f. Folly.
Suī, sĭbĭ. Himself, herself, itself. See 184.
Sŭm, essĕ, fuī. To be. See 204.
Sŭpĕrŏ, ārĕ, āvī, ātŭm. To conquer.
Supplĭciŭm, iī, n. Punishment.
Suŭs, ă, ŭm. His, her, its, their, his own, her own, its own, their own.
Sȳrācūsae, ārŭm, f. plur. Syracuse, a city of Sicily.

T.

Tăceŏ, tăcērĕ, tăcuī, tăcĭtŭm. To be silent.
Tărentŭm, ī, n. Tarentum, an Italian town.
Tarquĭniŭs, iī, m. Tarquin, a Roman king.
Tēlŭm, ī, n. Javelin, weapon.
Tĕmĕrĭtās, tĕmĕrĭtātĭs, f. Rashness.
Templŭm, ī, n. Temple.
Tempŭs, tempŏrĭs, n. Time.
Terră, ae, f. Land, earth.
Terreŏ, terrērĕ, terruī, terrĭtŭm. To frighten, terrify.
Tertiŭs, ă, ŭm. Third.
Thălēs, ĭs, m. Thales, a Grecian philosopher.
Thēbānŭs, ă, ŭm. Theban, belonging to Thebes (a city in Greece).

Thēbānŭs, ī, m.  A Theban.
Thĕmistŏclēs, ĭs, m.  Themistocles, a celebrated Athenian.
Thrăsȳbūlŭs, ī, m.  Thrasybulus, the liberator of Athens.
Tīcīnŭs, ī, m.  Ticinus, a river of Cisalpine Gaul.
Trēs, trĭă.  Three.  See 176.
Trīgintā.  Thirty.  See 175, 2.
Triumphŏ, ārĕ, āvī, ātŭm.  To triumph.
Trōjă, ae, f.  Troy, ancient city in Asia Minor.
Tū, tuī.  Thou, you.  See 184.
Tullĭă, ae, f.  Tullia, a Roman proper name.
Tullŭs, ī, m.  Tullus, a Roman king.
Tŭm, adv.  Then, at that time.
Turrĭs, turrĭs, f.  Tower.
Tuŭs, ă, ŭm.  Your, yours, thy, thine.
Tȳrannŭs, ī, m.  Tyrant.
Tȳrĭŭs, ă, ŭm.  Tyrian.

## U.

Ulyssēs, ĭs, m.  Ulysses, a Grecian king.
Unĭversŭs, ă, ŭm.  All, the whole, entire.
Unŭs, ă, ŭm.  One.  See 176.
Urbs, urbĭs, f.  City.
Usŭs, ūs, m.  Use.
Utĭlĭs, ĕ.  Useful.

## V.

Vălētūdŏ, vălētūdĭnĭs, f.  Health.
Vărĭĕtās, vărĭĕtātĭs, f.  Variety.
Vărĭŭs, ă, ŭm.  Various.
Varrŏ, varrōnĭs, m.  Varro, a Roman consul.
Vēr, vērĭs, n.  Spring.
Verbŭm, ī, n.  Word.

Vĕrēcundĭă, ae, f.  Modesty.
Vērĭtās, vērĭtātĭs, f.  Truth, verity.
Vērŭs, ă, ŭm.  True, real.
Vērŭm, ī, n.  Truth.
Vestĕr, vestră, vestrŭm.  Your.
Vestĭŏ, īrĕ, īvī, ītŭm.  To clothe.
Vĭă, ae, f.  Way, road.
Victŏr, victōrĭs, m.  Victor, conqueror.
Victōrĭă, ae, f.  Victory.
Victōrĭă, ae, f.  Victoria, Queen of England.
Vĭgĭlŏ, ārĕ, āvī, ātŭm.  To watch, be awake.
Vīlĭs, ĕ.  Cheap.
Vindex, vindĭcĭs, m. and f.  Vindicator, avenger.
Vĭŏlŏ, ārĕ, āvī, ātŭm.  To violate.
Vĭr, vĭrī, m.  Man, hero, soldier.
Virgŏ, virgĭnĭs, f.  Maiden, girl.
Virtūs, virtūtĭs, f.  Valor, virtue.
Vītă, ae, f.  Life.
Vĭtĭŭm, iī, n.  Fault, vice.
Vĭtŭpĕrŏ, ārĕ, āvī, ātŭm.  To find fault with, censure, blame.
Vīvŏ, vīvĕrĕ, vixī, victŭm.  To live, reside.
Vŏcŏ, ārĕ, āvī, ātŭm.  To call.
Vŏlŏ, ārĕ, āvī, ātŭm.  To fly.
Vŏluntārĭŭs, ă, ŭm.  Voluntary.
Vŏluptās, vŏluptātĭs, f.  Pleasure.
Vox, vōcĭs, f.  Voice.
Vulnĕrŏ, ārĕ, āvī, ātŭm.  To wound.
Vulnŭs, vulnĕrĭs, n.  Wound.
Vultŭr, vultūrĭs, m.  Vulture.
Vultŭs, ūs, m.  Countenance.

## X.

Xerxēs, ĭs, m.  Xerxes, a Persian king.

# ENGLISH-LATIN VOCABULARY.

### A.

A, an. *Not to be translated, as the Latin has no article.* See p. 12, note 1.
Acceptable. *Grātŭs, ă, ŭm.*
Admonish. *Admŏneŏ, admŏnērĕ, admŏnui, admŏnĭtŭm.*
Adorned. *Ornātŭs, ă, ŭm.*
Advise. *Mŏneŏ, mŏnērĕ, mŏnui, mŏnĭtŭm.*
After. *Post,* prep. with acc.
Against. *Contrā,* prep. with acc. Sometimes denoted by the Dative.
Alexander. *Alexandĕr, Alexandrī,* m.
All. *Omnĭs, ĕ.*
Always. *Sempĕr,* adv.
Announce. *Nuntiŏ, ārĕ, āvī, ātŭm.*
Appoint. *Creŏ, ārĕ, āvī, ātŭm.*
Army. *Exercĭtŭs, ūs,* m.
Arrival. *Adventŭs, ūs,* m.
At. *Denoted by the Ablative of Place, or of Time.* See 421 and 426.
Athenian. *Athēniensĭs, ĕ.*
Athenian, an Athenian. *Athēniensĭs, ĭs,* m. and f.
Athens. *Athēnae, ārŭm,* f. plur.
Attack. *Impĕtŭs, ūs,* m.
Await. *Exspectŏ, ārĕ, āvī, ātŭm.*

### B.

Battle. *Proeliŭm, ĭi,* n.
Battle-array. *Aciēs, ēī,* f.
Be. *Sŭm, essĕ, fŭī.*
Be silent. *Tăceŏ, tăcērĕ, tăcuī, tăcĭtŭm.*
Beautiful. *Pulchĕr, pulchră, pulchrŭm.*
Before. *Antĕ,* prep. with acc.
Bird. *Avĭs, ăvĭs,* f.
Birth-day. *Nātălĭs diēs,* m.
Blame. *Vĭtŭpĕrŏ, ārĕ, āvī, ātŭm.*
Book. *Lĭbĕr, lĭbrī,* m.
Boy. *Puĕr, puĕrī,* m.
Brave. *Fortĭs, ĕ.*
Bravely. *Fortĭtĕr,* adv.
Bravery. *Virtūs, virtūtĭs,* f.
Bring to a close. *Fīniŏ, īrĕ, īvī, ītŭm.*
Brother. *Frāter, frātrĭs,* m.
Brutus. *Brūtus, ī,* m.
By. *A, ăb,* prep. with abl. Often denoted by the Ablative alone. See 414.

### C.

Caius. *Cāiŭs, ĭī,* m.
Call. *Vŏcŏ, ārĕ, āvī, ātŭm.*
Camillus. *Cămillŭs, ī,* m.
Can, can have. See *may, may have.*
Carthage. *Carthāgŏ, Carthāgĭnĭs,* f.
Carthaginian. *Carthāgĭniensĭs, ĕ.*
Carthaginian, a Carthaginian. *Carthāgĭniensĭs, ĭs,* m. and f.
Cato. *Cătŏ, Cătōnĭs,* m.
Cicero. *Cĭcĕrŏ, Cĭcĕrōnĭs,* m

Citizen. *Cīvĭs, cīvĭs,* m. and f.
City. *Urbs, urbĭs,* f.
Cloud. *Nūbēs, nūbĭs,* f.
Commander. *Impĕrātŏr, impĕrātōrĭs,* m.
Concerning. *Dē,* prep. with abl.
Consul. *Consŭl, consŭlĭs,* m.
Contrary to. *Contrā,* prep. with acc.
Conversation. *Sermŏ, sermōnĭs,* m.
Corinth. *Cŏrinthŭs, ī,* f.
Corinthian. *Cŏrinthĭŭs, ă, ŭm.*
Corinthian, a Corinthian. *Cŏrinthĭŭs, ĭī,* m.
Cornelius. *Cornēlĭŭs, ĭī,* m.
Could, could have. See *might, might have.*
Country. *Pătrĭă, ae,* f.
Courage. *Virtūs, virtūtĭs,* f.
Crown. *Cŏrōnă, ae,* f.

### D.

Daily. *Quŏtĭdĭănŭs, ă, ŭm.*
Daughter. *Fīlĭă, ae,* f.
Day. *Dĭēs, dĭēī,* m. See 119, note.
Dear. *Cārŭs, ă, ŭm.*
Declare. *Indĭcŏ, indĭcĕrĕ, indixī, indictŭm.*
Delight. *Dēlectŏ, ārĕ, āvī, ātŭm.*
Desirous of. *Cŭpĭdŭs, ă, ŭm; ăvĭdŭs, ă, ŭm.*
Did. *Often the sign of the Imperfect, or of the Perfect tense, especially in questions.*
Diligence. *Dīlĭgentĭă, ae,* f.
Diligent. *Dīlĭgens, dīlĭgentĭs.*
Do. *Often the sign of the Present tense, especially in questions.*

### E.

Eight. *Octŏ.* See 175, 2.
Eighth. *Octāvŭs, ă, ŭm.*
Enemy. *Hostĭs, hostĭs,* m. and f.

Exercise. *Exerceŏ, exercērĕ, exercuī, exercĭtŭm.*
Exile. *Exsŭl, exsŭlĭs,* m. and f.
Expect. *Exspectŏ, ārĕ, āvī, ātŭm.*

### F.

Father. *Pătĕr, pătrĭs,* m.
Father-in-law. *Sŏcĕr, sŏcĕrī,* m.
Fertile. *Fertĭlĭs, ĕ.*
Fidelity. *Fĭdēs, fĭdeī,* f.
Field. *Agĕr, ăgrī,* m.
Fifth. *Quintŭs, ŭ, ŭm.*
Fifty. *Quinquāgintā.* See 175, 2.
Fight. *Pugnŏ, āre, āvī, ātŭm.*
Finish. *Fīnĭŏ, īrĕ, īvī, ītŭm.*
Five. *Quinquĕ.* See 175, 2.
Flee. *Fŭgĭŏ, fŭgĕrĕ, fŭgī, fŭgĭtŭm.*
Flower. *Flōs, flōrĭs,* m.
Fly. *Vŏlŏ, ārĕ, āvī, ātŭm.*
Foot. *Pēs, pĕdĭs,* m.
Fond of. *Amans, ămantĭs.*
For. *Prō,* prep. with abl. In the sense of *because of,* it is denoted by the Ablative alone (414); and in the sense of *for the benefit of,* by the Dative (384).
Fortify. *Mūnĭŏ, īrĕ, īvī, ītŭm.*
Four. *Quattuŏr.* See 175, 2.
Fourth. *Quartŭs, ă, ŭm.*
Friend. *Amīcŭs, ī,* m.
Friendship. *Amīcĭtĭă, ae,* f.
From. *A, ăb,* prep. with abl.
Fruit. *Fructŭs, ūs,* m.

### G.

Garden. *Hortŭs, ī,* m.
Gaul. *Gallŭs, ī,* m.
Gem. *Gemmă, ae,* f.
General. *Dux, dŭcĭs,* m. and f.
Gift. *Dōnŭm, ī,* n.
Glory. *Glōrĭă, ae,* f.
Gold. *Aurŭm, ī,* n.
Golden. *Aureŭs, ă, ŭm.*

Good. Bŏnŭs, ă, ŭm.
Goodness. Bŏnĭtās, bŏnĭtātĭs, f.
Govern. Rĕgŏ, rĕgĕrĕ, rexi, rectum.
Great. Magnŭs, ă, ŭm.
Greece. Graeciă, ae, f.
Grove. Lūcŭs, ī, m.
Guard. Custōdĭŏ, īrĕ, īvī, ītŭm.

## H.

Had. *Often the sign of the Pluperfect tense.*
Hannibal. Hannĭbăl, Hannĭbălĭs, m.
Happy. Beātŭs, ă, ŭm.
Have. Hăbĕŏ, hăbērĕ, hăbuī, hăbĭtŭm. Sometimes simply the sign of the Perfect tense; as, we *have* loved.
He, she, it. *Is, că, ĭd ; illĕ, illă, illŭd.* The pronoun is often implied in the ending of the verb.
He himself. Ipsĕ, ipsă, ipsŭm.
Hear. Audĭŏ, īrĕ, īvī, ītŭm.
High. Altŭs, altă, altŭm.
Himself. Suī (184); ipsĕ, ipsă, ipsŭm.
His. Suŭs, ă, ŭm.
Hope (verb). Spĕrŏ, ārĕ, āvī, ātŭm.
Hope (noun). Spēs, spĕī, f.
Hour. Hōră, ae, f.
Hundred. Centŭm. See 175, 2.

## I.

I. Egŏ, meī. See 184.
In. *In*, prep. with abl.
In behalf of. *Prō*, prep. with abl.
Instruct. Erŭdĭŏ, īrĕ, īvī, ītŭm.
Instructor. Praeceptŏr, praeceptōrĭs, m.
Into. *In*, prep. with acc.
Invite. Invĭtŏ, ārĕ, āvī, ātŭm.
Iron. Ferrŭm, ī, n.
Island. Insŭlă, ae, f.
It. See *he, she, it.*
Italy. Itălĭă, ae, f.

## J.

Judge. Jūdex, jūdĭcĭs, m. and f.
Justice. Justĭtĭă, ae, f.

## K.

Keep one's word. Fĭdĕm servārĕ. See p. 74, note 4.
Kindly. Bĕnignē, adv.
King. Rex, rēgĭs, m.
Knowledge. Scientĭă, ae, f.

## L.

Large. Magnŭs, ă, ŭm.
Latinus. Lătīnŭs, ī, m.
Lavinia. Lāvīnĭă, ae, f.
Law. Lex, lēgĭs, f.
Lead. Dūcŏ, dūcĕrĕ, duxī, ductŭm.
Lead back. Rĕdūcŏ, rĕdūcĕrĕ, rĕduxī, rĕductŭm.
Lead forth. Edūcŏ, ēdūcĕrĕ, ēduxī, ēductŭm.
Let. *Render by the Subjunctive.* See 196, I., 2.
Leader. Dux, dŭcĭs, m. and f.
Letter. Epistŏlă, ae, f.
Liberate. Lĭbĕrŏ, ārĕ, āvī, ātŭm.
Life. Vĭtă, ae, f.
Like. Sĭmĭlĭs, ĕ.
Love. Amŏ, ārĕ, āvī, ātŭm.

## M.

Macedonia. Măcĕdŏnĭă, ae, f.
Man. Hŏmŏ, hŏmĭnĭs, m. Vĭr, vĭrī, m. The latter is used as a term of respect; *a true* or *worthy man, a hero.*
Many. Multī, ae, ă, plur.
May, can. *Signs of the Present Subjunctive.*
May have, can have. *Signs of the Perfect Subjunctive.*
Me. See *I.*
Memory. Mĕmŏrĭă, ae, f.

Might, could, would, should. *Signs of the Imperfect Subjunctive.*
Might have, could have, would have, should have. *Signs of the Pluperfect Subjunctive.*
Mind. *Anĭmŭs, ī, m.*
Moat. *Fossă, ae, f.*
Money. *Pĕcūniă, ae, f.*
Month. *Mensĭs, mensĭs, m.*
More. *Sign of the Comparative degree.* See 160.
Most. *Sign of the Superlative degree.* See 160.
Mound. *Aggĕr, aggĕrĭs, m.*
Mountain. *Mons, montĭs, m.*
Much. *Multŭm, adv.*
My. *Meŭs, ă, ŭm.* See 185.

## N.

Name. *Nōmĕn, nōmĭnĭs, n.*
Nightingale. *Luscĭniă, ae, f.*
Noble. *Nŏbĭlĭs, ĕ.*
Not. *Nōn, adv.* Interrogative, *nonnĕ.*

## O.

Obey. *Pārĕō, pārērĕ, pārui, pārĭtŭm.*
Observe. *Servŏ, ārĕ, āvī, ātŭm.*
Occupy. *Occŭpŏ, ārĕ, avī, ātŭm.*
Of. *Denoted by the Genitive.* See 393.
Of itself. *Pĕr sē.*
On. *Often denoted by the Ablative of Time.* See 426.
One. *Unŭs, ă, ŭm.* See 176.
Oration. *Orātĭŏ, ōrātiōnĭs, f.*
Orator. *Orātŏr, ōrātōrĭs, m.*
Our. *Nostĕr, tră, trŭm.*

## P.

Parent. *Părens, părentĭs, m.* and f.
Philip. *Phĭlippŭs, ī, m.*
Pisistratus. *Pisistrātŭs, ī, m.*

Please. *Plăceŏ, plăcērĕ, plăcuī, plăcĭtŭm.*
Pleasing. *Grātŭs, ă, ŭm.*
Pleasure. *Vŏluptās, vŏluptātĭs, f.*
Plough. *Arŏ, ărārĕ, ărāvī, ărātŭm.*
Plunder (verb). *Spŏliŏ, ārĕ, āvī, ātŭm.*
Practise. *Exerceŏ, exercērĕ, exercui, exercĭtŭm.*
Praise (verb). *Laudŏ, ārĕ, āvī, ātŭm.*
Praise (noun). *Laus, laudĭs, f.*
Precept. *Praeceptŭm, ī, n.*
Predict. *Praedīcŏ, praedīcĕrĕ, praedīxī, praedictŭm.*
Present (noun). *Dōnŭm, ī. n.*
Publius. *Publĭŭs, ĭī, m.*
Punish. *Pūniŏ, īrĕ, īvī, ītŭm.*
Pupil. *Discĭpŭlŭs, ī, m.*
Put to flight. *Fŭgŏ, ārĕ, avī, ātŭm.*

## Q.

Queen. *Rēgĭnă, ae, f.*

## R.

Receive. *Accĭpĭŏ, accĭpĕrĕ, accēpī, acceptŭm.*
Reign, royal authority. *Regnŭm, ī, n.*
Renowned. *Clārŭs, ă, ŭm.*
Reside. *Hăbĭtŏ, ārĕ, āvī, ātŭm.*
Rhine. *Rhēnŭs, ī, m.*
River. *Amnĭs, amnĭs, m.*
Roman. *Rōmānŭs, ă, ŭm.*
Roman, a Roman. *Rōmānŭs, ī, m.*
Rome. *Rōma, ae, f.*
Romulus. *Rōmŭlŭs, ī, m.*
Rule. *Rĕgŏ, rĕgĕrĕ, rexī, rectŭm.*

## S.

Safety. *Sălŭs, sălūtĭs, f.*
Same. *Īdĕm, eădĕm, ĭdĕm.* See 186.
Say. *Īcŏ, dīcĕrĕ, dīxī, dictŭm.*

Save. *Servŏ, ārĕ́, āvī, ātŭm.*
Scipio. *Scīpĭŏ, Scīpĭōnĭs,* m.
Senator. *Sĕ́nātŏr, sĕnātōrĭs,* m.
Serve. *Servĭŏ, īrĕ́, īvī, ītŭm.*
Servius. *Servĭŭs, ĭi,* m.
Setting. *Occāsŭs, ūs,* m.
Shall, will. *Signs of the Future tense.*
Shall have, will have. *Signs of the Future Perfect tense.*
Shepherd. *Pastŏr, pastōrĭs,* m.
Should, should have. See *might*, *might have*.
Show. *Monstrŏ, āre̅, āvī, ātŭm.*
Sicily. *Sĭcĭlĭă, ae,* f.
Silent. See *be silent*.
Silver. *Argentŭm, ī,* n.
Sing. *Cantŏ, āre̅, āvī, ātŭm.*
Singing, a song. *Cantŭs, ūs,* m.
Six. *Sex.* See 175, 2.
Slave. *Servŭs, ī,* m.
Sleep. *Dormĭŏ, īre̅, īvī, ītŭm.*
Soldier. *Mīlĕs, mīlĭtĭs,* m.
Somebody, some one. *Ălĭquĭs, ălĭquă, ălĭquĭd,* or *ălĭquŏd.* See 191.
Son. *Fīlĭŭs, ĭi,* m.
Son-in-law. *Gĕ́nĕr, gĕ́nĕrī,* m.
Song. *Carmĕn, carmĭnĭs,* n.
Speak. *Dīcŏ, dīcĕ́rĕ, dīxī, dīctŭm.*
State. *Cīvĭtās, cīvĭtātĭs,* f.
Strengthen. *Firmŏ, āre̅, āvī, ātŭm.*
Sun. *Sōl, sōlĭs,* m.
Sunset. *Occāsŭs sōlĭs.*
Sword. *Glădĭŭs, ĭi,* m.

## T.

Take. *Căpĭŏ, căpĕ́rĕ, cēpī, captŭm.*
Take by storm. *Expugnŏ, āre̅, āvī, ātŭm.*
Tarquin. *Tarquĭnĭŭs, ĭi,* m.
Tell. *Dīcŏ, dīcĕ́rĕ, dīxī, dīctŭm.*
Temple. *Templŭm, ī,* n.

Ten. *Dĕ́cĕm.* See 175, 2.
Terrify. *Terrĕŏ, terrēre̅, terruī, terrĭtŭm.*
Than. *Quăm.* Often omitted, in which case the Ablative follows. See 417.
That. *Ĭllĕ, ĭllă, ĭllŭd.* See 186
The. *Not to be translated, as the Latin has no article.* See p. 12, note 1.
Their. *Sŭŭs, ă, ŭm.*
Then. *Tŭm,* adv.
Thing. *Rēs, rĕī,* f.
This. *Hĭc, haec, hŏc.* See 186.
Three. *Trēs, trĭă.* See 176.
Time. *Tempŭs, tempŏrĭs,* n.
To. *Ad, ĭn,* preps. with acc. *To* is sometimes denoted by the Accusative, and sometimes by the Dative. See 379 and 384
True. *Vērŭs, ă, ŭm.*
Truth. *Vērŭm, ī,* n.
Tullia. *Tullĭă, ae,* f.
Two. *Dŭŏ, duae, duŏ.* See 176.
Tyrant. *Tȳrannŭs, ī,* m.

## U.

Use. *Usus, ūs,* m.
Useful. *Utĭlĭs, ĕ.*

## V.

Valor. *Virtūs, virtūtĭs,* f.
Valuable. *Prĕtĭōsŭs, ă, ŭm.*
Very. *Sometimes the sign of the Superlative.* See 160.
Victoria. *Victōrĭă, ae,* f.
Victory. *Victōrĭă, ae,* f.
Violate. *Vĭŏlŏ, āre̅, āvī, ātŭm.*
Virtue. *Virtūs, virtūtĭs,* f.

## W.

Walk. *Ambŭlŏ, āre̅, āvī, ātŭm.*
War. *Bellŭm, ī,* n.

Way. *Vĭă, ae,* f.
Well. *Bĕnĕ,* adv.
Who, which (relative). *Qui, quae, quŏd.* See 187.
Who, which, what (interrogative)? *Quĭs, quae, quĭd?* *qui, quae, quŏd?* See 188.
Wide. *Lātŭs, ă, ŭm.*
Wife. *Conjux, conjŭgĭs,* f.
Will, will have. See *shall, shall have.*
Winter. *Hiems, hiĕmĭs,* f.
Wisdom. *Săpientiă, ae,* f.
Wise. *Săpiens, săpientĭs.*
With. *Cum,* prep. with abl. Often denoted by the Ablative alone. See 414.

Word. *Verbŭm, ĭ,* n. To keep one's word, *fĭdĕm servārĕ.* See p. 74, note 4.
Would, would have. See *might, might have.*
Wound. *Vulnĕrŏ, ārĕ, āvi, ātŭm.*
Write. *Scrībŏ, scrībĕrĕ, scripsī, scriptŭm.*

Y.

Year. *Annŭs, ĭ,* m.
You. *Tū, tui.* See 184.
Your. *Tuŭs, ă, ŭm; vestĕr, vestră, vestrŭm.*
Yourself. *Tū, tū ipsĕ.*

## Harkness's Elements of Latin Grammar.

This work is intended especially for those who do not contemplate a collegiate course, but it may be successfully used in any school where, for special reasons, a small grammar is deemed desirable. The beginner needs to store his mind at the outset with the laws of the language in such forms of statement as he can carry with him throughout his whole course of study. The convenience and interest of the student in this regard have been carefully consulted in the preparation of this manual. All the paradigms, rules, and discussions, have been introduced in the exact language of the author's Grammar, by which it may at any time be supplemented. While, therefore, in many schools this work will be found a sufficient Latin Grammar, it may be used in others, either as preparatory to the larger Grammar, or in connection with it.

No separate references to this volume will ever be needed in editions of Latin authors, as the numbering of the articles is the same as in the larger Grammar.

*From* Pres. COBLEIGH, *Tennessee Wesleyan University.*

"This work is very timely. I regard it as indispensable in many schools in the South."

*From* Prof. W. H. YOUNG, *Ohio University.*

"I most heartily commend this work. I have for some time felt its need. It seems to make your Latin course complete."

*From* Prof. C. G. HUDSON, *Genesee Wesleyan Seminary, Lima, N. Y.*

"I can heartily recommend it. I think that it is superior to all rivals."

*From* Prof. H. D. WALKER, *Orangeville Academy, Pa.*

"In my opinion, no work of Professor Harkness will be more widely used, or more valuable, than this. It supplies a want long felt by teachers. It is clear, thorough, and sufficiently extended for ordinary students."

*From* Prof. S. H. MANLEY, *Cornell College, Iowa.*

"I think it one of the finest compendiums of Grammar I have ever seen. It must prove of great service as a preparatory drill-book."

*From* Prof. L. F. PARKER, *Iowa College.*

"I feel under personal obligation for this new incentive and aid to classical study."

*From* H. F. LANE, *High School, Templeton, Mass.*

"It is *exactly* adapted to our wants. We use all of Harkness's books—Grammar, Reader, and Composition. We consider them emphatically 'the best.'"

*From* Prof. J. A. KELLER, *Heidelberg College, Ohio.*

"I was surprised to find so full an outline of Latin Grammar comprised within such narrow limits."

*From* Prof. M. B. BROWN, *Notre-Dame University.*

"In my opinion, it is just the book which has long been needed. It is a book to be learned *entire*, and is complete as far as it goes. Prof. Harkness deserves the thanks both of students and teachers."

*From* Rev. B. G. NORTHROP, *Secretary of Board of Education, Conn.*

"I am highly pleased with Harkness's Elements of Latin Grammar. Its brevity commends it for beginners and for all contemplating a partial Latin course of study."

*D. APPLETON & CO.'S PUBLICATIONS.*

# HARKNESS'S LATIN GRAMMAR.
## 12mo, 355 pages.

Although this work has been published but a short time comparatively, it is recommended by and introduced into a large number of Colleges and Classical Schools, among which are the following:

BOWDOIN COLLEGE, Brunswick, Me.
BATES COLLEGE, Lewiston, Maine.
LEWISTON FALLS ACADEMY, Auburn, Me.
DOVER HIGH SCHOOL, Dover, N. H.
DARTMOUTH COLLEGE, Hanover, N. H.
NORWICH UNIVERSITY, Norwich, Vt.
GLENWOOD LADIES' SEMINARY, Brattleboro, Vt.
AMHERST COLLEGE, Amherst, Mass.
TUFTS COLLEGE, Medford, Mass.
PHILLIPS ACADEMY, Andover, Mass.
STATE NORMAL SCHOOL, Framingham, Mass.
HIGHLAND SCHOOL, Worcester, Mass.
NEWTON HIGH SCHOOL, Newton, Mass.
PUBLIC HIGH SCHOOL, Springfield, Mass.
ROXBURY LATIN SCHOOL, Roxbury, Mass.
LAWRENCE ACADEMY, Groton, Mass.
AUBURNDALE FEMALE SEMINARY, Auburndale, Mass.
SPENCER ACADEMY, Spencer, Mass.
JAMAICA PLAIN HIGH SCHOOL, Jamaica Plain, Mass.
BROWN UNIVERSITY, Providence, R. I.
UNIVERSITY GRAMMAR SCHOOL, Providence, R. I.
PUBLIC HIGH SCHOOL, Providence, R. I.
FRIENDS' BOARDING SCHOOL, Providence, R. I.
WARREN HIGH SCHOOL, Warren, R. I.
PROVIDENCE CONFERENCE SEMINARY, East Greenwich, R. I.
WESLEYAN UNIVERSITY, Middletown, Ct.
FREE ACADEMY, Norwich, Ct.
NEW LONDON ACADEMY, New London, Ct.
YALE COLLEGE, New Haven, Ct.
ROCHESTER UNIVERSITY, Rochester, N. Y.
MADISON UNIVERSITY, Hamilton, N. Y.
COLLEGE OF THE CITY OF NEW YORK.
CORTLAND ACADEMY, Homer, N. Y.
OSWEGO HIGH SCHOOL, Oswego, N. Y.
HAMILTON COLLEGE, Clinton, N. Y.
HOBART FREE COLLEGE, Geneva, N. Y.
CANANDAIGUA ACADEMY, Canandaigua, N. Y.
NEWTON HIGH SCHOOL, Newton, N. J.
HAVERFORD COLLEGE, West Haverford, Pa.
CLASSICAL AND MILITARY SCHOOL, Columbia, Pa.
SHURTLEFF COLLEGE, Upper Alton, Ill.
IOWA STATE UNIVERSITY, Iowa City, Iowa.
UNIVERSITY OF MICHIGAN, Ann Arbor, Mich.

# Harkness's Latin Grammar.

*From Rev. Prof. J. J. OWEN, D. D., New York Free Academy.*

"I have carefully examined Harkness's Latin Grammar, and am so well pleased with its plan, arrangement, and execution, that I shall take the earliest opportunity of introducing it as a text-book in the Free Academy."

*From Mr. JOHN D. PHILBRICK, Superintendent of Public Schools, Boston, Mass.*

"This work is evidently no hasty performance, nor the compilation of a mere book maker, but the well-ripened fruit of mature and accurate scholarship. It is eminently practical, because it is truly philosophical."

*From Mr. G. N. BIGELOW, Principal of State Normal School, Framingham, Mass.*

"Harkness's Latin Grammar is the most satisfactory text-book I have ever used."

*From Rev. DANIEL LEACH, Superintendent Public Schools, Providence, R. I.*

"I am quite confident that it is superior to any Latin Grammar before the public. It has recently been introduced into the High School, and all are much pleased with it."

*From Dr. J. B. CHAPIN, State Commissioner of Public Instruction in Rhode Island.*

"The vital principles of the language are clearly and beautifully exhibited. The work needs no one's commendation."

*From Mr. ABNER J. PHIPPS, Superintendent of Public Schools, Lowell, Mass.*

"The aim of the author seems to be fully realized in making this 'a *useful* book, and as such I can cheerfully commend it. The clear and admirable manner in which the intricacies of the Subjunctive Mood are unfolded, is one of its marked features.

"The evidence of ripe scholarship and of familiarity with the latest works of German and English philologists is manifest throughout the book."

*From Dr. J. T. CHAMPLIN, President of Waterville College.*

"I like both the plan and the execution of the work very much. Its matter and manner are both admirable. I shall be greatly disappointed if it does not at once win the public favor."

*From Prof. A. S. PACKARD, Bowdoin College, Brunswick, Maine.*

"Harkness's Latin Grammar exhibits throughout the results of thorough scholarship. I shall recommend it in our next catalogue."

*From Prof. J. J. STANTON, Bates College.*

"We have introduced Harkness's Grammar into this Institution. It is much more logical and concise than any of its rivals."

*From Mr. WM. J. ROLFE, Principal Cambridge High School.*

"Notwithstanding all the inconveniences that must attend a change of Latin Grammars in a large school like mine, I shall endeavor to secure the adoption of Harkness's Grammar in place of our present text-book as soon as possible."

*From Mr. L. R. WILLISTON, Principal Ladies' Seminary, Cambridge, Mass.*

"I think this work a decided advance upon the Grammar now in use."

*From Mr. D. R. HAGER, Princ. Eliot High School, Jamaica Plain, Mass.*

"This is, in my opinion, *by far the best Latin Grammar ever published*. It is admirably adapted to the use of learners, being remarkably concise, clear, comprehensive, and philosophical. It will henceforth be used as a text-book in this school."

# Harkness's Latin Grammar.

*From* Prof. C. S. HARRINGTON *and* Prof. J. C. VAN BENSCHOTEN, *of the Wesleyan University.*

"This work is clear, accurate, and happy in its statement of principles, is simple yet scholarly, and embraces the latest researches in this department of philological science. It will appear in our catalogue."

*From* Mr. ELBRIDGE SMITH, *Principal Free Academy, Norwich, Ct.*

"This is not only the best Latin Grammar, but one of the most thoroughly prepared school-books that I have ever seen. I have introduced the book into the Free Academy, and am much pleased with the results of a month's experience in the class-room."

*From* Mr. H. A. PRATT, *Principal High School, Hartford, Ct.*

"I can heartily recommend Harkness's new work to both teachers and scholars. It is, in my judgment, the best Latin Grammar ever offered to our schools."

*From* Mr. I. F. CADY, *Principal High School, Warren, R. I.*

"The longer I use Harkness's Grammar the more fully am I convinced of its superior excellence. Its merits must secure its adoption wherever it becomes known."

*From* Messrs. S. THURBER *and* T. B. STOCKWELL, *Public High School, Providence.*

"An experience of several weeks with Harkness's Latin Grammar enables us to say with confidence, that it is an improvement on our former text-book."

*From* Mr. C. B. GOFF, *Principal Boys' Classical High School, Providence, R. I.*

"The practical working of Harkness's Grammar is gratifying even beyond my expectations."

*From* Rev. Prof. M. H. BUCKHAM, *University of Vermont.*

"Harkness's Latin Grammar seems to me to supply the desideratum. It is philosophical in its method, and yet simple and clear in its statements; and this, in my judgment, is the highest encomium which can be bestowed on a text-book."

*From* Mr. E. T. QUIMBY, *Appleton Academy, New Ipswich, N. H.*

"I think the book much superior to any other I have seen. I should be glad to introduce it at once."

*From* Mr. H. ORCUTT, *Glenwood Ladies' Seminary, W. Brattleboro', Vt.*

"I am pleased with Harkness's Latin Grammar, and have already introduced it into this seminary."

*From* Mr. CHARLES JEWETT, *Principal of Franklin Academy.*

"I deem it an admirable work, and think it will supersede all others now in use; in the division and arrangement of topics, and in its mechanical execution, it is superior to any Latin Grammar extant."

*From* Mr. C. C. CHASE, *Principal of Lowell High School.*

"Prof. Harkness's Grammar is, in my opinion, admirably adapted to make the study of the Latin language agreeable and interesting."

*From* Mr. J. KIMBALL, *High School, Dorchester, Mass.*

"It meets my ideal of what is desirable in every grammar, to wit: compression of general principles in terse definitions and statements, for ready use; and fulness of detail, well arranged for reference."

## Harkness's Cæsar.

This edition of Cæsar's Commentaries, intended to follow the Latin Reader, aims to introduce the student to an appreciative study of Latin authors. The text is the result of a careful collation of the several editions most approved by European scholars. The notes are intended to guide the faithful efforts of the learner, and to furnish him such collateral information as will enable him to understand the stirring events recorded in the Commentaries, and such special aid as will enable him to surmount real difficulties of construction and idiom. They will thus, it is hoped, render an acceptable service both to the instructor and the learner, by lightening the burden of the one, and by promoting the progress of the other. The dictionary has been prepared with special reference to the wants of the student.

The Life of Cæsar, the Map of Gaul, and the diagrams and illustrations which accompany the notes, will greatly add to the value of the work.

*From Pres. AIKIN, Union College, N. Y.*

"This edition of the Commentaries is admirably suited, not merely to give the student an acquaintance with his immediate text-book, but also to develop those habits of investigation, that thoughtfulness in regard to the scope of the whole subject, and that style of vigorous, tasteful, and idiomatic rendering, which are among the rarest, as they are certainly among the most important, results of classical study."

*From S. H. TAYLOR, LL. D., Phillips Academy, Andover, Mass.*

"The notes are prepared with a judicious appreciation of the wants of the pupil. They show the hand of the finished scholar, as well as of the experienced teacher."

*From Prof. W. A. PACKARD, Princeton College, N. J.*

"The notes are models of what the beginner needs to interest and guide him. The text is furnished with the best illustrations in the way of maps and plans."

*From Prof. W. T. JOHNSON, Notre-Dame University, Ind.*

"This is certainly an excellent text-book—superior to any other edition of the Commentaries now in use."

*From Pres. McELDOWNEY, Albion College, Mich.*

"This is the most valuable edition of Cæsar with which I am acquainted."

*From Prof. H. W. HAYNES, University of Vermont.*

"Never before have I seen such a lucid and simple explanation of Cæsar's bridge across the Rhine."

*From Prof. C. S. HARRINGTON, Wesleyan University, Conn.*

"The student who uses this edition must read Cæsar with a lively relish."

*From Prof. W. A. STEVENS, Denison University, Ohio.*

"The notes are gotten up on the right principle, and are greatly superior to those of similar works in England."

*From Prof. J. E. GINTNER, Otterbein University, Ohio.*

"This is the only edition of Cæsar recommended to our classes."

*From A. D. SANDBORN, Wilton Seminary, Iowa.*

"I know of no work of the kind in which the notes so fully meet the wants of both teacher and pupil. I am delighted with the life of Cæsar."

*From Prof. S. HASSELL, State Normal University, Del.*

"This edition of Cæsar is superior to all others published in this country. The biographical sketch of the Roman commander is a splendid production."

# Arnold's First Latin Book;

Remodelled and Rewritten, and adapted to the Ollendorff Method of Instruction. By ALBERT HARKNESS, A. M. 12mo, 302 pages.

Under the labors of the present author, the work of Arnold has undergone radical changes. It has been adapted to the Ollendorff improved method of instruction, and is superior to the former work in its plan and all the details of instruction. While it proceeds in common with Arnold on the principle of imitation and repetition, it pursues much more exactly and with a surer step the progressive method, and aims to make the pupil master of every individual subject before he proceeds to a new one, and of each subject by itself before it is combined with others; so that he is brought gradually and surely to understand the most difficult combinations of the language. An important feature of this book is, that it carries along the Syntax *pari passu* with the Etymology, so that the student is not only all the while becoming familiar with the forms of the language, but is also learning to construct sentences and to understand the mutual relations of their component parts.

Special care has been taken in the exercises to present such idioms and expressions alone as are authorized by the best classic authors, so that the learner may acquire by example as well as precept, a distinct idea of pure Latinity.

It has been a leading object with the author so to classify and arrange the various topics as to simplify the subject, and, as far as possible, to remove the disheartening difficulties too often encountered at the outset in the study of an ancient language.

*From* W. E. TOLMAN, *Instructor in Providence High School.*

"I have used Arnold's First Latin Book, remodelled and rewritten by Mr. Harkness, in my classes during the past year, and find it to be a work not so much remodelled and rewritten as one *entirely new*, both in its plan and in its adaptation to the wants of the beginner in Latin."

*From* WM. RUSSELL, *Editor of the First Series of the Boston Journal of Education.*

"The form which this work has taken under the skillful hand of Mr. H. is marked throughout by a method purely elementary, perfectly simple, gradually progressive, and rigorously exact. Pupils trained on such a manual cannot fail of becoming distinguished, in their subsequent progress, for precision and correctness of knowledge, and for rapid advancement in genuine scholarship."

*From* GEORGE CAPRON, *Principal of Worcester High School.*

"I have examined the work with care, and am happy to say that I find it superior to any similar work with which I am acquainted. I shall recommend it to my next class."

*From* J. R. BOISE, *Professor of Ancient Languages in Michigan University.*

"I have examined your First Book in Latin, and am exceedingly pleased both with the plan and execution. I shall not fail to use my influence toward introducing it into the classical schools of this State."

## Second Latin Book.

Comprising an Historical Latin Reader, with Notes and Rules for Translating, and an Exercise Book, developing a Complete Analytical Syntax, in a series of Lessons and Exercises, involving the Construction, Analysis, and Reconstruction of Latin Sentences. By ALBERT HARKNESS, A.M., Senior Master in the Providence High School. 12mo, 362 pages.

This work is designed as a sequel to the author's "First Latin Book." It comprises a complete analytical syntax, exhibiting the essential structure of the Latin language, from its simplest to its most expanded and elaborate form.

The arrangement of the lessons is decidedly philosophical, gradually progressive, and in strict accordance with the law of development of the human mind. Every new principle is stated in simple, clear, and accurate language, and illustrated by examples carefully selected from the reading lessons, which the student is required to translate, analyze, and reconstruct. He is also exercised in forming new Latin sentences on given models. This, while it gives variety and interest to what would otherwise be in the highest degree monotonous, completely fixes in the mind the subject of the lesson, both by analysis and synthesis.

The careful study of this volume, on the plan recommended by the author, will greatly facilitate the pupil's progress in the higher departments of the language. Such is the testimony of the numerous institutions in which Harkness's improved edition of Arnold has been introduced.

*From J. A. SPENCER, D. D., late Professor of Latin in Burlington College, N. J.*

"The present volume appears to me to carry out excellently the system on which the late lamented Arnold based his educational works; and in the Selections for Reading, the Notes and Rules for Translating, the Exercises in Translating into Latin, the Analyses, etc., I think it admirably adapted to advance the diligent student, not only rapidly, but soundly, in an acquaintance with the Latin language."

*From PROF. GAMMELL, of Brown University.*

"The book seems to me, as I anticipated it would be, a valuable addition to the works now in use among teachers of Latin in the schools of the United States, and for many of them it will undoubtedly form an advantageous substitute."

*From PROF. LINCOLN, of Brown University.*

"It seems to me to carry on most successfully the method pursued in the First Book. Though brief, it is very comprehensive, and combines judicious and skilfully-formed exercises with systematic instruction."

*From J. J. OWEN, D. D., Professor of the Latin and Greek Languages and Literature in the Free Academy, New York.*

"This Second Latin Book gives abundant evidence of the author's learning and tact to arrange, simplify, and make accessible to the youthful mind the great and fundamental principles of the Latin language. The book is worthy of a place in every classical school, and I trust will have an extensive sale."

*From PROF. ANDERSON, of Lewisburg University, Pennsylvania.*

"A faithful use of the work would diminish the drudgery of the student's earlier studies, and facilitate his progress in his subsequent course. I wish the work a wide circulation."

*D. APPLETON & CO.'S PUBLICATIONS.*

# Arnold's Latin Course:

I. FIRST AND SECOND LATIN BOOK AND PRACTICAL GRAMMAR. Revised and Carefully Corrected, by J. A. SPENCER, D. D. 12mo, 359 pages.

II. PRACTICAL INTRODUCTION TO LATIN PROSE COMPOSITION, Revised and carefully corrected by J. A. SPENCER, D. D. 12mo, 356 pages.

III. CORNELIUS NEPOS. With Questions and Answers, and an Imitative Exercise on each Chapter. With Notes by E. A. JOHNSON, Professor of Latin, in University of New York. New edition, enlarged, with a Lexicon, Historical and Geographical Index, etc. 12mo, 350 pages.

---

Arnold's Classical Series has attained a circulation almost unparalleled, having been introduced into nearly all the leading educational institutions in the United States. The secret of this success is, that the author has hit upon the true system of teaching the ancient languages. He exhibits them not as dead, but as living tongues; and by imitation and repetition, the means which Nature herself points out to the child learning his mother-tongue, he familiarizes the student with the idioms employed by the elegant writers and speakers of antiquity.

The First and Second Latin Book should be put into the hands of the beginners, who will soon acquire from its pages a better idea of the language than could be gained by months of study according to the old system. The reason of this is, that every thing has a practical bearing, and a principle is no sooner learned than it is applied. The pupil is at once set to work on exercises.

The Prose Composition forms an excellent sequel to the above work, or may be used with any other course. It teaches the art of writing Latin more correctly and thoroughly, more easily and pleasantly, than any other work. In its pages Latin synonymes are carefully illustrated, differences of idioms noted, cautions as to common errors impressed on the mind, and every help afforded toward attaining a pure and flowing Latin style.

*From* N. WHEZLER, *Principal of Worcester County High School.*

"In the skill with which he sets forth the *idiomatic peculiarities*, as well as in the directness and simplicity with which he states the facts of the ancient languages, Mr. Arnold has no superior. I know of no books so admirably adapted to awaken an *interest* in the study of the language, or so well fitted to lay the foundation of a correct scholarship and refined taste."

*From* A. B. RUSSELL, *Oakland High School.*

"The style in which the books are got up are not their only recommendation. With thorough instruction on the part of the teacher using these books as text-books, I am confident a much more ample return for the time and labor bestowed by our youth upon Latin must be secured. The time certainly has come when an advance must be made upon the old methods of instruction. I am glad to have a work that promises so many advantages as Arnold's First and Second Latin Book to beginners."

*From* C. M. BLAKE, *Classical Teacher, Philadelphia.*

"I am much pleased with Arnold's Latin Books. A class of my older boys have just finished the First and Second Book. They had studied Latin for a long time before, but never *understood* it, they say, as they do now."

www.ingramcontent.com/pod-product-compliance
Lightning Source LLC
Chambersburg PA
CBHW020250170426
43202CB00008B/307